Santa Fe

MW00488819

Get a better deal on local crafts...

Palace of the Governors, see Shopping

Let the kids run wild.

Inn at Loretto, see Accommodations

Dress up for an open-air aria...

Santa Fe Opera, see Nightlife and Entertainment

Sample startling Indian art...

Wheelwright Museum of the American Indian, see Diversions

Hang with *chic*-os and *chic*-as...

The Double A, see Dining

Have your spring wedding...

Santuario de Nuestra Señora de Guadalupe, see Diversions

See the flour of Santa Fe's youth...

Maria's New Mexican Kitchen, see Dining

Dine well for less *dinero*...

Pastability, see Dining

Ski in the high desert...

Santa Fe Ski Area, see Getting Outside

Where to learn what the Navajo know...

Museum of Indian Art and Culture, see Diversions

Sleep in a designer's digs...

Spencer House, see Accommodations

Have *buenos nachos...*

Coyote Cafe, see Dining

irreverent guides

Santa Fe

BY

JOHN VILLANI

A BALLIETT & FITZGERALD BOOK

MACMILLAN • USA

what's so irreverent?

It's up to you.

You can buy a traditional guidebook with its fluff, its promotional hype, its let's-find-something-nice-to-say-about-everything point of view. Or you can buy an Irreverent guide.

What the Irreverents give you is the lowdown, the inside story. They have nothing to sell but the truth, which includes a balance of good and bad. They praise, they trash, they weigh, and leave the final decisions up to you. No tourist board, no chamber of commerce will ever recommend them.

Our writers are insiders, who feel passionate about the cities they live in, and have strong opinions they want to share with you. They take a special pleasure leading you where other guides fear to tread.

How irreverent are they? One of our authors insisted on writing under a pseudonym. "I couldn't show my face in town again if I used my own name," she told me. "My friends would never speak to me." Such is the price of honesty. She, like you, should know she'll always have a friend at Frommer's.

Warm regards,

Michael Spring

Michael Spring
Publisher

a disclaimer

Prices fluctuate in the course of time, and travel information changes under the impact of the varied and volatile factors that influence the travel industry. Neither the author nor the publisher can be held responsible for the experiences of readers while traveling. Readers are invited to write to the publisher with ideas, comments, and suggestions for future editions.

about the author

As one of the Southwest's most widely published freelance writers, **John Villani** has covered Santa Fe's arts scene since the late 1980s for newspapers in Santa Fe and Albuquerque. His work currently appears in *Southern Accents*, *Art Business News*, *Home Garden*, *Cooking Light*, *Southwest Art*, *The Christian Science Monitor*, *New Mexico*, and the *Albuquerque Journal*. He writes on the subjects of visual arts, performing arts, travel, food, interior design, gardening, and eco-tourism.

photo credits

Page i: by Jack Parsons; Page ii: by Jack Parsons; Page iv: top and center by Jon Villani, bottom courtesy of Coyote Cafe; Page v: top and bottom by John Villani; Page vi: top and bottom by John Villani; Page vii: top courtesy of Santa Fe Opera (by Hans Fahrmeyer), middle by John Villani, bottom courtesy of Double A (by Tim Street-Porter); Page viii: top and bottom by John Villani.

Balliett & Fitzgerald, Inc.
Series editor: Holly Hughes / Executive editor: Tom Dyja / Managing editor: Duncan Bock / Production editor: Howard Slatkin / Photo editor: Maria Fernandez / Editorial assistants: Jennifer Leben, Iain McDonald Macmillan Travel art director: Michele Laseau

Design by Tsang Seymour Design Studio

All maps © Simon & Schuster, Inc.

Air travel assistance courtesy of Continental Airlines

MACMILLAN TRAVEL
A Simon & Schuster Macmillan Company
1633 Broadway
New York, NY 10019

Copyright © 1996 by Simon and Schuster, Inc.

ISBN 0-02-860883-6
ISSN 1085-472X

special sales

Bulk purchases (10+ copies) of Frommer's Travel Guides are available to corporations at special discounts. The Special Sales Department can produce custom editions to be used as premiums and/or for sales promotions to suit individual needs. Existing editions can be produced with custom cover imprints such as corporate logos. For more information write to: Special Sales, Simon & Schuster, 1633 Broadway, New York, NY 10019.

Manufactured in the United States of America

contents

THE LOWDOWN

introduction

Around here, there's a bit of local wisdom that says, "Santa Fe either embraces you or spits you out." That's a damn useful chunk of advice. To many, we are a refuge. People come to Santa Fe because of romantic dreams, half-true notions that this city can somehow help them find answers to life's questions. And for some (myself included), this town really does change lives forever. It's a magical blend of place, people, culture, and history.

When I arrived here on a crystalline day in January 1989, an eight-inch snowfall the previous evening had left Santa Fe's wiggly streets and sloping adobe walls shrouded in a mantle of powdery white. It was intoxicating. I wandered over to the portal of the Palace of the Governors and bought a great-looking bracelet for $55 from one of the Native American jewelers there. Later that evening I had my first taste of chiles rellenos, and knocked them back with a locally brewed Santa Fe Pale Ale. Within a week I had a girlfriend, a government job, and an apartment in a historic home once lived in by a New Mexico governor. For some fortunate folks, Santa Fe's embrace is irresistible.

A friend of mine aptly describes Santa Fe as "a candy store—everything you could want is right here, and all you've got to do is ask for it." Fair enough, but on the other hand, be careful what you ask for, because you just may get it...and all the headaches that come with it.

Santa Fe is still reeling from a turbocharged, traumatic period of population growth. Since the late 1980s real-estate values have skyrocketed, as urban refugees from both coasts have hooked their hopes, dreams, and equity onto places such as Sun Valley (ID), Bozeman (MT), Jackson (WY), Durango (CO), Moab (UT), Bisbee (AZ), and here. When you have a lot of newcomers trying to wedge their way into a small western town, the demand for permanent housing rises so high that local residents can be priced out of the market, and eventually property taxes get jacked up to exorbitant heights. A tremendous amount of resentment is then directed at the outsiders, who are rightly perceived as the source of many problems.

All of this real-estate runaround goes counter to New Mexican tradition: our communities grew up as a mosaic of Spanish colonial land grants. The property within those grants has for centuries been divided, subdivided, and handed down from one Hispanic family's generation to the next—that's why the houses in Santa Fe's historic areas are built so close together. And these people don't take kindly to the concept of selling their homes and land. The very notion that today's boomers would tack a realtor's listing price onto this enduring legacy is incomprehensible to longtime New Mexicans. Selling your land is seen as rejecting your friends, family, and heritage. In most parts of the culturally diverse Southwest, when fast-growing communities divide along political, social, and economic lines, they also divide along ethnic lines. Hispanics and Native Americans almost always become the have-nots while Anglo newcomers usually become the haves. It's not a pretty situation and can lead to all sorts of trouble in a small community like ours. Crime is becoming a significant problem in Santa Fe, and according to authorities like our mayor, it's largely because of the community's glaring economic inequities. Tourism has its costs as well. Sure, all those new downtown hotels look great, and the Plaza has an inspiring range of shops selling everything from $800 cowgirl boots to $10,000 Navajo rugs. But downtown Santa Fe no longer serves the needs of local residents. Woolworth's is still there, but that's it—just try to find a drugstore or a gas station, or even a place that will sell you a hammer and nails. With rents approaching $120 per square foot, those businesses have either moved down Cerrillos Road or closed for good.

Having given you this reality check from a resident's standpoint, I'll still tell you to expect a fantastic visit. Our official motto is "The City Different," and Santa Fe certainly tries to measure up to that. Living at 7,000 feet, high in the southernmost reaches of the Rocky Mountains, we're greeted nearly every day of the year by crystal-clear, deep blue skies. From downtown street corners we can see the 12,000-foot peaks of the Sangre de Cristo Mountains, and on most days the larger buildings at Los Alamos National Laboratory, 40 miles distant, are visible from the rooftop bar at La Fonda hotel. Daily life here comes packaged with stunning views.

And living near the mountains doesn't only mean great things to look at. During winter, I can log in four solid hours of morning work, then throw my skis into the back of my truck and head up the Sangre de Cristo Mountains to the Santa Fe Ski Area. I'll buy a half-day ticket, hit the slopes by 12:30, and be off the mountain and back at my desk by 4:30, just in time to return the afternoon's accumulation of phone messages. Later that evening I'll splash around in one of the outdoor hot tubs at 10,000 Waves to loosen up my thigh muscles, and wonder how I ever ended up living in a place this beautiful. In late spring I love to take day-long white-water rafting trips down the killer rapids in the Taos Box hellhole of the Rio Grande, and later sit underneath the cottonwoods at Embudo Station sipping one of Preston Cox's smashing, microbrewed red chile ales. Summers are perfect for oiling up the gears on my mountain bike and flying down one of the many trails winding through the lodgepole pines in Santa Fe National Forest, or for half-day hikes up Atalaya Trail at the edge of St. John's College. From the top of the trail I can almost make out the Sierra Madre Mountains in Chihuahua, Mexico.

Even after seven years, whenever I drive the High Road to Taos I'm still amazed at the way the landscape changes between Santa Fe and places just north of town. Be ready for spectacular views of mesas, mountains, farmland, and desert. Stop in to see the beautiful adobe church in the Hispanic farming village of Chimayo, or at any of the four Native American pueblos along the High Road; throw in a side trip to the hot springs at Ojo Caliente and a meal of red chile enchiladas at Angelina's restaurant in Española and you've sampled some of the best this corner of the country offers. Another thing that's different down here is New Mexico's eloquent twist on American food. Enchiladas, sopapillas, tamales, bizcochitos, green chile stew, and tortillas—in this part of the country these are basic, no-frills staples of life. If you really want to take a bite out of New Mexico, pull up to a small-town cafe and order up a green chile cheeseburger. Yes, make reservations at those fancy Santa Fe restaurants with their national reputations and Europe-trained chefs. But also take the time to stop in at the funked-out, family-operated cafes. While the sign outside the restaurant may be in Spanish, the kitchen language spoken inside is transcendently international.

This is also a truly multicultural corner of the world, multicultural to the bone. My Venezuelan grandfather would have fallen in love with Santa Fe's cultural diversity and its Spanish colonial-cum-Indian pueblo architecture. The desk clerk checking you into your hotel could be a Hopi, Zuni, San Ildefonso, or Navajo Indian. Look around town and you'll quickly notice that our state's largest ethnic group is Hispanics, descendants of Spanish settlers who colonized (and Christianized) this region long before any Englishman set foot on Plymouth Rock. Today the heirs of those conquistadors are Santa Fe's firemen, business owners, taxi drivers, lawyers. New Mexico is also the nation's 48th-poorest state when it comes to per-capita income (thank God for Mississippi!), so in this part of the country, what passes for economic development can take some pretty strange forms, like the recent rush to develop gambling casinos on Indian-owned lands. Most of the nearby Indian Pueblos are expanding their profitable casino operations, so if you want to take a crack at craps or the dollar slots, there are plenty of places within a 30-minute drive from the Plaza. On the other hand, if your notions about experiencing Native America don't include showgirls and bingo, try visiting a pueblo on one of their many feast days (local newspapers print schedules). Usually special ceremonial dances are held in the pueblo's central plaza on such occasions, replete with traditionally costumed dancers. Don't take photographs and don't applaud the dancers—that's against the rules. Just enjoy the ceremonies and take your memories home with you.

As a writer, I particularly appreciate another thing that makes Santa Fe different: its widespread support for creative pursuits. I still marvel at the incredible assemblage of talented, traveled, sage men and women I meet in the course of my daily life. Even many of the doctors, dentists, and CPAs here consider themselves artists (and several are accomplished enough to have their work exhibited in serious art galleries). Having so many arty folks around means there's a built-in support system for creative types. Talented people come here from all over the world to open the store or gallery of their dreams, and you should try to get to know some of them. They won't make it difficult.

Your economic impact is welcome, and folks living here actually will expend considerable effort to help make your Santa Fe experience pleasant, even unforgettable. Just keep in mind that you've gotta accept the different ways things are done. Nobody moves too fast (except when driving on Cerrillos Road). If we wanted to move fast, we would be living somewhere else, like Dallas or Phoenix or New York or L.A. Most of us have lived in places like that and we moved here to *escape* the pace of life in big cities. Believe me, things get done here—it just takes a little more time than you're used to.

No matter what your agenda, there really are countless ways to enjoy the authentic Santa Fe. Fun places to stay, unusual spots to dine, clubs where you can shake your wild thing, gallery openings where you can observe local flora and fauna… it really is like a candy store! My best advice is to take things slowly, let this place work its way into your psyche, and don't try to battle its mannerisms or offbeat pace. Take the time to linger an hour or so over one of Santa Fe's incredibly colorful sunsets, or spend a while listening to the tales spun by mariachi singers. A margarita in front of a blazing fire, a basket of chips and salsa shared with friends, a whiff of piñon pine, or an afternoon walk along Canyon Road… these are the experiences from which Santa Fe's life is spun.

Santa Fe Neighborhoods

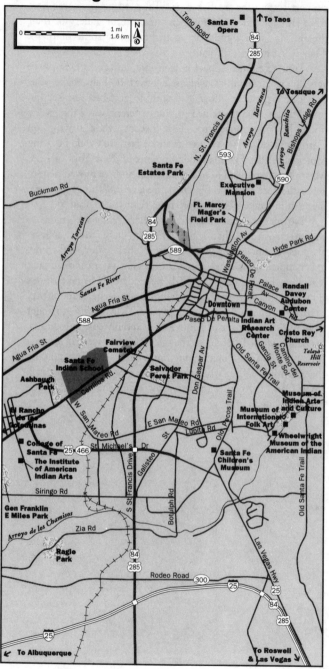

you probably didn't know

How can I pick up an artist or a wealthy art collector?... Try gallery-hopping on one of the city's typically frantic Friday evenings. Year round, this is when most opening receptions are scheduled, and the scene always draws a buzzing crowd of local art collectors, hangers-on, artists and their friends, writers, and curious visitors. Those in the know count on being served cheap wine and some sort of nibbles, so dinner plans afterward are a must. Sometimes there's an after-party at a gallery owner's, friend's, or collector's home, but it's more likely to be an eclectic group of friends, old and new, congregating at one of the town's more affordable restaurants. Tip: Shortly after engaging a local person in conversation, be direct! Just pop the question: "So, where's everybody going later?"

How can I start a meaningful conversation, anywhere at any time?... Simply mention your therapist, and you've gained a Santa Fe person's ear. Flip through the Yellow Pages and you'll find that massage therapists, acupuncturists, relationship counselors, psychotherapists, and chiropractors outnumber the city's lawyers, which is both reassuring and disconcerting. People living in Santa

Fe tend to invest their time and money in the pursuit of therapeutic goals that are physically and psychically removed from mainstream America's. If some local person shows enough interest in you to strike up a conversation, it's crucial that you respond in a suitable manner. Under no circumstances should you ever discuss your job, or the stress associated with your job, or the glories of living in a lakefront condo. Instead, try, "The reason I'm here is that I'm looking to clear my mind/reorganize my life/find a spiritual path, and my therapist advised me to find a peaceful, healing place to do that hard, personal work. Santa Fe just seemed like the right place to start my quest for fulfillment."

Why don't Santa Fe drivers use their turn signals?... One sure way to get yourself cut off and dissed by our local drivers is to commit the faux pas of using your turn signal. Almost nobody here gives a tinker's damn about signaling where and when they may or may not want to turn off a road. Why would they ever care to let anyone else driving on the road know what they're up to? Even the city's cops share this phobia about tipping their hand to oncoming drivers, so don't expect local folks to suddenly shape up and start behaving like they lived in Spokane or something.

How will Santa Fe's altitude affect me?... It makes you get drunk a lot quicker, which can save you big bucks when dining at the Coyote Cafe. Seriously, alcohol consumed here has a stronger kick for visitors who live most of their lives at sea level, or even in relatively low-altitude places like Denver (mile-high wimps). Combined with the incredibly low humidity in this corner of the water-starved Southwest, the direct sunshine will give your skin a beating—bring plenty of lotion and lip balm for moisturizing your kisser and the inside passages of your nose (I know it sounds gross, but it works). Wear sunblock and a hat, and yes, drink lots and lots of water, day and night.

Hispanic, Latino, Chicano—which is which?... Here in the Land of Enchantment the commonly used term "Hispanic" broadly means anyone whose ethnic origins are rooted in a Spanish-speaking country. "Latino" could serve the same purpose, and in many parts of Texas and Arizona that's indeed how most folks use it. But in New Mexico—a land that was colonized by European Spaniards—the term "Hispanic" refers more specifically to European heritage, while "Latino" refers to South or Central American heritage. Then there's "Chicano," which is broadly used in Texas, California, Arizona, and Colorado; in New Mexico, it's used only for people of Mexican descent. Got it all straight now?

Red or green?... New Mexico's largest agricultural crop is chile (misspelled in Texas as "chili"), and for hundreds of years local cooks have served thick, chile-based sauces alongside or atop all sorts of dishes. If you walk into a Santa Fe restaurant and order a dish such as enchiladas, the waitperson will automatically ask you, "Want that red or green?" "Red" refers to red chile, "green" to green chile. Everybody knows this language, so the sooner you learn it the better. Sometimes the red is hotter, sometimes the green is hotter...you'll just have to ask your waiter which is which. As a general rule, green chile goes with dishes featuring chicken or whole chiles, while red chile gets ladled over pork, beef, and tacos. Breakfast burritos can go either way, so if you can't make up your mind, just ask for "Christmas," and you'll get both.

What happened to "Santa Fe style"?... Howling coyotes and pastel-painted furniture have nearly disappeared from our shops and homes—and not a moment too soon. Long a running joke among local residents, the entire Santa Fe style movement of the late 1980s and early 1990s was a contrived rip-off of this region's authentic carved folk art and its primitive, Spanish colonial–hybrid home furnishings. For a taste of the real stuff at affordable prices, try looking for furniture at places like **El Paso Import Company** for Mexican primitive–style tables and chairs. If you have deeper pockets, there are many craftspeople—including **Collaborations**, **Dell Woodworks**, and **Southwest Spanish Craftsmen**—who hand carve elegant reproductions of Santa Fe's traditional pieces. (See Shopping.)

What's with Santa Fe's mayor?... Debbie Jaramillo, elected in 1994, is a Hispanic woman with outspoken views about nearly every hot-button topic in Santa Fe. A grassroots political activist, she defeated a pro-business candidate to take the city's top political job; her reputation is that of a woman who "speaks for the people." Most of the time, that puts her at odds with the real-estate developers, business boosters, and hotel builders who want to see Santa Fe become even more of a southwestern theme park than it already is. Her good deeds, which include shaking up the city's inbred police department and incompetent school administration, have required more guts than any of our political hacks has shown in the past.

Where does northern New Mexico end?... New Mexico is oriented toward its northern and southern points; the Rio Grande, which flows from north to south, is New Mexico's spine as well as its lifeblood. When you're standing in Santa Fe, you're in northern New Mexico. Albuquerque, the state's largest city, is an hour's drive south of Santa Fe, but most New Mexicans feel it's also part of northern New Mexico. All of this disgusts the residents of Taos, an hour's drive north of Santa Fe, which seems to the rest of us to be $1/3$ Native American, $1/3$ Hispanic, and $1/3$ part of Colorado. Taoseños feel theirs is the only place in the state that can truthfully claim to be northern New Mexico, and the rest of us are just deluded.

Now, if you really want to get confused about where northern New Mexico begins and ends, talk to someone in Las Cruces, the state's third-largest city, about a half hour's drive north of the U.S.–Mexico border. To them, anything on the other side of Elephant Butte Lake (about 40 miles north of 'Cruces) is "El Norte." But we in the rest of the state know that the folks in 'Cruces eat too much hot chile and most of their brains have turned into salsa.

What's the frequency, Kenneth?... Even though most of this parched state is oriented toward its north–south axis, the downtown area of The City Different is oriented on an east–west axis. Walking around downtown and on Canyon Road, you'll be ready to swear on a stack of bibles that you're going north here, south there, and maybe back north again a little later… you're 100 percent certain. Guess what? All you are is disoriented, just like we locals are 365 days a year! Some call this effect the "Santa Fe vortex," others call it "the place's energy." (I chalk it up to whatever made us destroy too many of our precious brain cells before we reached the age of 30.) So just go ahead and stumble around, feeling certain that east is north, north is west, and west is south. After all, nobody here gives a damn.

Why is this man trying to walk me to my car?...

Around here, it is standard practice to accompany women to their vehicles whenever locals have gathered at a bar for a few drinks or a party has broken, and for good reason. One of the unfortunate realities in the Southwest is that criminals and local bad guys of all ethnic backgrounds prey upon women. Purse-snatchings, rapes, sexual assaults, and harassment take place no matter the season, around Canyon Road, the downtown Plaza area, supermarket parking lots, hotel rooms, you name it. Women should not put themselves in a vulnerable position. Also, always remove valuables, suitcases, and fanny packs from your rental cars (or at least lock them in the trunk). Smash-and-grab vehicle thefts are as much a problem in Santa Fe as in any metropolitan area.

Doesn't anybody around here have a job?... It must

look to outsiders like we don't work too hard—like we're a bunch of superannuated slackers who lead lives of maximum inefficiency. Maybe that's on target. After all, if you could measure the "black sheep factor," Santa Fe would register an outrageously high number of residents who were once the outcasts of their families, schools, or social groups. You know, the overly sensitive/creative/shy types who stood on the sidelines while their faster-developing counterparts burned themselves out on careers, marriages, and mortgages by the time they reached 35. Most of the people living here are self-employed (and others are independently wealthy, which really helps in a town this expensive). Jobs in Santa Fe are scarce and low-paying, so many locals are either in creative professions (painters, screenwriters, jewelers, craftspeople, etc.) or have set themselves up as one-person consulting businesses for clients around the country. For those who work at regular jobs, it's a common practice to hold down several low-wage, part-time positions just to make a half-decent living.

And that's the way we like it. We came here to find peace of mind and creative inspiration, and to live somewhere where the stable, successful life of a creative professional is the rule, not the exception.

accomm

1

odations

Santa Fe is pretty
damn quiet at
night. Yeah, local
kids like to cruise
the Plaza for a
few hours in the
evening, and if

the New Mexico legislature is in session the streets near the Roundhouse (our bizarre-looking, round capitol) can be clogged with lobbyists, politicians, and citizen activists. For the most part though, downtown hotels and B&B inns are pretty peaceful places once the sun goes down. A restful night's sleep is no problem.

The same can't be said for Cerrillos Road, the city's main artery, which carries substantial traffic from 7am to 9pm and moderate traffic the rest of the time. If you choose to stay at one of the many hotels lining this commercial strip, be sure to ask for a room away from the main drag—otherwise, you're likely to be awakened at 1am by police sirens, 18-wheelers, or high school kids thumping down the road in muscle cars with stereos the size of refrigerators.

Around downtown Santa Fe there always seems to be a new hotel under construction, which I assume testifies to the city's enduring popularity. Recently, though, most of these new hotels have been rather unglamorous affairs geared to travelers on a $90 to $150 nightly budget, a fairly mid-range price for Santa Fe. The city's soaring number of bed-and-breakfast inns offer a better deal at this price level, often serving up the kind of handsome environments and luxurious amenities that seasoned travelers dream about—accommodations that would cost twice as much if you were to stay in a similarly stylish setting at one of the downtown area's plusher hotels. So for Santa Fe high style on the cheap, bed-and-breakfast inns are your answer. A few are better than others for matters such as privacy, location, and decor, so call ahead to any place you're considering to request a brochure.

Hotel-wise, the more stylish downtown places will cost anywhere from $125 to $350 per night in summer, which is our high season. Even the plainer hotels aren't much less expensive—they just have a lower top end. Like fancy hotels everywhere, the more expensive places will, in some cases, offer you so much charm and luxury that you may not feel like exerting yourself in Santa Fe's 7,000-foot altitude. That would be a shame, no matter how much you want a great poolside suntan. There's so much more to Santa Fe than the inside of a glossy hotel room.

Is There a Right Address?

There are two primary areas where you'll find overnight accommodations: downtown and along Cerrillos Road. With few exceptions (noted later in this chapter), the place to look for stylish lodgings within easy reach of Santa Fe's great restaurants and art galleries is in the downtown Plaza area. The hotels on downtown's fringe shuttle guests into the center of town in minivans; for the rest, all you'll need is a good pair of Reeboks. The street layout in Santa Fe's older neighborhoods has more in common with a series of donkey paths than with the logic-driven grid pattern common to most cities; winding, weaving, twisting, and circling dirt roads were what lent this place its initial dose of funky, unpredictable charm. The downtown area's hotels and B&B inns are mostly concentrated in this rendition of a city planner's worst nightmare. But that's a plus for visitors, because it places most of Santa Fe's attractions within a short walk from your rented room.

With all the charm of a Tucson commercial strip, the 5 miles of Cerrillos Road are widely thought of as the biggest eyesore north of El Paso. Lacking the '50s kitsch of Albuquerque's Central Avenue (good ol' Route 66) or any other redeeming qualities, Cerrillos Road is where folks looking to save a buck can find not only cheap places to sleep but also unpretentious, affordable restaurants, liquor stores with New Mexico's notorious drive-up windows, supermarkets, and shopping malls. Cruise Cerrillos and you'll find basic rack joints such as Motel 6, HoJo's, Quality Inn,

Roots, Hispanic style

Ten years before the Pilgrims ever set foot upon Plymouth Rock, a bunch of Spanish conquistadores, farmers, and bureaucrats set up shop in a place the local Native American people called the "dancing ground of the sun." That settlement grew up to be Santa Fe, a multicultural experiment in community living if there ever was one. In many ways it's still a relic of that colonial past. The sons and daughters of those paper-pushers from Spain, along with the sons and daughters of the Native American populace, stuck around trying to survive in this forsaken outpost, and after a few decades of bloody battles, they began to intermarry by the score—which is why a pure-blooded Spaniard would say that Santa Fe's Hispanics look more mestizo and Mexicano than European. But Santa Fe's Hispanic people remain proud of their Spanish roots, calling themselves Spaniards first, Hispanics a distant second. This is in contrast to the southern part of the state, where the Hispanics are mostly of Mexican descent (same goes for Texas, Arizona, and California). And our representation of Cubans and Puerto Ricans is miniscule—just try finding a decent Caribbean restaurant in this state and you'll see what I mean!

SANTA FE | ACCOMMODATIONS

Hampton Inn, LaQuinta, and all the others. Keep in mind that if you stay at one of these places, you'll definitely need a rental car, a fat taxi budget, or at least bus fare to get you in and out of downtown.

Of course, being a few minutes from Canyon Road and the Plaza isn't everyone's cup of tea (especially for repeat visitors), and several upscale hotels and B&B inns on the outskirts of town have done quite well by catering to other needs.

Winning the Reservations Game

Santa Fe is a tourism-dependent community, so a few variables inevitably come into play with respect to how hotels and B&B inns set their room rates. Every hotel in the downtown area raises its rates during the midsummer rush, and most hotels break down their rates according to expected demand at different times of the year. In other words, the same $90 room you rent for a ski vacation in February will cost you $200 if you want to visit in July and August during the Santa Fe Opera's season. Between those dates, the cost of this room rises or falls, depending on the demand indicated by past tourism patterns.

But things seldom go according to plan, here or elsewhere in the universe. Santa Fe's been known to have economic mini-slumps materialize out of nowhere, usually the result of economic trends in other parts of the nation. If you're able to hit one of these down periods at the time of your visit, you can save as much as 20 percent off the listed "rack rate" on a downtown hotel room. Of course, that doesn't work to your benefit if you've reserved and guaranteed payment for a room six months (or even one month) ahead of time. You've got to have the flexibility to grab a discount when it comes up. That usually means no more than three weeks' advance notice for booking a stay at a downtown hotel.

Discounting room rates is part of a strategy called "yield management," in which hoteliers knock down room rates in order to raise the hotel's percentage of occupancy to a desired level. Once that percentage has been reached, the hotel goes back to quoting rack rates, and no amount of sweet talk from you is going to change their minds. In Santa Fe, hotel managers generally use two different methods of yield management, depending on the time of year. In the off-season (generally November to April), they'll offer special rates to visitors who make their reservations early, thereby raising the hotel's occupancy level to that magic desired rate. During the summer, however, they'll be poker-faced about discounts, denying their very existence until panic starts to set in (usually a few weeks out from what looks like a slump in occupancy), when they'll suddenly start throwing discounts at anyone smart enough to ask for one. Moral of the story: reserve far ahead in winter, gamble with last-minute calls in summer.

And year-round, the only way to get a discount is to ask for it, straight out. Yes, you risk getting laughed at if the hotel is sitting pretty. But unless you ask for a discount, nobody taking reservations for the hotel is going to volunteer that there's one available. You have a better chance of getting a discount for a stay anytime Sunday through Wednesday, since weekends are usually fairly busy around here (especially during the ski season and summer).

Another way to get a discounted rate at a downtown hotel is to belong to an affinity travel group such as AARP or AAA that has discount policies with the national hotel chains. Don't expect to get these discounts at locally owned downtown hotels. Corporate rates are rare in Santa Fe; they are usually available only through the national chains. Bucket shops are practically nonexistent, owing to the city's small size and the absence of a commercial airport.

As for squeezing a discounted rate from one of the B&B inns, you won't generally find them offering even a seasonal discount. (B&Bs tend to maintain year-round rates, raising them every couple of years to adjust for inflation.) Instead, just try mentioning ruefully to the B&B owner or manager that the rate they've quoted seems a bit high for your budget. If that owner or manager is staring at a reservations sheet with some glaring gaps in occupancy, he or she will almost always drop their rates anywhere from 10 to 20 percent, depending on how hard up they are. As with hotels, midweek stays are when you'll most likely find B&B discounts. Don't expect any B&B discounts for affinity groups or corporate travelers, but if you plan on staying five days or more do ask for a discount, as most owners will sweeten the deal for longer stays (it saves them having to cast about to fill your room with other guests).

A Note on Santa Fe Style

The nationwide clamor over Santa Fe architecture and interior design has simmered down in the past few years, thank God. But most visitors still come here looking to surround themselves with whitewashed adobe walls, weather-beaten wood furniture, Mexican tile floors, and Navajo rugs. Our distinctive interior styles use thick, round wooden beams, called *vigas*, to hold up an adobe (or pseudo-adobe) structure's ceiling; between the vigas are thinner beams, called *latillas*, laid perpendicular to the vigas. The round hearths common to Santa Fe homes are called *kiva* fireplaces, named after the round kiva structures used by southwestern Native American tribes for religious ceremonies. Traditional adobe construction uses dried bricks made of compressed mud and straw, but because of new construction codes and the high cost, hardly anyone uses genuine adobe to build their adobe-style homes. Surprise—it's really just painted stucco!

The Lowdown

Most overrated... Okay, the award goes to the **Inn of the Anasazi** for one reason only: no views. Everything else here lives up to the hotel's high standards, but for my money, when I'm staying in a town known for spectacular hundred-mile vistas, I wanna see something from my room, dammit! All the cute twig shutters and gorgeous lighting are supposed to draw your eye to the plush interiors, but without any sort of a view it all means diddly, especially when it's the most expensive place around. The **Inn at Loretto** has the exact opposite problem—its beautiful exterior (it looks like Taos Pueblo on the outside) and mountain-view rooms are sabotaged by interior design schemes so cheesy you'll think you've been shanghaied to the Lubbock Hilton. **Hotel Santa Fe** gets dissed for its supposed suites, not much more than closet-sized jokes. They're crammed with undersized furniture, which is supposed to make the rooms look normal-sized (thanks guys, but it doesn't work). After a few days, your shins will be bruised from bumping into furniture and you'll feel like you've been running some sort of lab-rat maze. But the worst offender is **Camas de Santa Fe**, a B&B that took over a structure formerly used as a suite of medical offices and (get this) *didn't change the room sizes!* Who told these people that examination cubicles could do double-duty as rooms for people on vacation? When you walk into this place, you feel like you should pee into a specimen jar. If you've made the mistake of booking a room here, my best advice (after you get over the shock) is to run down Cerrillos Road to **El Rey Inn** and beg for mercy.

Adobe abundance... If the Santa Fe vacation of your dreams hinges on having an environment lifted straight from the pages of an interior design magazine, there's probably no better place than downtown's **La Posada de Santa Fe** and its pricy but stylish adobe cottages. Sprawled across six gorgeous green acres of lawns, gardens, and cottonwood groves, almost all of this hotel's quarters have authentic details like fireplaces, hand-carved doors, smooth adobe walls, handcrafted furniture, and much more. Also downtown—and much more urban in tone—the **Inn of the Anasazi**'s rooms are less spacious and more expensive than La Posada's adobe cottages, but do have a certain romantic, gold-plated adobe feeling. Check out the intricate masonry, which replicates the look of an ancient Indian cliff dwelling.

B&B inns are smartly tailoring themselves to fill anyone's adobe expectations, and in the downtown area nobody does it better than **Dos Casas Viejas**, a gated refuge owned by a prominent interior designer and her dentist husband. A stunning lap pool, private walled patios, kiva fireplaces, luxurious bedding and bath linens, Santa Fe furniture right out of a designer's showroom—it has upped the ante for everybody. More modest in price but chock-full of flair is the **Adobe Abode**, a converted traditional home in a quiet residential area. It lives up to the adobe part of its name a whole lot better since it recently added a new series of adobe rooms, decorated with a hip sense of fun in kitschy fantasy themes ranging from buckaroo to fiesta madness. Not too chic, not overdone. The friendly owner is a dedicated fan of Santa Fe's restaurant scene, which makes her inside tips worth paying attention to. **Water Street Inn** has its full quotient of adobe-style rooms, complete with viga ceilings, kiva fireplaces, antique furniture, air-conditioning, and a sun-splashed breakfast deck. An afternoon happy hour with New Mexico wines, large sundecks, and nearby restaurants make up for what Water Street Inn lacks in gardens and grounds. The Queen Anne–style **Preston House**, within walking distance of the Plaza, has a newer adobe outbuilding with a few stylish southwestern rooms and several very plain territorial-style rooms—be careful to ask for one of the more authentic southwestern rooms if you book here.

If you don't need to be so close to downtown, one of Santa Fe's most exquisite gems is the **Galisteo Inn** in the quiet community of Galisteo, a short drive south of town. Three-foot-thick adobe walls, viga ceilings, soaring cottonwood trees, shaded hammocks, a swimming pool, sauna, riding stables, and expanses of green lawn give this place maximum peace and quiet without sacrificing authenticity. Its prices are reasonable and there's even a great restaurant right on the premises.

Country charm... Lace curtains, European antiques, overstuffed furniture, and patterned wallpaper all set **Spencer House**, in downtown's residential area, apart from the rest of the city's B&B scene. Surrounded by a small, well-tended garden, and owned by one of the buyers for a chi-chi Santa Fe home furnishings store, Spencer House recently received an award from the city fathers for its restoration efforts. Some of the rooms have a showroom feel, which may or may not be conducive to making your own style of mess. **Grant Corner Inn** is a bit closer to the Plaza and more expensive; its rendition of country charm is more reminiscent of an inn on the coast of Maine, with creaky floors, brass beds, and both private and shared baths. In a league of its own is the older, Queen Anne–style main building of the **Preston House**, located on a quiet, dead-end street just a minute's walk from the Plaza. This turn-of-the-century former banker's home has an atmosphere unlike anyplace else in town, with stained-glass windows, fireplaces, oriental carpets, lacy curtains, porch swings, shaded gardens, and a resident cat who acts like he owns the place. It's hardly what you'd expect in a Santa Fe B&B, which is just what makes it a great getaway spot. A short walk from the Plaza in another direction brings you to the South Capitol neighborhood and the **Don Gaspar Compound**, a setting that could easily be in the Pacific Northwest or New England. Guests stay in a neatly restored pair of brick cottages with antique furniture, artworks, polished floors, and French doors—perfectly authentic Santa Fe Victorian, a style that mostly disappeared four decades ago, around the time adobe style became the city's preferred architectural theme. Owned by a Colorado couple whose other B&B property outside Durango has been written about in nearly every major design and gardening magazine, the Don Gaspar Compound has gardens that have to be seen, smelled, and walked around in to be believed—5-

foot lilies, 4-foot irises, sprinkling water fountains, roses, and all the rest.

Historic Santa Fe style... Back in the years when railroads had a strong hold on the Southwest's economy, anyone wanting to visit Santa Fe had exactly one hotel to choose from, **La Fonda** (which in Spanish means "The Inn"). Located in the heart of Santa Fe at what once was the terminus of the Santa Fe Trail, La Fonda has a massive, dark lobby that sends shivers up the spine of Wild West history buffs and romantics. Locals enjoy repeating stories about the different lunatics and drunken cowboys who have ridden their horses through the lobby, sauntering up to La Fonda's bar and ordering a round of drinks for both pony and pilot. Artists, presidents, outlaws, hookers, politicians, movie producers, and atomic-era spies have trod La Fonda's hallowed ground since the late 1500s. The present incarnation has enough art galleries, cocktail lounges, restaurants, and gift shops to keep even the most jaded tourist occupied for hours. If somehow you get bored, try checking out something I occasionally like showing to out-of-town guests: the hotel's guest book. I'm always surprised by the worldwide roster of people who stay at La Fonda, and the wonderful things they write about Santa Fe in the guest book's margins. Best of all, nobody will hassle you if you need to stop in and use the hotel lobby's restrooms. That's the kind of place La Fonda is (and the kind of place Santa Fe is, come to think of it).

Hotel St. Francis has witnessed life as everything from an overnight flophouse to a twilight haunt of senior citizens who rent rooms and never leave. All that's changed in the past few years, as a recent top-to-bottom renovation has given this downtown grande dame a new lease on life. The lobby's afternoon tea service, the bar's hopping nighttime crowd, and the restaurant's fabulous cuisine have turned Hotel St. Francis into one of Santa Fe's meeting places. The staff is friendly and well-meaning, and the lobby's concierge desk is one of the town's best places to pick up brochures, maps, and tidbits about what's going on. Its guest rooms are not especially known for great decor, but what the hell—they're convenient to everything in town.

A couple of downtown B&B inns—the Queen Anne–style **Preston House** and the adobe-style **Pueblo**

Bonito—are great places to sample the city's eclectic architectural past, when Victorians sat side-by-side against adobe homes and territorial mansions. Pueblo Bonito was once an apartment complex; comprised of several buildings with private entrances, it offers large rooms with southwestern decor, a big hot tub, and funky flair (but if you stay here be sure to request a room away from noisy Galisteo Street).

For modern pop history, down Cerrillos Road is the locally favored **El Rey Inn**. The architectural theme is authentic enough, but the real attraction (besides the bargain prices) is its 1940s, Route 66 feeling. You half expect Neal Cassidy to pull Ford up to the registration area and lay in for a few nights. A nicely tuned, well-run place to stretch out in, the El Rey Inn is well worth taking a look at, especially if you like living up to those cat's-eye Ray-Bans.

Economical Santa Fe style... History, adobe, country, pshht. If your idea of a great vacation includes not splurging for the equivalent of a pair of Guccis every time you lay your head on a pillow, take a look at downtown locales such as **Garrett's Desert Inn**, just two blocks from the Plaza, which runs only $84 a night in high season (the place even has a swimming pool and a first-rate French cafe serving pastries, quiches, and bouillabaisse). Don't expect a lot in the way of decorative flair, just a place to conserve your cash assets. Also downtown, **El Paradero** is a large adobe B&B that not too many years ago was a farmhouse on the edge of town. Today it's an eclectic collection of rooms with a surprising amount of style, either shared or private baths—and it's just a five-minute walk from the Plaza. Rooms rent for as little as $70 nightly during high season, and that's with breakfast included. On Cerrillos Road at the **Santa Fe Motel**, rooms with kitchenettes cost a comparatively paltry $85 in summer and a bit less during ski season. Down the road, **El Rey Inn** is a deservedly popular 1930s motor court that's been turned into a surprisingly sophisticated alternative to the pricier places downtown. The 86 rooms here range from Spanish colonial–style casitas with scads of local artworks to doubles that go for as little as $72 at the height of summer season. There's a pool, refreshing gardens, and guests from all over the globe; the neighboring Pantry restaurant serves one of Santa Fe's greatest breakfast burritos. For those on a super-tight budget there's always the **Silver Saddle Motel**, a Cerrillos Road joint so authentically funky that an avant-garde German documentary filmmaker decided it merited at least 60 minutes' worth of international silver-screen fame. Located next door to the Jackalope import mercado (see Shopping) and across the street from Little Anita's restaurant, the Silver Saddle Motel delivers lots of rough edges for as little as $50 nightly; some rooms have kitchenettes. Your fellow hotel guests will include loads of curious Germans who have fallen in love with the joint from the 1992 movie. A remodeled, sixties-style motel, the **Pecos Trail Inn**, is farther afield, a five-minute drive from the Plaza; it has somewhat stylish surroundings, as well as a pool and adjacent jogging trail. Prices run $79 nightly during summer season, while rooms with kitchenettes are $89.

Escape from Santa Fe style... Every now and again the crush of so-called style in this town makes me want to scream. That's when I know it's time to visit my wacko brother and sister-in-law in Spokane, or at least head out the door to Albuquerque for a meal at the Olympia Cafe, a world-class Greek diner. If I got spooked so severly I had to abandon the adobe-and-brick duplex I call home, I'd probably grab a room at one of the downtown chain hotels such as the **Picacho Plaza Hotel**, a Radisson operation that looks, both inside and out, as if it could be transplanted into any suburban environment. In summer, bizarrely enough, there are nightly performances by Maria Benitez, one of America's foremost flamenco dancers, and her diverse troupe of flamenco pros drawn from nightclubs in places like Buenos Aires and Barcelona. The **Residence Inn**, a midwestern-bland Marriott property just five minutes' drive southeast of the Plaza, is great for the reluctant traveler, or for those who absolutely must log in a few hundred frequent flyer miles each time they travel. On the other hand, if you want an upscale, sophisticated B&B antidote to Santa Fe style, take a look at the **Territorial Inn**'s 10 antique-filled rooms in what once was a two-story home. Not quite southwestern, not quite New England, and not quite frilly country inn, they're just a block and a half from the Plaza. Also downtown are the **Grant Corner Inn** with its New England–frilly decor, and the prosperously residential Queen Anne–style **Preston House**.

Location, location, location... **La Fonda** gets the top rating when it comes to Plaza-area hotels—it's right at the southeast corner of the Plaza. (Being the first hotel in town, it grabbed the prime spot right off the bat.) Every room has a view stretching somewhere across the downtown area's rooftops; the best look out onto the spires of the St. Francis Cathedral and the Sangre de Cristo Mountains. Its massive lobby is a real public gathering place, with even a candy shop at one end and a decent bar at the other; sign up here for river-rafting trips, day tours of Indian pueblos, or just meet the local characters who hang out in the lobby's leather chairs, waiting for the good old days to return. If you can't swing a reservation at La Fonda, the next best thing is **La Posada de Santa Fe** for its gracious, parklike setting of individual casitas clustered around the hotel's gardens, swimming pool, and terraces. This is also one of the quietest settings you'll find in the downtown area, a key consideration for those who like sleeping with their bedroom windows cracked open.

Worst locations... No contest here: the worst location for any Santa Fe hotel is Cerrillos Road, our ticky-tacky strip of schlock that looks transported straight from Spokane, or somewhere with even less charm (I shudder at the thought). **El Rey Inn**, the **Santa Fe Motel**, and just about every other place in town where you can sleep for a reasonable price falls into this category. Downtown, the **Inn on the Alameda** couldn't be in a worse spot—whatever bonehead designed this place apparently forgot that when you plop a hotel at one of the busiest intersections in town, you should face the hotel *away* from the street. Most of Inn on the Alameda's expensive rooms front right onto asphalt parking lots that connect to Alameda Street, where traffic backs up from 7am to 6pm, waiting to get through the light at Paseo de Peralta. Maybe long-distance truckers love this sort of arrangement, but for anyone on vacation it's a noisy nightmare. The **Eldorado Hotel** deserves a special mention for its horrific architecture and dumb-as-a-stump siting. This 219-room behemoth blocks off what used to be downtown's spectacular vistas of the distant Jemez Mountains with an ugly building that has more in common with contemporary prison design than it ever will with the spirit of Santa Fe. This is what happens when second-rate architects are told to maximize a tight piece of property's income potential and "…uhh, oh yeah, make it look like Santa Fe, kinda." Tiny swimming pool, too-huge bar, and the absence of a lobby make this place the design laughingstock of New Mexico. One more lousy decision on downtown location goes to the **Inn of the Anasazi**, a fine hotel built on downtown's worst lot. You can pay 300 bucks a night to sleep in a room with shutters permanently shielding you from the concrete walls on the opposite sides of dark passageways. It was sheer stupidity to put this great hotel on this awful piece of property—someone's arms and legs should be broken for screwing up on this decision.

Swanky inside… Bump into your favorite Hollywood movie stars and East Coast CEOs downtown at the **Inn of the Anasazi**, Santa Fe's most expensive, most obsequious, and most amenity-loaded pleasure palace. The moment you pull up in front of this southwestern-to-the-max hotel, you'll be surrounded by bellhops and parking valets, a sure sign that it's time to pull out those $5 bills you've stashed for tips and Tecates. The staff here is used to dealing with egos a mile wide and temper tantrums thrown by bossy out-of-towners. If you can successfully negotiate your way around such obnoxious fellow guests, the Inn of the Anasazi can be an extraordinary place to stay, with its treasure trove of locally created works of art, complex masonry intended to replicate the appearance of an ancient Indian cliff dwelling, heralded restaurant, and plush guest rooms. Cushy bathrobes, European shampoos, fireplaces, CD stereo systems, and pillows stuffed with the softest goose down are what you can expect to get here, all served up in an interior environment that's breathtaking. The only expense spared in building this downtown hotel was finding a decent plot of land, which means the Anasazi's guests have to do without mountain views or even windows overlooking the pedestrian action on Washington Avenue. **La Posada de Santa Fe** runs well below the Inn of the Anasazi when it comes to those service and amenity details worth paying big bucks for, yet it's still a great hotel at any price. The emphasis here is on handcrafted furnishings, tile floors, floor-to-ceiling drapes, skylights, and private patios, amenities that other hotels can only dream about offering. The bar in La Posada's historic Staab House restaurant is one of my favorite places to hang out on a cold winter night, with its Victorianesque wingback chairs, oriental rugs, and huge fireplaces, but not because of its drinks, which tend to be overpriced and weak.

A great way to find affordable rooms with beaucoup interior élan, 200-thread linens, and stylish furniture is to look at B&B inns such as **Dos Casas Viejas**, which is owned by a nationally prominent interior designer (expect hand-carved furniture in each room, hand-pressed sheets gracing its four-poster beds), as well as **Spencer House**, which is owned by a linen and home furnishings buyer who circles the globe for his commercial clients (expect French this, English that, Ralph Lauren the other). The newer **La Tienda Inn** has an interior design scheme blending fine black-and-white photography and exquisite lithographs with an uncluttered, yet thoroughly tasteful and stylish (read: expensive) selection of furnishings. It's all incorporated into several buildings—formerly a grocery store, private residence, and small apartments—at the edge of Santa Fe's historic barrio. La Tienda is affordable and is still one of the town's best-kept secrets, yet it's fast becoming a favorite with visiting artists as well as Hollywood types looking to stay off the main tourist track. Nearby, the **Water Street Inn** has much more of a southwestern flair to its interiors, with hand-carved furnishings and Mexican tiled baths, as well as sensuously curved adobe walls and kiva fireplaces. The big attraction for interior design fans is the Water Street Inn's extensive use of elegant Mexican textiles by the Xochi design house—tightly woven, intricately patterned fabrics used in nearly every square inch of the inn's bed coverings, pillowcases, drapery, and upholstery. Xochi fabrics are expensive, but worth it—you'll be tempted to touch and feel your way around these well-appointed interiors.

Garden paradises... Look around Santa Fe and you'll notice that the predominant color of the landscape in this water-hungry part of the nation is a bland, oft depressing, brown. City dwellers may think it all looks cute and different, but take my word for it: Those of us who live here know the color of dirt and blown dust when we see it. So splotches of green lawn, towering cottonwood trees with their shade-throwing canopies, stone fountains gurgling streams of water, and bountiful floral beds are roundly appreciated for breaking up the visual monotony of our adobe wonderland. Nearly every B&B inn and hotel in town has at least some semblance of a garden or lawn, usually along the lines of the tiny, tidy affairs we locally paid folks keep for our own peace of mind. But if it's verdant majesty you're looking for, there are a few worthy places to keep in mind. First and foremost is **Bishop's Lodge**, a sprawling resort just minutes outside of downtown Santa Fe, in a fold of the foothills of the Sangre de Cristo Mountains where natural springs and flowing streams provide fresh, snowmelt-fed running waters year-round. This is one of the only places in Santa Fe where you can be soothed by the sound of water cascading over rock-lined stream bottoms. Generations of gardeners have worked this land since it was an actual retreat for the Santa Fe bishops of the late 1800s, and they've turned it into a profusion of manicured lawns, eye-dazzling flower beds, shady trees, and rose gardens. In town, the adobe cottages of **La Posada de Santa Fe** spread over six landscaped acres of manicured lawns, flower borders filled with perennials and annuals, climbing roses atop lattice trellises, and dozens of large, terra-cotta pots filled with geraniums, all underneath an ancient canopy of cottonwood and pine trees.

The gardens surrounding **Don Gaspar Compound** are another, smaller oasis in this southern Rocky Mountain desert. Designed by an iris breeder who splits his time between gardening and tending to his B&B guests, this tiny paradise of wildly exotic, colorful, and fragrant flowers is laced with brick pathways leading to secluded resting spots with stone benches, Parisian cafe tables, and lawn chairs. Don Gaspar Compound is the type of place design magazines lust after, and it's not a bad place to work on the finer points of your own lust.

Luscious love nests... For years, Santa Fe locals have made the mountainside hot tubs and serene massage rooms of **10,000 Waves** one of their prime places for fast, readily accessible psychic getaways. An hour of pampering in this Japanese spa setting does wonders for your body and soul—and it's an incredibly scenic place to seduce somebody else's body and soul. I've always wondered what it would be like to never leave 10,000 Waves, and you now can do the next best thing: Luxuriate for a few days at one of the spa's new Houses of the Moon accommodations. Five minutes' drive from the Plaza and reasonably priced, these casitas and apartments come with discounted rates on any of 10,000 Waves' hot tubs or body treatments. The decor is a lovely blend of American mountain lodge and Japanese country home, with futon sofas, peeled-pine furniture, Japanese lanterns, natural cotton bedding, and European tiled baths. Farther away to Santa Fe's south is the **Galisteo Inn**, a historic hacienda in the quiet community of Galisteo, a 20-minute drive from Santa Fe's Plaza. Some of the nation's most famous artists own homes and ranches in the Galisteo area (the Inn itself pays a good deal of attention to the art on its walls), and if you stay a few nights at the Inn you'll get a taste of what the attraction of this area's all about. Massive adobe walls, wood floors that creak as you amble through the spacious interior—you really get the feeling of being off somewhere in the hinterlands of the rural Southwest. And the inn has a really superb restaurant, so you can just snuggle up and stay put if you want to. Much closer to the Plaza, **La Posada de Santa Fe** lays on privacy and self-contained comfort, both so important for capturing romantic moods. It combines adobe southwestern architecture in its casitas with a Victorian main building and restaurant. For the in-town B&B crowd there's perhaps no better spot for lighting your inner fires than the **Preston House**, an impeccably well preserved Queen Anne relic from the late 1800s. The rooms here look as if they could have been lifted straight from the pages of *Little Women*.

Great breakfasts, brunches, and teas... For some visitors, the day's first meal just isn't breakfast unless their plates are heaped with fried eggs, breakfast burritos, strips of bacon, and hash browns. The **Grant Corner Inn** has such great hearty breakfasts that it even attracts locals; its legendary summer Sunday brunch sprawls across the inn's classic veranda and out onto its front lawn, where string quartets serenade munching guests behind a white picket fence. To sneak a peek at how the city's political power-brokers operate, or just watch local businesspeople schmooze over their toast and jelly, make a breakfast reservation at **La Fonda**'s glass-ceilinged courtyard restaurant. The service isn't great and the food won't impress anyone, but this is where Santa Fe has, for decades, had its fate decided by the state's fat cats and backroom deal-makers. On Sundays the **Eldorado Hotel**'s lobby restaurant serves up an immense brunch buffet that always fools me into thinking I have the appetite of an NFL linebacker—I start piling my plate full of eggs benedict, sausage links, cinnamon rolls, and a slice of beef tenderloin. Pianist Eleanor Steinert, a grand-motherly type who can occasionally can be found party-ing on Santa Fe's Friday-afternoon gallery circuit, always works the keyboard at the El Dorado brunch. With sum-mer seating outdoors on a flagstone patio, the Sunday brunch at **La Posada** is a favored spot for romancing cou-ples, after-church families, and savvy visitors. The brunch covers everything from oysters to omelettes, depending on the time of year, and always starts off with a glass of champagne. **Bishop's Lodge** has a Sunday brunch service that's a tad on the expensive side but is nothing short of amazing in its selection of desserts, fresh seafood, and New Mexican dishes. Linger underneath the cotton-woods, reading the *New York Times* and sipping a cham-pagne morning glory.

For afternoon tea service, the **Hotel St. Francis** is the best place in town to see and be seen, although the newly arrived coffee boutiques and latte carts at the **Plaza Real** and the **Hilton of Santa Fe** are gaining ground(s) as well as loyal customers. Plaza Real's front-deck espresso stand is one of Santa Fe's best people-watching hangouts. One interesting B&B selection that afternoon teetotalers talk about is the kinda funky, kinda tiny, kinda eclectic **Castillo Inn**, a five-room downtown B&B owned by British ex-pat Jane Crawford, who bakes up a daily selec-tion of fresh scones and brews teas from Harrods. Even if you're not a guest at the inn you can take your beloved tea here just by calling ahead and making a reservation.

Taking care of business... A centralized downtown location is one big reason why the **Plaza Real**, a newer hotel, has lots of loyal clients, but then there's also its friendly staff and its vastly more favorable prices than those of the neighboring La Fonda and Inn of the

Anasazi. The tiny Plaza Real bar pours strong drinks for folks to unwind with, and in summer the sprawling patio on Washington Avenue is super for people-watching, especially when you've got a gin and tonic in hand. Closer to the state office building complexes, the **Inn of the Governors** is a longtime favorite of politicos and lobbyists, who keep its Mañana piano bar one of the city's hopping nightspots. Inn of the Governors has gorgeous territorial-style architecture, a small swimming pool, and lots of off-street parking to go with the room decor, which ranges from sublime southwestern to commercialized silliness. **Hotel Santa Fe** is a safe bet for business travelers, offering somewhat small suite accommodations with a bit of adobe flair. Half owned by the Picuris Pueblo (note the Pueblo-style architecture and lots of great art by Native Americans) and half-owned by a group of Santa Fe investors, Hotel Santa Fe has a great staff that makes up in competence for anything the hotel lacks in room size and decor. Among B&Bs, the best business traveler bets are the New Englandy **Grant Corner Inn**, for its cozy restaurant and central location (just don't book its third-story rooms, which are somewhat claustrophobic), and the **Dancing Ground of the Sun**, for suite-like rooms with kitchenettes—either sprawling casitas or southwestern-style rooms. Historic, territorial-style charm makes this small B&B a great find for downtown stays requiring a little elbow room.

Horse lovers' havens... In many parts of the Southwest, folks heading out for a few days or even weeks of vacation bring their horses along, usually trailering them in expensive rigs hooked to the backs of humongous pickups. Upon arriving at their destination, they saddle up for days of fantastic rides into remote wilderness areas, or maybe even use the steeds as sure-footed transportation into and out of prime hunting areas.

Several places around Santa Fe still cater to the western horsey set (which these days tends to be wealthy oilmen from Texas and Oklahoma, or wealthy farmers and ranchers from Colorado, Kansas, and southern New Mexico). For those of us who don't happen to own a few hundred thousand dollars' worth of Arabians, tack, trailers, and pastures, it's good to know that these resorts and inns not only have the stables and corrals needed to board their guests' traveling horses, but also have a few ponies of their own that you can rent by the hour for fabulous trail rides. Even if you don't know how to ride, there's always a wrangler or two on hand to accompany you on your trip, teaching you a few saddle-worthy tricks along the way.

Santa Fe's most prestigious resort for the horsey set is **Rancho Encantado**, a 168-acre guest ranch in the hills of Tesuque, just a 15-minute drive from Santa Fe's Plaza. Besides its expansive stables, which board horses year-round for both visitors and local residents, this hotel and casita complex has a large swimming pool, tennis courts, and lots of authentic cowboy/southwestern style. It's also a great place to stay if you hanker to socialize with the wealthy western types who return here year after year. The ranch has a restaurant and bar, which is a big plus when you're on the fringes of town. Another main stop for the Santa Fe–bound horse lover is **Bishop's Lodge**, which borders the Santa Fe National Forest. The stables here don't operate year-round, but they're geared to serve the resort's guests during the summer months, with miles of trails winding up into the Sangre de Cristo Mountains. If saddle sores start crimping your riding style, there's a great swimming pool and several tennis courts to keep you busy. Two other options for traveling horse people are a couple of B&B inns to the south of Santa Fe, the **Galisteo Inn** and small **Open Sky**. Both have adjoining, independently owned stables and boarding facilities, and each offers day rides for guests. Open Sky's rooms are a bit less stylish than those at the Galisteo Inn, but it's also less expensive; it's set on a broad, flat mesa where you get all the awe-inspiring, 50-mile views one expects from a place with a name like this.

Art lovers' havens... As you'd expect in an energetic arts community like Santa Fe, there's art everywhere. Not all of it is great art, but at least there's enough to accommodate everyone's tastes. One of my favorite experiences with art in hotels happens in **La Fonda**'s historic lobby, where an original Georgia O'Keeffe painting is cemented into the plaster wall right behind the front desk. But if it's great art in your room that you want, try staying at the **Inn of the Anasazi**, where hundreds of original works by some of the Southwest's top Native American, Hispanic, and Anglo artists are displayed throughout the public

SANTA FE | ACCOMMODATIONS

spaces and within its plush guest quarters. This place is so used to pampering guests, you can even request having the art in your room changed during your stay, just in case your eyes get tired of seeing the same thing two days in a row. Stroll through the lobbies and first-floor hallways of **La Posada** and the **Eldorado Hotel** to check out some great works of art by deceased and contemporary Santa Fe artists, but don't expect anything visually intriguing on the walls of their guest rooms. At least La Posada is tastefully decorated elsewhere; inside the Eldorado, things get too southwestern for most people's tastes, with lots of ready-made kitsch furniture and pastel colors. **La Tienda Inn** has a tastefully framed and artfully displayed collection of black-and-white photography as well as early-20th-century Gustave Baumann lithographs, adding an inspired tenor to this B&B's already gorgeous interiors.

Gym dandies... While plenty of Santa Fe hotels have their requisite workout rooms with an exercycle, stair machine, and universal gym, only the **Picacho Plaza Hotel** can lay straightfaced claim to being the best choice for hardbodies intent on keeping up their aerobic or bodybuilding regimens. Rooms here come with full use of the adjoining Santa Fe Spa, the city's best-equipped health club. The tiny pool at Santa Fe Spa is practically useless, however, and there are no tennis courts or outdoor track, so if it's lap swimming and racquet sports that keep you in shape check out the facilities at **Rancho Encantado**, the only authentically western-style guest ranch/hotel in the region, and the **Bishop's Lodge** resort, both of which cater to the pool and tennis set. The large, subtly southwestern rooms at Bishop's Lodge would make you swear you've time-warped back to Santa Fe in the 1950s. On the B&B scene, both the hacienda-like **Galisteo Inn** and the small but classy **Dos Casas Viejas** have lap pools, while Galisteo Inn's rural location also makes it a great place for runners looking to log a few miles on Galisteo's nearly deserted dirt roads.

Privacy lovers' havens... You want to get away from it all, you don't want any run-ins with your fellow guests, and you basically want anonymity. Take a look at the spread-out casitas at both **La Posada de Santa Fe**, for in-town stays amid manicured grounds, or at ranch-style

Rancho Encantado, if you don't mind a short drive into town. At Rancho Encantado you can practically park your rental car outside your front door, which means nobody's going to see you unless you want to be seen. Another in-town hotel that offers good, but not great, privacy is the **Inn on the Alameda**—it has lots of private entrances and some tiny courtyards, but you'll have to request a room not facing busy Alameda Street if you want nighttime peace and quiet. Fireplaces, rounded walls, tile floors, and all the region's interior design tricks make this a stylish, but over-priced, place for downtown stays. A better bet downtown would be the upscale B&B inn **Dos Casas Viejas**, tucked behind a gate on Agua Fria Street; the owners' huge collection of novels makes it an especially unforgettable vacation hideout. Or try endearingly funky **Pueblo Bonito**, where there are several private entrances (it used to be apartments), and a few rooms with fireplaces. For intro-spective getaways, the handful of individual casitas at the **10,000 Waves** spa make a zen-like retreat; also a ways out of town, **Galisteo Inn** offers rural peace in an adobe hacienda. The owners at any of these B&B inns will be happy to bring breakfast service to your room on a tray, provided you give them some advance warning.

There are also several places renting condominiums for nightly and extended stays. Their prices tend to be as high as the city's more expensive hotels, but you do get a lot in the way of southwestern style, space, and adobe-wall privacy. **Campanilla Compound** is a few blocks from the Plaza in one direction, while **Las Brisas** is a few blocks in the opposite direction. While Campanilla is just slightly pricier, they are much the same in decor, complete with kitchens and laundry rooms. The units at Las Brisas are located on a busier street, but it's in the classy South Capitol neighborhood, a great place for walks, bike rides, and frisbee throwing in a park.

Family values... What you folks need is a swimming pool and lots of space for those kiddies to run around and work off all that pent-up energy. What you don't need is rooms decorated with fragile antiques, snooty staff, or fellow guests who are hellbent on peace and quiet. Downtown chain hotels—the **Hilton of Santa Fe**, the Best Western affiliate **Inn at Loretto**, and the cheaper **Garrett's Desert Inn**, which isn't a chain but has all the requisite charm of one—all have pools, sturdy furnishings, and on-site restaurants where kids can splurge on burgers and fries. Unfortunately, none of them has open green space—for that, you'll have to venture out of the downtown area, to the family-oriented **Bishop's Lodge** or **Rancho Encantado**. Both of these resorts have horse trails and hiking trails as well as open lawns where kids can yell, run around, and act like their favorite superheroes. Both also have large swimming pools, with plenty of space for moms and dads who want to work on their suntans while keeping an eye on their splashing young ones.

For those who hate surprises... Downtown, the **Picacho Plaza Hotel**, a Radisson, tends to book busloads of package tourists. Its resolutely average room decor holds no surprises, for them or for you—but a nearby highway means you need to be careful about where the front desk staff wants you to sleep. Tour groups also herd in and out of downtown's other larger chain hotels, the **Inn at Loretto** and **Hilton of Santa Fe**, as well as the hulking 219-room **Eldorado Hotel**, which is what passes for a mega-hotel in Santa Fe. Only the Eldorado has the interior space to absorb the tour masses—it's a great place for librarians' conventions and weddings, which doesn't change the fact that the Eldorado should be knocked down and started over again. On Cerrillos Road, the **High Mesa Inn**, a reasonably priced Best Western operation, is usually packed with tour groups. If you call ahead, the front desk staff will tell you whether or not they're expecting a tour during the time you're considering a stay. This big hotel is next to a McDonald's and across the street from a Chevron station; if it's charm you want, go elsewhere.

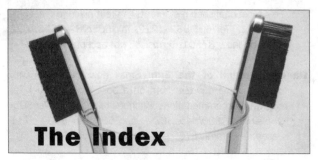

The Index

$$$$	over $160
$$$	$100–$160
$$	$75–$100
$	under $75

Prices reflect high–season rates for a double room.

Adobe Abode. Divided into two distinct environments, a traditional-style home and a newer adobe addition, Adobe Abode has the convenience and personable staff most B&B fans find important.... *Tel 505/983–3133, fax 505/986–0972. 202 Chapelle St., 87501. 6 rms. $$$*

Bishop's Lodge. Resort with riding trails, tennis courts, swimming pool, skeet-shooting range, hiking trails, and restaurants, on the landscaped grounds of an authentic old clerical residence. Convenient to the Plaza, the Santa Fe Opera, Shidoni Foundry, and the funky Tesuque Village Market.... *Tel 505/983–6377, 800/732–2240, fax 505/989–8739. Box 2367, 87504-2367, on Bishop's Lodge Road (3 mi from the Plaza). 88 rms. $$$$*

Camas de Santa Fe. Small rooms at too-high prices, but at least it's close to downtown. Make this your last resort.... *Tel 505/984–1337. 323 E. Palace Ave., 87501. 15 rms. AE, DC not accepted. $$*

Campanilla Compound. Live like a Santa Fe local (sorta) at one of these downtown condos, decorated and constructed in a typically southwestern motif. Great for longer stays as well as for folks who want lots of room for entertaining.... *Tel 505/988–7585, 800/828–9700. 334 Otero St., 87501. 14 units. $$$$*

Castillo Inn. Run by a engaging British gal, Castillo Inn is kitty-corner to the back door of Josie's, one of downtown Santa

Fe's most cherished restaurants. A great place to feel comfortable.... *Tel 505/982–1212, fax 505/982–7323. 622 Castillo Place, 87501. 5 rms. AE not accepted. $$*

Dancing Ground of the Sun. Small downtown B&B with casitas; some quarters front on a busy street, so ask for courtyard accommodations. Kitchens in casitas.... *Tel 505/986–9797, 800/645–5673, fax 505/986–8082. 711 Paseo de Peralta, 87501. 5 casitas, 2 rms. $$$$*

Don Gaspar Compound. A couple of renovated homes surrounded by phenomenal gardens, a short walk from the Plaza in the historic, tree-shaded South Capitol neighborhood.... *Tel 505/986–8664, fax 505/986–0696. 623 Don Gaspar Ave., 87501. 6 rms., 2 casitas. $$$*

Dos Casas Viejas. Thick adobe walls and linens chosen right from the pages of an interior designers' sourcebook make this the classiest B&B in Santa Fe's downtown area. A 10-minute walk from the Plaza, even closer to the great shopping around Santa Fe's Guadalupe Street district.... *Tel 505/983–1636. 610 Agua Fria St., 87501. 5 rms. AE not accepted. $$$$*

El Paradero. Unpretentious B&B—a convenient, basic place to stay in the Guadalupe district. Breakfast patio, comfortable common areas, and off-street parking.... *Tel 505/988–1177. 220 W. Manhattan Ave., 87501. 14 rms. AE not accepted. $*

El Rey Inn. A surprise for this commercial strip, this place is not just affordable, it's downright stylish. Swimming pool, lovely gardens, beaucoup southwestern style, and easy walks to some of Santa Fe's most authentic, locals-only restaurants.... *Tel 505/982–1931, fax 505/989–9249. 1862 Cerrillos Rd., 87501. 86 rms. $*

Eldorado Hotel. Downtown Santa Fe's biggest architectural nightmare, this monstrous hotel squats on a prime piece of real estate.... *Tel 505/988–4455, 800/955–4455, fax 505/995–4543. 309 W. San Francisco St., 87501. 219 rms. $$$$*

Galisteo Inn. Secluded, historic adobe hacienda has a lap pool, towering cottonwoods, and a fantastic restaurant serving regional and innovative contemporary dishes. Rural location in a Hispanic village 20 miles south of the Plaza.... *Tel 505/466–4000. HC 75, Box 4, Galisteo, NM 87540. 12 rms. $$*

Garrett's Desert Inn. Affordable and downtown, this fairly mundane motel has a pool and is an easy walk to the Plaza. The bonus here is a great French cafe.... *Tel 505/982–1851, 800/888–2145, fax 505/989–1647. 311 Old Santa Fe Trail, 87501. 82 rms. $$*

Grant Corner Inn. A block from the Plaza and surrounded by art galleries, this New Englandesque B&B has everything going for it: charm, location, great food.... *Tel 505/983–6678. 122 Grant Ave., 87501. 11 rms. $$$*

High Mesa Inn. A chain hotel with a pool and lots of generic-style rooms, the High Mesa Inn is a favorite of tour groups, RV types, and families with lots of kids.... *Tel 505/473–2800, 800/777–3347, fax 505/473–4905. 3347 Cerrillos Rd., 87501. 210 rms. $$*

Hilton of Santa Fe. This downtown hotel's best feature is its El Cañon tapas-and-wine bar. The rooms make a bow to regional decor, the restaurant is competent, the staff is well trained, the location is good, but the experience falls short of great.... *Tel 505/988–2811, 800/336–3676, fax 505/986–6439. 100 Sandoval St., 87501. 158 rms. $$$*

Hotel St. Francis. The stylish lobby and a popular bar adjoining a highly regarded restaurant make this downtown hotel a good choice for anyone who wants a lively setting.... *Tel 505/983–5700, 800/529–5700, fax 505/989–7690. 210 Don Gaspar Ave., 87501. 75 rms. $$$*

Hotel Santa Fe. Big, locally owned downtown hotel is co-owned and largely staffed by the Picuris Pueblo. Somewhat small suite rooms and no restaurant.... *Tel 505/982–1200, 800/825–9876, fax 505/984–2211. 1501 Paseo de Peralta, 87501. 158 rms. $$$*

Inn at Loretto. This downtown outpost of the Best Western chain has a great location to go along with its swimming pool and several art galleries. Don't expect much by the way of charm once you're in its rooms, though.... *Tel 505/988–*

*5531, 800/727–5531, fax 505/984–7988. 211 Old
Santa Fe Trail, 87501. 137 rms. $$$*

Inn of the Anasazi. This top-end downtown hotel excels in most
categories. The restaurant is one of the best in Santa Fe, the
staff is flawless, the art-loaded interior is a design dream,
the rooms are tasteful, and there are fireplaces every-
where.... *Tel 505/988–3030, 800/688–8100, fax 505/
988–3277. 113 Washington Ave., 87501. 59 rms. $$$$*

Inn of the Governors. A small pool, late-night piano bar,
uneven restaurant, and the omnipresence of busy Alameda
Street make this downtown hotel a gamble.... *Tel 505/982–
4333, 800/234–4534, fax 505/989–9149. 234 Don
Gaspar Ave., 87501. 100 rms. $$$*

Inn on the Alameda. Close to the entrance of Canyon Road,
this southwestern-style hotel is wedged into one of Santa
Fe's busier street corners. Jacuzzis, no restaurant.... *Tel
505/984–2121, 800/289–2122, fax 505/986–8325.
303 E. Alameda St., 87501. 66 rms. $$$*

La Fonda. The grande dame of Santa Fe hotels, La Fonda is
right on the downtown Plaza. There's a rooftop pool over the
parking garage, and a rooftop bar that's one of the city's
best places to watch summer sunsets.... *Tel 505/982–
5511, 800/523–5002, fax 505/988–2952. 100 E. San
Francisco St., 87501. 153 rms. $$$*

La Posada de Santa Fe. Downtown's most authentic, most
spacious, and best landscaped hotel, La Posada has a
great Victorian-era bar, weekend brunches on a tree-shaded patio, a pool, and gardens everywhere, all within a two-
minute walk of the Plaza.... *Tel 505/983–6351, 800/727–
5276, fax 505/982–6850. 330 E. Palace Ave., 87501.
119 rms. $$$*

La Tienda Inn. An old grocery store and a neighboring apart-
ment building have been turned into this sleek B&B. A few
minutes walk from the Plaza and close to many of the best
restaurants in Santa Fe.... *Tel 505/989–8259, 800/889–
7611. 445 W. San Francisco St., 87501. 7 rms. $$$*

Las Brisas. Time-share condos convenient to downtown.
Pullout sofas, laundry, and kitchens.... *Tel 505/982–*

5795, fax 505/982–7900. 624 Galisteo St., 87501. 11 units. $$$

Open Sky. Straddling the line between a ranch and a more traditional B&B, Open Sky is located south of Santa Fe with views stretching 50, 60, or more miles into the horizon. There's a horse stable down the road a bit, with rides and wranglers (guides) for a small fee. 15 miles from the Plaza.... *Tel 505/471–3475. Rte. 2, Box 918, 87505. 3 rms. $$*

Pecos Trail Inn. Motel with low prices, semi-low style, and a location a few miles off the Plaza; it has a popular southwestern restaurant and a sometimes-busy bar, as well as a pool and an adjacent jogging trail.... *Tel 505/982–1943. 2239 Old Pecos Trail, 87501. 16 rms. $*

Picacho Plaza Hotel. Great views, incredible workout facilities, and an unexceptional restaurant are this Radisson hotel's main drawing cards.... *Tel 505/982–5591, 800/333–3333, fax 505/988–2821. 750 N. St. Francis Dr., 87501. 135 rms. $$$*

Plaza Real. One of downtown's more affordable places, and certainly its friendliest hotel. No pool or restaurant, but does serve breakfast and has rooms with private entrances. Close to all the good restaurants.... *Tel 505/988–4900, 800/279–7325, fax 505/988–4900. 125 Washington Ave., 87501. 56 rms. $$$*

Preston House. Frilly Queen Anne–style B&B with a later southwestern addition, within a few minutes walk of the Plaza.... *Tel 505/982–3465. 106 Faithway St., 87501. 15 rms. $$*

Pueblo Bonito. Once a private home, then an apartment complex, now a great B&B, Pueblo Bonito has adobe style and a close-to-downtown location.... *Tel 505/984–8001. 138 W. Manhattan St., 87501. 20 rms. $$*

Rancho Encantado. Authentically western-style guest ranch/hotel, within a 15-minute drive of the Plaza. Pool, tennis, horseback riding, hiking, lots of land for roaming around, and a good restaurant.... *Tel 505/982–3537, 800/722–9339, fax 505/983-8269. Rte. 4, Box 57C, 87501. 88 rms. $$$*

Residence Inn. This Marriott hotel is a 10-minute drive south of the Plaza, has a pool, and offers room decor that would make your granny happy.... *Tel 505/988–7300, 800/331–3131, fax 505/988–3243. 1698 Galisteo St., 87501. 120 rms. $$$*

Santa Fe Motel. You'll never confuse this downtown motel with someplace fancy, but you won't pay an arm and a leg for it, either. Close to restaurants.... *Tel 505/982–1039, 800/999–1039. 510 Cerrillos Rd., 87501. 22 rms. $$*

Silver Saddle Motel. This funky Cerrillos Road spot fills up fast with an eclectic group of well-traveled bargain hunters. Proximity to several locals-only restaurants.... *Tel 505/471–7663. 2810 Cerrillos Rd., 87501. 26 rms. $*

Spencer House. With romantic rooms and design flair from top to bottom, this small B&B is close to downtown. Its co-owner is one of Santa Fe's most in-demand decorators.... *Tel 505/988–3024. 222 McKenzie St., 87501. 4 rms. $$*

10,000 Waves. Part of an extremely popular Japanese spa, these rooms and casitas are perfect places for quiet and isolation, yet are just a 10-minute drive from the Plaza. All rooms come with a 10% discount on the Waves' hot tubs and massages.... *Tel 505/982–9304. Box 10103, 87504. 5 rms. $$*

Territorial Inn. This downtown B&B has tremendous charm as well as a fantastic location. Hot tub.... *Tel 505/989–7737. 215 Washington Ave., 87501. 10 rms. $$*

Water Street Inn. Superbly decorated, this sun-filled B&B is a friendly and convenient downtown alternative to the hotel circuit.... *Tel 505/984–1193. 427 W. Water St., 87501. 8 rms. $$$*

Downtown Santa Fe Accommodations

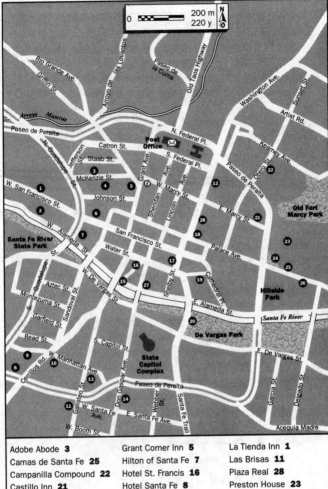

Adobe Abode **3**	Grant Corner Inn **5**	La Tienda Inn **1**
Camas de Santa Fe **25**	Hilton of Santa Fe **7**	Las Brisas **11**
Campanilla Compound **22**	Hotel St. Francis **16**	Plaza Real **28**
Castillo Inn **21**	Hotel Santa Fe **8**	Preston House **23**
Dancing Ground	Inn at Loretto **19**	Pueblo Bonito **13**
of the Sun **24**	Inn of the Anasazi **18**	Santa Fe Motel **9**
Don Gaspar	Inn of the Governors **27**	Spencer House **4**
Compound **14**	Inn on the Alameda **15**	Territorial Inn **12**
El Paradero **10**	La Fonda **17**	Water Street Inn **2**
Eldorado Hotel **6**	La Posada	
Garrett's Desert Inn **20**	de Santa Fe **26**	

42

Greater Santa Fe Accommodations

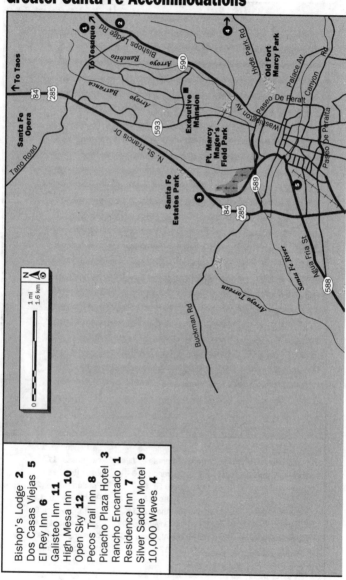

Bishop's Lodge **2**
Dos Casas Viejas **5**
El Rey Inn **6**
Galisteo Inn **11**
High Mesa Inn **10**
Open Sky **12**
Pecos Trail Inn **8**
Picacho Plaza Hotel **3**
Rancho Encantado **1**
Residence Inn **7**
Silver Saddle Motel **9**
10,000 Waves **4**

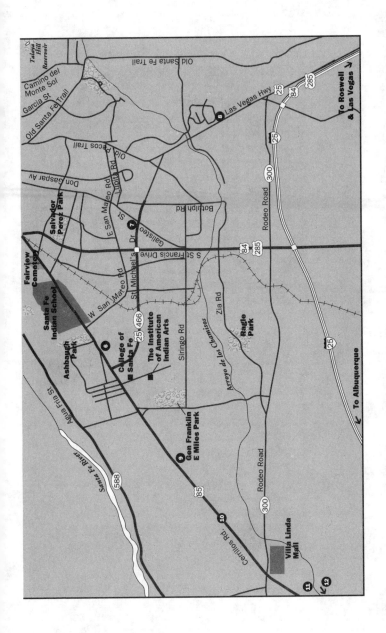

My old motto: I eat, therefore I exercise. My motto since moving to Santa Fe: I eat chiles rellenos, therefore

I exercise but... still gain weight.

Santa Fe's food rep is 100 percent truth. As a matter of fact, New Mexico's food rep is 100 percent truth. After working my jaws up one side of the Land of Enchantment and down the other, I can honestly say that when it comes to the broad culinary category most folks refer to as "Mexican food," there's nothing as good as the distinctly regional cooking of New Mexico.

Want some evidence? Let me take you on a mini-tour of my blue jeans collection: the size 32s over on the far left are what I wear when I'm eating lots of salads and skiing about three times a week. The size 34s in the middle are what I wear when I'm living on chips, salsa, an occasional plate of Maria's fajitas, and am running about three times a week. The 36s right in front are what I wear when I'm eating Dave's chiles rellenos, The Shed's enchiladas, Tiny's sopapillas, Tia Sophia's breakfast burritos... and am running six days a week and pulling about 20 minutes of sit-ups. The sweatpants over there... well, just forget it. After living here for seven years I stay away from Mexican, Tex-Mex, and southwestern restaurants whenever I travel (except when I eat my way through Mexico). I mean, why bother eating food that I can get cheaper and better at home? If you live in Philly, do you order a cheesesteak at Miami Subs? Of course not!

Local Tastes

Okay, I see you've got your fork in one hand and knife in the other, but first, let's do an introductory language lesson, because, as the nun who taught me algebra used to say, terminology is important. Tex-Mex food is the slop served at truck stops in west Texas. You know, the gooey, cheesy, sauce-laden crap, like the junk those national chain restaurants serve up when you are dumb enough to order nachos at a place named after an Irish poet. And you know "Mexican" as well... the hard-shell tacos served at happy-hour buffet tables, which you're supposed to fill with lettuce, cheese, and some soy product passed off as ground meat.

After you've had Tex-Mex and pseudo-Mexican, sitting down to an authentic northern New Mexico meal will make the hair stand straight up out of your head and your toenails curl up tighter than a periwinkle. It is, I assure you, like nothing you've ever tasted before. The regional cooking of this corner of the Southwest is much lighter, more aromatic, more straightforward, and much more sophisticated than what everyone else out there refers to as Mexican food. Yes, we do use cheese in our food—but not a lot of it, and that's an important difference. And we eat certain things that you don't find in those so-called Mexican restaurants, things like bowls of posole and baskets of sopapillas dripping with honey (gringos, see "What's a..." to learn what the hell these dishes taste like). In the morning we like our eggs and bacon and spuds all rolled up in a tortilla, and if you want to get the day off to a hot start you ladle some red chile sauce over that rolled tortilla and call the entire number a breakfast burrito. Let's face it, the world of Mexican foods isn't exactly kind to your waistline, but northern New Mexico's take on it isn't that bad for your arteries and thighs, at least.

But what about heat—the sort of self-induced nuclear implosion that happens after you whoosh a few forkfuls of spicy food down your gullet? Well, here's the good news: Our home-grown secret ingredient, the state's largest agricultural crop, is one of the best things ever to push its way out of this blessed planet's soil—the blissful, dreaded chile pepper. The chile peppers we grow here in New Mexico come in all sizes and all levels of spiciness, from cucumber-mild to intergalactic-rocket-fuel-hot. So if you don't want a hole burned in your tongue, just ask for mild

What's a...

Carne Adovada: chunks of roasted pork or beef marinated in a spicy red chile sauce. **Chile Relleno:** batter-fried green chile pepper stuffed with cheddar cheese and sometimes other ingredients such as chicken, goat cheese, or mushrooms. **Empanada:** fruit-filled, hand-sized pie that's been deep-fried. **Fajitas:** grilled chicken, pork, or beef with grilled vegetables such as peppers, onions, and tomatoes, meant to be eaten with flour tortillas. **Huevos Rancheros:** fried eggs, tortillas, refried beans, melted cheese, and red chile on top—a gut-buster of a breakfast. **Natillas:** vanilla custard (not to be confused with flan, which is a caramel custard). **Posole:** hominy stew made from the same stuff grits are made from, except in New Mexico we don't grind the hominy into a powder. **Quesadilla:** grilled flour tortillas stuffed with cheese and sometimes chicken or exotic ingredients like smoked duck. **Sopapilla:** side dish of fried bread in the shape of a small pillow, meant to be eaten with honey. **Tamale:** cornmeal stuffed with chicken/beef/pork/ anything else imaginable, wrapped in a corn husk and usually a paper outer wrapper. **Tostadas:** crisply fried corn tortillas with refried beans, melted cheese, and other fixings on top.

SANTA FE | DINING

chiles. Mind you, when somebody in New Mexico mentions the word "chile," what they're talking about is the pepper itself, and not a bowl of something with beans, ground beef, and chopped onion. That stuff's called and spelled "chili," and it's what you find served at ski lodges in the dead of winter, or at black-tie balls in the godawful suburbs of Dallas. If someone in New Mexico offers you a dish prepared with chile, or if they offer you a bowl of chile, what you'll get is chile peppers... either whole, chopped, or cooked into a sauce.

To be on the safe side, whenever I'm offered chile in a New Mexican restaurant, I always ask the waitperson if the chile's "really hot today." You'll get an honest assessment by someone who spends quite a bit of time dealing with this issue, so trust the reply. "Medium hot" to our New Mexican taste buds translates into three stars on a Szechwan menu's five-star rating scale. If it's hot chile, that's five stars, and if it's mild chile, that's one star or just a tiny bit hotter (but not a full two stars). Just to make things more difficult, the chile served in New Mexico's restaurants comes in two colors—red and green—and the red's not necessarily hotter than the green (see You Probably Didn't Know).

Chile primer

Don't make the mistake of assuming all chile is wickedly hot, 'cause the truth of the matter is that these types of peppers come in all shapes, sizes, and intensities. In late summer, gunnysacks of freshly picked chiles, red or green, are hauled northward from the massive chile fields outside of Hatch, New Mexico, and vendors set up chile roasters (they look like mesh oil drums) along roadside stands. It's a New Mexico tradition to buy and eat fresh-roasted chiles in dishes like green chile stew. Sometimes the red's hotter, sometimes the green's hotter...that's why it's important to ask. Me, I always pick the hotter one.

(The red peppers are what we use in chile ristras, those strings of several dozen chiles hanging from nearly every doorway and portal in the state.) Either the red or the green, or even both, may be found at any given restaurant. When ordering, ask which is hotter, then ask for either red or green chile sauce ladled atop your food, or request it on the side. Myself, I get a thrill from the yin and yang of ordering my food "Christmas"—red and green together.

Green-chile stew is another highlight on anybody's gourmet tour of the Southwest. It's served at just about every New Mexico–style restaurant, especially from the start of chile harvest season in September through the end of ski season in April. The most popular version of green-chile stew is served with shredded chicken, but a vegetable configuration with chunks of potatoes is a great alternative for non-carnivores. And as my Aunt Emma likes to say, forewarned is forearmed: It's best to ask the waiter about the hotness level of the green-chile stew before you even consider ordering it.

Chiles rellenos are, in my humble opinion, a gift from the gods. Long pods of green chiles grown in the ideal climate of New Mexico's Hatch Valley are stripped of their tough outer skin, cored and seeded, then filled with mild cheese such as longhorn, cheddar, or asadero. Rolled and breaded in corn-meal, then either grilled, deep fried, or pan fried, they're, they're… the best thing going if you've gotta wear clothes.

What to Wear

About the only time I give a second thought to which clothes I'm throwing on for lunch or dinner at a Santa Fe restaurant is when my hand reaches into my jungle of a closet and snags a white shirt. The scenario goes like this: "Hmmmm… those red chile stains are a bitch to pull off linen, so maybe tonight I'll wear something blue." Around here, half the population thinks of professional working attire as a torn pair of paint-splattered jeans you wear while banging around in the studio; suits and ties are mandatory only for funerals or weddings. Our regional style of dress is defined by one word: whatever.

When to Eat

Because Santa Fe's the capital of New Mexico, there are thousands of wage slaves hitting our streets at the middle of each day, looking for places to eat and nearby parking spaces. Lunchtime in Santa Fe's restaurants can be a great time for people-watching, with tourists, local politicians, artists, secretaries, and lawyers all crammed into the same grazing grounds. But to avoid this crunch, locals will try to arrive at their favorite lunch spots between 11:30 and noon, or they'll just wait until 1:30 and draw the entire affair out until the middle of the afternoon.

Outside of the hotels, not that many places serve break-fast, but the ones that do will take the affair seriously and serve from 7am until 10 or even 11am. The biggest obstacle course Santa Fe's going to throw in your way is dinner, especially if, like me, your idea of vacation dining involves sitting down for cocktails around 9pm and scraping that last morsel of dessert off your plate somewhere in the neighborhood of midnight. Here in Santa Fe we are, I'm afraid, still laboring under the legacy of being a town that rolls up its sidewalks well before the witching hour. Yeah, you can drink at many places right up until 2am, but when it comes to nighttime meals, Santa Fe likes seeing its chefs, waitstaff, and bussers get a good night's rest. With a few exceptions, 5pm is when things start, and restaurants in this town generally close at 10pm. (Cafe Oasis, Pranzos, and San Francisco Street Bar & Grill all stay open later—see below.) That doesn't mean you should expect to be seated and fawned over if you sashay through a restaurant's doors at 9:59pm. At most places you'll be expected to have your dessert ordered and check paid by 10. In the seven years I've lived here, there have been dozens of times when my 9:30 appearance at a Santa Fe restaurant has been greeted with an "I'm sorry, our kitchen's closed... we can serve you dessert and maybe some bread, if that's alright." If you prefer to dine late, the smartest thing is to call ahead and ask what time the restaurant seats its last table.

El Tipper-Ero

Service in Santa Fe restaurants can be abysmal... just absolutely a mess, even in a place that charges you $20 a plate for pasta. That's why I always tip 20 percent for great service, which is such a rarity around this town. (You practically fall down on your knees in praise whenever you're lucky enough to land a friendly, efficient, and knowledgeable waiter or waitress for your table.) For straightforward service that delivers the meal and drinks in a timely manner with just minor glitches, 15 percent is the norm. But I wouldn't hesitate to throw down 10 percent or even less for bad service.

The Lowdown

Best green-chile cheeseburgers... Green-chile cheeseburgers are such a part of New Mexico's fast-food culture that even Wendy's have them on its menu down here. But God forbid you'd ever drive down Cerrillos Road to go anywhere other than **Baja Taco** for a slab of ground beef, melted cheese, and green chile on a bun. This place is take-out and drive-through only, but there are a few concrete tables set up outside its front door. If you want to rub shoulders with some locals while standing in line and waiting for your burgers, get there between 5:30 and 6:30pm, when prices drop 25 percent for happy hour. The three top green-chile cheeseburger sit-down places in town are **Dave's Not Here**, **Bobcat Bite**, and **San Francisco Street Bar & Grill**. Dave's Not Here, a 15-minute walk from the Plaza in an older residential area, is a locals' hangout famous for its huge portions of burgers, rellenos, burritos, etc. The chile's hot, the tables are crowded together, the waitresses are fast, the prices are right, and the food's always great. Bobcat Bite, a 10-minute drive from the Plaza, is strictly a classic lunch spot, with counter stools, a few tables, and a flawless reputation for enormous, perfect burgers. Try the grilled cheese sandwich, the pork-chop platter, or the awesome grilled ham and cheese if it ain't your burger day. San Francisco Street Bar & Grill is right next to the Plaza, and is a fine alternative if you're staying downtown. It's the only one of the top three that's got a liquor license, a bar pouring a half-dozen or so microbrews, and lots of room (great for non-smokers). Their reuben sandwich is also great, along with some corkscrew fries and a Tecate. A good late-night choice, since it's open all the way to 11pm (that's way late for Santa Fe).

You'll get a respectable bang for your green-chile cheeseburger buck at **Tommy's Bar & Grill**, a downtown bar that's smart enough to make sure its food's as memorable as its drinks, while **Cowgirl Hall of Fame**, in the Guadalupe district, serves perfectly fine salads and burgers (skip its barbecue—anyone who knows from barbecue wouldn't eat that here). **Zia Diner**, also in the Guadalupe, a good place for homestyle meals, has a stellar green-chile meat loaf with enormous scoops of mashed potatoes, as well as pies that'll have you screaming for a side of vanilla ice cream. Or, if you're really in an artery-destroying mood, wolf down the chicken-fried steak and polish it off with an authentic, 1950s-style milkshake.

Real rellenos... Whenever I'm in a rellenos kind of mood, the first place I head for is **Dave's Not Here**. Their chiles rellenos are prepared so perfectly, the cook piles them in huge stacks atop the kitchen counter, awaiting the hordes of locals who appear promptly at 11:30am doin' their Pavlovian best to satisfy their innermost urges. Tied for first place at the top of my rellenos list is **Maria's New**

Mexican Kitchen, a decades-old Santa Fe institution that's hands-down the best northern New Mexico–style restaurant in town, maybe even the entire state. Maria's is a favorite with people who have eaten New Mexico's food all their lives and know great from simply good: It serves authentic, simple, flawlessly presented food, at prices so reasonable you'll think someone made the mistake of placing a 10-year-old menu on your table. When Santa Fe locals argue about which restaurant in town is best, Maria's always finishes in the money, whether it's for those awesome lemon-juice margaritas, or for the freshly made tortillas mixed and pressed by a Mexican woman right there in one corner of the restaurant's dining room. Besides Maria's erotically light rellenos, there are huge guacamole salads with a side of pico de gallo, the best damn fajitas north of Puerto Vallarta, burritos the size of fireplace logs, and on and on.

Best Frito pies... Frito pies aren't pies at all. I haven't the vaguest notion of why this local treat's called a pie—it was probably the idea of some fifth-grader who didn't know pie from pudding. But hey, don't let silly little details get in the way of enjoying northern New Mexico's meal-in-a-bag—hot red chile poured over a split-open bag of corn chips, sprinkled with shredded cheese and chopped onion. Just get yourself down to the Plaza, find **Woolworth's**, walk up to the lunch counter, and order one (small or large, it's your stomach's call, but the small's big enough for me). Sure, there are a few other places around Santa Fe serving Frito pies (**Dave's Not Here**, that funky neighborhood joint with the great green-chile burgers, comes immediately to mind), but for those of us living here, the best of all Frito pies in the known world are the ones spooned up at Woolworth's. Eat 'em while sitting across the street on one of the dozens of wrought-iron benches scattered around the Plaza.

Institutions... Tops on this list is one of the oldest restaurants in the Southwest: the **La Fonda** hotel's La Plazuela dining room (see Accommodations). Here you'll find everyone: families brunching after Sunday church services, high-school kids dressed in their prom-night best, sleazy politicians cutting up pieces of the local taxpayers' pie, blue-haired ladies who 50 years ago spent their wedding night at the hotel. The food's manageable and filling, but gourmet heaven the La Fonda ain't. Instead, sit somewhere where you can scope out the crowd, watch the sunshine filtering through the skylight play off the tile floors, enjoy the guitarist strumming away at dinner, and try to imagine how many meals have been served here since the days when Billy the Kid made his living as a local dishwasher (I swear, it's true!), or at least since the hotel's present incarnation opened its doors in the 1920s. On the grounds of what once was the best little whorehouse north of El Paso (a title now reserved for New Mexico's state capitol), **The Palace** is the downtown favorite hangout for (guess who) political hacks, lobbyists, and assorted hangers-on. Rich colors saturate each wall; the bad art's mounted in ornate, gilded frames; every piece of exposed wood's been varnished and stained until it resembles marble; and the waitstaff's been plying these same fertile tipping fields since LBJ was a Texas congressman. The food's about what you'd expect—chateaubriand, grilled salmon, lamb chops—all fine but unmemorable. Caesar salads are the house specialty, prepared tableside with a nice flourish (note the thousand stains from dressing dripped on the red carpets). **The Compound** has a rep for being the "fanciest" restaurant hereabouts; you'll detect a certain air of snobbery here—this is one place where you'll want to make an effort to dress up. Its adobe-walled setting right off Canyon Road is one of the prettiest in town, and in the kitchen, sauces are king, from Old-World cream and pepper to newer incarnations using wine and herbs. Not especially great food, and certainly not worth the price, but competent. Expect to be seated at a table next to an elderly couple on your left and, on your right, a party of four Japanese tourists who fell for a recommendation in an old Santa Fe guidebook.

The **Pink Adobe** has been around for 50 years, and as impossible as this sounds, it's still one of the hippest and most enjoyable places in town, drawing as much of a local crowd as it does tourists. Composed of two buildings (one's a bar, the other's for dining), the Pink serves fine steaks, gumbos, green-chile stew, and New Mexican dishes. The staff's informal and extremely competent, and I suspect the Pink's going to be around a lot longer than any of us. Even though it's been around for less than a decade, the **Coyote Cafe** has exerted so strong an influence on

Santa Fe's dining scene that it's got to be considered an institution. The restaurant's owner, Mark Miller, has opened Coyote clones in Las Vegas and Austin, and lately he's turned his attention to Washington, D.C., opening Red Sage and an Asian diner called Raku. The food at Coyote's uniformly great, and this is one place where the high prices are unquestionably worth it—from great cocktails and dozens of tequilas to the red chile onion rings surrounding the cowboy-cut rib steak.

The restaurant that wouldn't die... For years, **Josie's Casa de Comida** was one of the best northern New Mexico–style dining spots in town, if a bit eccentric— they made people line up outside the front door after scrawling their names on a who's-next blackboard. The prices, the blue corn enchiladas, the pies, the posole... all outstanding. When Josie tried calling it quits, her loyal fans blocked all the entrance ramps to I-25 and Josie was forced to dip her tootsies back into the Santa Fe restaurant scene by opening a catering-only operation in her old downtown location. Well, before long, she had those same food addicts lining up outside her back door, begging for food to go, which she happily prepared and sold out the door. And wouldn't you know but within a few months she'd been "convinced" to open up a small, corner room (with four tiny tables) so folks wouldn't have to eat in their cars! Today, it looks like the tiny room's all we're going to get, but if you want to taste the true cuisine of Santa Fe in a totally eclectic atmosphere, get yourself over to Josie's and beg to be let inside the back door... just tell them Tommy Macione sent you.

Historic surroundings... A century ago, Franciscan priests planted rows of fruit and fir trees on the hundreds of ranch acres known today as **Bishop's Lodge** (see Accommodations), a verdant, overgrown niche in the Sangre de Cristo foothills that's a true rarity in this parched part of the country. The structure that served as a summer residence for Archbishop Lamy has been renovated and expanded, and several new buildings have been scattered around the property, but Bishop's Lodge still evokes that bygone Santa Fe. The lodge's restaurant is best known for spectacular weekend brunches—everything from Maryland crab cakes to Norwegian lox to Chimayo chile, served on a lovely patio—mind-boggling affairs that lure you into eating far, far, more than you ever intended to, and sleeping it all off after a warm stroll in the sun. Guys need to wear jackets at dinner, which by local standards is a nice experience, even if the food here doesn't exactly knock your socks off. For historic settings, not much in town beats **Upper Crust Pizza**, a fairly respectable slice-and-a-brew joint added on to an ancient adobe structure that for years was promoted as "the oldest house in North America." That place has since turned into an ice-cream shop, but Upper Crust still does its hand-tossed pizza thing, putting a veggie/healthy spin on things with feta cheese, whole wheat crusts, and piles of green chile. It's right across an alleyway from the San Miguel Mission, which (oy vey, local legend again) is rumored to be the oldest church in the 50 states. **Santacafe** has the charming historic setting of a centuries-old adobe, and it does have one of the very best patio dining rooms in town—I'd gladly take a date there any night of the week. But somehow, Santacafe leaves me santacold. It's always rated as one of the very best restaurants in town, but I can't for the life of me figure out why. Don't get me wrong: Santacafe's wonderful in all ways, from its neo-Asian/nouveau-southwestern food to the uncluttered decor to the European stall johnnies. But its food is not what I consider over-the-rainbow great, and the staff's attitude can be a real pain in the ass. **On Water**, on the other hand, is one of Santa Fe's most under-appreciated dining experiences. Located in the St. Francis Hotel, a historic downtown landmark that not so long ago was a down-at-the-heels eyesore, On Water projects a balanced, unpretentious sense of its stylish self. When it first opened, its food tended toward the cutesy side of nouveau, but now it's hit its stride, with innovative ways of grilling meats and seafood. Don't miss having a drink in On Water's classy, wood-paneled bar, at least. I'm reluctant to recommend the Staab House dining room of the **La Posada de Santa Fe** hotel (see Accommodations) because its food is so unpredictable. Dining on the exquisite patio during a warm summer evening can be intoxicating, provided the kitchen isn't a disaster zone. But it's still a lovely place to order a chef's salad, a glass of pinot grigio, and fritter away a couple of summer hours. This 19th-century Victorian structure is one of the few places in Santa Fe with its own resident ghost, Mrs. Julia Staab (her room, 256, is upstairs), so maybe that explains why the restaurant seems to be fighting some sort of curse.

Is **El Farol** historic? Does Georgia O'Keeffe's ghost prowl the Plaza at night? The answer to both is a definite yes, and for decades some of Santa Fe's most notorious drunks, sleazebags, and other artists have made El Farol their hangout of choice (probably because it's within stumbling distance of their studios). This place has its own legend and lore—one of my faves is the tale about the naked woman who rode her horse inside here one sunny summer afternoon. This old adobe looks like it could fall down around you at any minute, especially when the dance floor is thronged on weekends with sweaty bodies, but the main attraction here is the food, which is wonderful, if a bit on the expensive side. El Farol serves Spanish tapas, elegantly prepared and unfailingly delicious, as well as Spanish wines and some standards. If you come on a night where there are flamenco guitarists playing in the bar, you'll swear you're in Montevideo or Salamanca.

Decor to die for... Owned by local art dealer Gerald Peters, **La Casa Sena** displays an eye-popping collection of paintings by some of the Southwest's most sought-after artists, deceased and living. Not only is this restaurant superbly decorated, but it's also got drop-dead architecture to match—from the fully tricked-out, authentic adobe dining rooms to the huge, tree-shaded patio with dozens of wrought-iron tables. And here's the kicker: The food—sophisticated, nouveau southwestern cuisine—is to die for. From the moment you're seated at one of La Casa Sena's serenely spotlit tables through the last crumb of dessert, you'll feel like you've been swept away to restaurant heaven. There's also an incredibly comprehensive wine list, quality linens, stemware and fresh flowers on each table, and a well-trained staff making on-target recommendations. Another place where the food's a surefire bet is the **Inn of the Anasazi** (see Accommodations), a pricy downtown hotel whose dining room is some sort of architectural blend of cowboy-saloon-meets-Indian-ruins… yet somehow it works in a magical way. There are a few paintings by contemporary Native American artists in the dining room and many more in the hotel's reception areas and hallways; everything from the individually painted tableware to the cushions on the dining room chairs ingeniously entertain your senses. The Anasazi's tabs aren't cheap, but its wine list is a wonderfully affordable surprise loaded with California cabernets and Northwest pinot noirs—and the food will leave you speechless. It's a must-do on any serious culinary itinerary of the Southwest.

Pranzo, a popular two-story northern Italian restaurant, exhibits lots of great art from the Munson Gallery as well as the work of a few individual local painters. Located in Sanbusco Center, within walking distance of downtown hotels, Pranzo is usually jammed for weekday lunches, though parking is hardly ever a problem. The pasta dishes are straightforward, the wine list has lots of good bargains, and the wood-burning pizza oven stays hot until 11pm, making this one of Santa Fe's few late-night alternatives. There's also contemporary art on the walls of **Paul's**, partly from the owner's private collection and partly on consignment. This quiet, superbly competent restaurant doesn't do a lot of advertising, yet has a solid word-of-mouth reputation. Its biggest shortcoming is its downtown location—just a block from the Plaza, yet somehow situated so that the surrounding stores overwhelm it. The dining area still has some of the personality of a retail store, which is what this space used to be, but that's cancelled out by the restaurant's affordable prices and great service. Paul's slant on food is equal parts southwestern, European, and nouvelle, and its classically trained owner/chef masterfully makes this complex mosaic of spices and flavors burst to life. At **Garduno's**, a downtown restaurant that some folks consider a bit too Tex-Mex for this region, the very large landscape paintings of Dale Terbush monopolize most of the wall space, which isn't surprising considering that he designed much of the place. My favorite meal here is lunch, when the kitchen stages a massive fajita bar/buffet. Don't forget to try the salsa—it's killer!

For locally made, affordable art, stop in for a cappuccino and a scone at the **Aztec Cafe**, a slackers' and artists' hangout that regularly mounts some of Santa Fe's most innovative group and one-artist exhibitions. The photography shows here are exceptionally good, but Aztec's crowd is so colorfully youthful you may have trouble doing anything but watching the parade. At **Cloud Cliff Bakery**, another favorite artist hangout, the art on the walls is always great, the affordable food is always good, the bread, baked on-site, is the best in the state, and the coffee's taken seriously. Owned by a German who believes as strongly in community involvement as he does in serving good food, Cloud Cliff is willing to mount exhibitions that commercial art galleries shy away from. The art rotated through here is so good that it even sells to local people; twice annually there are shows featuring contemporary metal artists, from sculptors to architectural metalsmiths. Cloud Cliff is one of the Santa Fe crowd's favorite breakfast spots on weekends—breakfast service here lasts for four hours, which is plenty of time to drag your sleepy butt over to Second Street for a cup of great java. The food's superb and cheap (don't forget to take home a loaf of what they call levain bread). **Natural Cafe**—one of Santa Fe's most popular vegetarian restaurants, though I (the fiery food lover) find the food underspiced—has a great selection of changing art exhibits on its walls, and it's an especially favored exhibition site for weavers and textile artists. The **Pink Adobe**, a longtime hangout for artists and other ne'er-do-wells, happens to be owned by a woman who is herself an accomplished painter, and every corner of the Pink's rabbit warren of interior dining rooms is loaded with her artwork. The food's great too—the gypsy stew is a local legend, and the apple pie with brandy sauce is irresistible.

For outdoor people-watching... Dining alongside one of the busier streets in any town seems like a bad choice, unless that street is Canyon Road (or Via Veneto) and the restaurant's **Geronimo**. Set in a historic adobe across from the Turner-Carroll Gallery, Geronimo attracts as many local loyalists as it does tourists, all of them enamored of its kitchen's masterful Southwest-meets-West-Coast cuisine. And now that Geronimo's stopped being so complicated in its ingredients and presentations, even my Aunt Dede can safely order from one end of its menu to the other. The front portal seats nearly 30 streetside diners, who can scope out the endless pedestrian action along Canyon Road. **Coyote Cantina**—attached by a second-floor stairway to its sister, the Coyote Cafe—is a great downtown alternative if you want to sit outside somewhere for beer and a quesadilla. The service can be spotty and the prices are on the high side, but one thing you don't have to worry about is the quality of the food. My favorite seat is one of the dozen or so wooden stools along the adobe wall that overlooks Water Street. You can flick fire ants onto unsuspecting passers-by on the street below, comment on the summer flesh show across the street, get a great buzz from Mexican brews, and have yourself a good ol' time. The downtown coffeehouse **Galisteo News** has a fabulous people-watching patio at the intersection of Galisteo and Water streets. If you're here during the warmer months of the year, make sure you don't leave town without stopping by the streetside vending cart known as **Roque's Carnitas**. Parked at the end of the portal of the Palace of the Governors at the intersection of Washington and Palace (kitty-corner to the Plaza), this place is so easy to find that even those numbskull, I-know-zip-about-Santa-Fe-but-I-think-I-can-fool-my-readers travel writers from the *New York Times* and *Travel & Leisure* have been able to "discover" it. The cart's operated by a friendly couple (he's Roque, she's Mona) who sell a taco-like carnita that's filled with grilled, marinated beef or chicken smothered in salsa, onions, and green chile. Grab a carnita and a soda, stroll over to the Plaza, find a park bench, and kick back and enjoy.

Al fresco... **On Water** has a small but memorable patio behind tall adobe walls, just a few inches removed from the nearby downtown street. Overgrown with vines, trees, and potted plants of all sizes and colors, this is one of Santa Fe's best places to seduce the love of your life, provided the weather's right. The innovative American food is usually satisfying, too. If my folks were in town I'd make plans to splurge on lunch or dinner at **La Casa Sena**, downtown in Sena Plaza. Sitting outside on the flagstone patio, shaded by ancient trees, listening to the gurgling fountain splashing water over its three tiers... they'd love it. Then there's the back patio at the **Corn Dance Cafe**—one of Santa Fe's most exquisite outdoor dining spots, with rickety ramadas, wobbly tables, a splashing fountain, even an occasional neighborhood cat slinking through the coyote fence. This pleasant adobe restaurant is run by an elegant Indian woman from Oklahoma, who has earned it a regional reputation for contemporary interpretations of the traditional foods of Native American tribes from New York to Alaska. As much as possible, Corn Dance deals with Native American suppliers for the buffalo, shrimp, free-range chicken, and trout that are staples on its menu, which means things might not be available if they didn't get delivered on time.

Open-air casual... One of the largest outdoor patios in Santa Fe is behind the **Cafe Oasis**, a fun and funky throwback to flower-power days. This sprawling, Christmas-lit patio is the backyard of a former private home remodeled into a series of quirky, personality-plus dining environments (ask for the Mystic Room and you'll dine sitting on pillows with your food on a low table). The menu covers chicken, seafood, and vegetarian dishes, the servers are young and hippie-ish, the smoker's room is absolutely bizarre—and the Oasis is open from early morning 'til 11pm. On Canyon Road, **Celebrations** is a seductive spot that works, of all things, a Cajun interpretation into the cuisine of the Southwest. One tiny patio is sheltered from the street by a rickety old coyote fence; another covered patio with an outdoor fireplace is an absolute gem of a spot to enjoy a bowl of chile gumbo and a tall glass of iced tea. Service here is always fast and well-informed, but because Celebrations is the only low-priced restaurant on Canyon Road, be ready to wait in line if you arrive at lunch hour. **Cowgirl Hall of Fame** in the Guadalupe district won't win any awards for its food, but the drinks are strong enough and the beer's cold enough to keep its large patio lively and wildly popular during the warmer months. When homesick Texans get a hankerin' for a corn dog (you know, like the stuff you get at county fairs) and a Lone Star, Cowgirl's will fix you right up... and if you're just drinkin' nobody's gonna mind. It has enough bathrooms to make you forget where you're going, and a whole lot of good-looking waitresses.

Il Vicino, a cosmopolitan-style pizza joint with wood-burning ovens, serves outdoors on a brick patio—a great place to dine unless there's a wind-tunnel effect off the backside of the adjacent Eldorado Hotel. In that case, stay indoors and enjoy Il Vicino's stylish, spotless decor. Il Vicino brews its own microsuds at its Albuquerque location, and ships them fresh and cold to us here; it also has a good wine selection. **India Palace**, which is downtown at the edge of a parking lot, has a sort of improvised patio environment, but its delicious food from the Subcontinent is served by the nicest, most well-meaning waitstaff in town. **Carlos' Gospel Cafe** is downtown in a dumb location, but somehow I find my way down to its unshaded brick patio several times each summer, which shows how much I enjoy Carlos' egg-salad sandwiches on thick-sliced whole wheat bread, and his famous hangover stew. **Old Santa Fe Trail Books & Coffeehouse**, a book-lined hangout in what once was a private home, has a great patio divided into a wind-shielded area and another section that's open to all nature's elements. The food here tends toward superb salads and sandwiches, and the cappuccino machine makes first-rate stuff. **Fox's Bar & Grill** may sound like a topless joint, but it's really a sports bar on the second floor of an office building. Its outdoor patio is one of Santa Fe's best places to watch summer sunsets—especially if your idea of heaven includes a cold brew, a humongous burger, onion rings, and a blazing magenta sky.

For committed carnivores... With its red banquettes straight out of the Kansas City airport lounge designer's guidebook, the **Bull Ring** falls short on steak-house ambiance, though local movers and shakers gravitate here anyway. The waitstaff looks perpetually bored, and the food's just not that great. Still, that doesn't stop them from charging some of the higher prices in town. If its a great cut of meat you're lusting after, try **Tiny's**, where the atmosphere's friendlier and the quality of the food exceeds the expectations you'll have from its low prices. The steaks are some of the best in town, the waitresses smile a whole lot, and everything on the menu's as unpretentious as it is succulent. Strictly for locals-in-the-know, Tiny's is far enough away from the Plaza that you won't run into tourists, yet close enough to downtown and the state office buildings that it consistently draws large crowds of regulars.

Mexican like in Mexico... If you've ever been to Mexico then you're probably familiar with the magical way Mexican restaurants serve dishes we consider to be "Mexican food"—there's something about the lingering taste of freshly squeezed lime juice over a plate of grilled shrimp or the elegant way squash blossoms are folded into a banana leaf tamale. Well, here in Santa Fe we're lucky to have a neighborhood Mexican restaurant, **Felipe's Tacos**, where the food is just as unpretentious, affordable, and luscious as anything south of the Rio Grande. From the moment you walk into Felipe's and catch the sounds of Mexican musicians blaring on the radio, you'll know you're someplace unexpectedly different. Mexican sodas are in the cooler, *menudo* (tripe) is served on Saturdays, families who have moved to El Norte for job opportunities file in throughout the day, and there's one of the best serve-yourself salsa bars I've ever tasted my way through, with real, freshly made salsas. If that's not enough, there's fresh guacamole served with every dish and the place is spotlessly clean. On Cerrillos Road, the **Old Mexico Grill** does a not-bad job with Mexican classics—they have a fine touch with seafood, as well as an appreciation for grilled, marinated meats. The large bar serves many, many cervezas and a host of tequilas, too. One of the stranger locations for a great, affordable restaurant is in the storage yards of the wacky Jackalope store (see Shopping), but that's exactly where you'll find an authentic version of a south-of-the-border taco stand: **Jackalope Cafe**, a wonderful outdoor patio shaded by tall cottonwoods that's a fine place to grab a casual bite to eat and a Mexican beer in summer.

Cheap eats... Attached to a seedy Texaco station at the lower end of Cerrillos Road, **Horseman's Haven** doesn't look like much from outside—if it weren't for the horde of pickups and Harleys invariably parked outside the front door, you'd probably never give the place a second look. But once you're inside it's a haven, all right... a haven of huge portions of great food at incredibly low prices. A gigantic burger basket with fries just cracks the $4 level, the ice tea's served in a humongous plastic tumbler, the enchiladas are first-rate, and the kitchen's run by a mom-and-pop couple who keep the place immaculate and friendly. **Tortilla Flats** is a Cerrillos Road restaurant with an outstanding local reputation for northern New Mexico–style dishes. Everything from the bowls of green-chile stew to the sopapillas served alongside entrees are done right, by anyone's standards. If you're smack in the middle of downtown, there's always **The Shed**, a Santa Fe institution with years of rock-solid reputation for great northern New Mexican food at great prices; it's located inside the historic hacienda-cum-shopping-center Sena Plaza. The red chile enchiladas with blue corn tortillas are flawless, the desserts are impossible to resist, and if you can wrangle a table on the patio, do it and enjoy a step back in time. It's frequently crammed with tourists—show up early if you don't want to wait in line for a table. If the line's too long, slip around the corner to the **Burrito Company**, which isn't nearly as good but is much larger and faster, and does serve a reasonable version of local cuisine.

If you've got some lingering concerns about the amounts of salt, chemical additives, and cholesterol you're pouring into your system, get thyself over to **Healthy Dave's Cafe**, an organic, vegetarian cafe inside the hulking belly of the Design Center on upper Cerrillos Road. This is the home of incredibly luscious nutburgers, heaping mounds of fresh hummus, perfect salads, and fresh fruit liquados…and it's casual, friendly, and unpretentious to boot. Eating Japanese in Santa Fe need not cost you an arm and a leg, if you search out the bargain-basement sushi in the fresh-food cases at **Wild Oats** and **Alfalfa's**, our pair of chic yet wonderful natural food markets. Each restaurant contracts with local sushi chefs who set up station from mid-morning through late afternoon, slicing, rolling, stuffing, and placing in plastic jewel boxes the freshest of sushi, with an emphasis on vegetarian innovations. Grab yourself a $4 to $6 assortment, a pair of chopsticks (they're free), a bottle of ginger ale, and head for the outdoor picnic tables at either market.

Good deals for full meals… Downtown, **Whistling Moon Cafe** has a contemporary Middle Eastern menu and an unpretentious manner, though it serves such perfectly prepared dishes, it has every right to act snobby. The waitstaff's snappy, experienced, and sassy; the tables are close but not crowded; wines are well-selected but not sky-high. Also downtown, **Poulet Patate** reaches for a weekend-in-Provence feeling with herbed rotisserie chickens and *vins ordinaire*. Okay, the atmosphere is a tad on the *très cher* side, and I've heard more than one of my pals mutter sideways about the small portions of everything but the chicken—but ooh la la, what chicken! Great house wine, too. When it comes to great food in a strange atmosphere, nobody in town takes the cake (make that tiramisu) like **Pastability**, one of the best restaurants in town and one of the best bargains anywhere. In true trattoria fashion, you've got to sit outside the restaurant, but instead of being on a sidewalk with a view of, say, the Grand Canal, you'll be on the painted floor inside the cavernous Design Center, a former car showroom turned into a commercial mall. No matter, just order a bottle of barbera, a bowl of rigatoni, and use your imagination. Owned by a bona fide Florentine who spent the better part of his youth as a cruise-boat chef, it serves truly first-rate Tuscan food. Italian wines (good ones) cost less than $20 a bottle, the pastas are all in the $6 to $8 range, and the sauces are perfection.

Overrated... Having been raised in a family that owned and operated French restaurants, I'm always delighted to try bistro fare as well as the more glorified renditions of French cuisine. Disappointment, however, awaited me at **Encore Provence**, an overpriced and overwrought French restaurant snuggled inside a historic former home, one of the prettiest settings in town. Everything here seems to fall short—small portions, timid seasoning, fussy presentation, and an attitude that's so damn Parisian it made me want to scream. Unless you're stopping by to pick up a dozen of its excellent bagels for your weekend brunch guests, **Bagelmania** is another place that's best avoided at mealtime. The place tries too hard to be what it can't be: a true-to-life New York deli with food just like your Jewish grandma used to make. I mean, a whole lot of us have lived in New York at one point or another in our lives (myself and half the rest of Santa Fe, it seems), so we know the difference between latkes and pastrami, and Bagelmania just doesn't cut the deli mustard—you'd be better off trying some of the great delis in Albuquerque. I'll never understand why local hotel concierges keep recommending the **Grant Corner Inn** (see Accommodations) to folks who want to dig into their eggs and hash browns right at the stroke of noon. I've had several meals here, and all of them have been unsatisfactory, from the moment I've sat down at a less-than-clean table to the minute I see my eggs sitting in a puddle of warm water to the second an overeager waitperson slides the check underneath my elbow. If the Grant Corner Inn cared as much about the food it serves as it does about the gardens surrounding the inn, I'd be happy to give it another try. My dining experiences have also been less than satisfactory at **El Nido**, a Tesuque hangout that primarily draws its crowd from nearby second-homeowners too lazy to drive five more minutes into Santa Fe, and from the summertime pre-opera audience. This place needs to stop trying to pass itself off as a seafood joint, or else the owners need to take a trip to Seattle to find out what the hell they're up against (you don't become "known" for seafood just by having five kinds of frozen fish on the menu). The menu lacks any sense of inventiveness, the service is impersonal and barely competent, and the food just doesn't justify the prices El Nido charges.

I'm sorry to say it, but the **Bull Ring** is more of a pretender than it is a true steak house. Sure, the joint's bar oozes with testosterone-inspired decor, and there are a few wonderful paintings hung on the walls of its two brightly lit dining rooms. But this place is just too damn prettified to take seriously as a steak house. It's a shame the Bull Ring didn't stay in its more personable former location on Old Santa Fe Trail. On two of the three times I've eaten here I've been tempted to send back my steaks for the unforgivable sins of being too fatty and gristly. The salads are great, the bread stinks, and the butter comes to your table hard as a rock. At **Julian's**, the prices are so high you may wonder if somehow you're being charged for a course or two you never received. Everything at this northern Italian restaurant is calculated to offend nobody... but if you ask me that's a hell of a dumb way to run a restaurant. One of the most confusing places in town is **La Tertulia**, located within easy walking distance of the Plaza in the gorgeous confines of a former convent, but perpetually plagued with uneven food and idiotic service. On some nights, this northern New Mexico restaurant can be magical; on other nights everything seems amiss from the very get-go—you'll wonder if some crazy nun locked in the basement has been allowed to take control of the kitchen....

Authentic northern New Mexican, top flight... If you love oysters, visit Apalachicola. If a muffuletta's your thing, New Orleans is the place to be. But if red chile, enchiladas, sopapillas, green-chile stew, and chiles rellenos are what you need to survive, has Santa Fe got some restaurants for you. And the really good news is that the best of them are incredibly cheap. Deciding which restaurant serves the best local foods could drive you nuts, but

I'll give the award to **Maria's New Mexican Kitchen**, a former roadhouse that used to be known as the place where prison guards ate—until the state penitentiary was moved 15 miles south of town. The walls of Maria's gorgeous and slightly funky cantina have murals by Alfred Morang, a well-known artist who, during his lifetime, was said to have loved scotch as much as he did painting. A five-stool bar and 10 dining tables are crammed up against the cantina's storied adobe walls; the restaurant's much bigger, with two other dining areas as well as a woman making fresh tortillas in a glassed-in booth off to the side. Maria's margaritas are second to none (I know, I know... so shoot me, for chrissake), and the owner puts together an extraordinarily affordable and wonderfully eclectic wine list that would be right at home in the most expensive of restaurants. And Maria's food, from one end of the menu to the other, is fabulous. If Maria's didn't have such great ambiance and dynamite margaritas, I'd have given top spot to **Tomasita's**, in the Guadalupe district adjacent to the old train depot. Legions of loyal followers line up for up to an hour on weekend nights, waiting for a seat in the noisy dining room. Tomasita's has the best salsa, the best green-chile stew, the best green-chile chicken enchiladas, and the fastest service in town. Waiters here know how to run and hustle, so the key to enjoying yourself here is to let your server know early on that you're here to relax, not to have your table turned over inside of 60 minutes. I have to rate **Cafe Pasqual's** right up there at the top of my list as well. The food's always great, in giganto portions, and the atmosphere makes me feel as if I'm sitting in some funky joint in the older part of Puerto Vallarta. The owner of Pasqual's has written her own cookbook divulging her secrets about blending northern New Mexico–style cooking with the classic traditions of Oaxaca. If only the prices weren't so high, Pasqual's would probably attract more locals than it does tourists... but the place is almost always thronged, so what's the difference?

Authentic northern New Mexican, runners-up...
Diego's Cafe, set in a shopping center, isn't going to win any awards for its ambiance, but it is within walking distance of the Plaza and its food and prices continue to attract hordes of locals. It's owned by a local family of

restaurateurs, and their experience shows in the smooth way things run here. Towering plates of nachos and awesome green-chile chicken enchiladas are sure winners. My only gripe with Diego's is that it's so busy, the staff often falls behind in keeping the floors and tables clean. **Cordelia's** is one of the best-kept secrets in town, but I have friends living at nearby pueblos who make a point of eating here whenever they make the drive into Santa Fe. The problem with Cordelia's is that it closes before 9pm most nights, and more than a few times I've pulled into the parking lot only to find the lights out and the staff departed. Concealed behind a Cerrillos Road motel, it's also one of Santa Fe's hardest-to-find restaurants. But if you can make your way here when it's open, you'll find a funky, spotless interior with a gurgling fountain, very friendly waitstaff, completely satisfying northern New Mexico food, and prices so ridiculously low you'll think someone made a mistake in adding up your check. To get a taste of what a Santa Fe coffee shop is like, drop in at **Tia Sophia's**, a very down-to-earth downtown place where the waitresses seem to know everyone by name, and the crowd looks like it's been coming here forever. Tia Sophia's claim to fame is its breakfast and lunch service. Eating here is like sitting down to a meal at mom's place… if your mom's from this corner of the country, that is. The red chile's famous for being too hot to handle, the cups of coffee are perpetually topped off, and the breakfast burritos are the best in town. The **Guadalupe Cafe**, a place that's been around more than a few years, has a decent local following that's always filled out with groups of tourists who come here, newspaper articles in hand, wanting to try the food. I end up having a couple of meals here throughout the year, but the decor is minimal and the food doesn't grab my undivided attention. For a more substantial local dining experience down by the Plaza, my recommendation is to try to wedge yourself in the back door at **Josie's Casa de Comida**, a funky little lunch-only place that's been trying (unsuccessfully) to keep a lid on its business for the past few years. Or get on line at **The Shed**, a Sena Plaza restaurant that starts seating those in the know at 11:30am, and for darn good reasons: fantastic food, exquisite surroundings, and astounding prices. The Shed's located in a 1700s-era hacienda, and it's somewhat miraculous that this place is still able to do what it does at the prices it charges. Its spotless reputation is well deserved, and if you miss eating here at least once during your Santa Fe stay you'll kick yourself all the way to the airport.

Authentic northern New Mexican on Cerrillos Road... If I'm arranging a lunch interview or just want to meet a friend to get caught up on things, I'll often suggest that we grab the always-great food at **La Choza**, an upper Cerrillos Road bargain eatery that's always packed with locals. La Choza is a surprising place, with fair prices, lots of authentic atmosphere, friendly waitstaff, and easy parking (actually, it's not such a surprise when you know that its owners also operate other successful restaurants in town, such as Tomasita's and Diego's Cafe—see above). Order the red chicken enchiladas with blue corn tortillas and you can't go wrong. One of the least appreciated restaurants in town is **The Pantry**, a Cerrillos Road joint with absolutely no atmosphere but an incredibly competent kitchen cranking out authentic, huge portions of local foods at great prices. Located within a short stroll of the El Rey Inn (see Accommodations), The Pantry's a great place to go for its huge breakfast burritos and dynamite sopapillas... there's always a squeeze bottle of honey on your table, and the salsa and chips are hands-down the best in Santa Fe. A slightly different experience unfolds at the **Old Mexico Grill**, a shopping-center restaurant on Cerrillos Road that's on a continual search for authenticity in classic Mexican and traditional northern New Mexican specialties. One of the best things going here is the huge bar and its bulging shelves filled with every variety of tequila known to modern man. The Old Mexico Grill is well worth a visit, even if you're just having a few turbocharged margaritas. But the food here is fairly priced and a sure bet, using lots of hard-to-find imported ingredients most commonly associated with restaurants south of the border.

Before the opera and other special nights... Though it's 15 miles south of town in the village of Galisteo, there's no place around that matches the **Galisteo Inn** (see Accommodations) for its impossibly romantic ambiance, elegant and innovative cuisine, gracious waitstaff, and a complete feeling of being disconnected from the Santa Fe life-support system. Though only a 20-minute drive from town, this refuge manages to do all things extremely well, inside the historic setting of a 1700s hacienda surrounded by towering cottonwood trees, manicured lawns, and more adobe walls than you can shake a stick at. Wonderfully prepared foods are Southwest- and California-influenced; the wine list could use some updating, but that's a minor flaw compared to the top-to-bottom, first-rate dining experience awaiting you. Downtown, **Cafe Escalera** has a decidedly contemporary feel, making little if any bow to the local design or food aesthetics. It's staffed by the best waitpeople in town, has fabulous breads, and the Mediterranean/southwestern food is totally sublime, which explains why this great restaurant is almost always packed with a top-notch crowd. Don't pass up the opportunity to sit at the bar and wait for your table—the Escalera's perfect martinis are huge, a fantastic opener for what's invariably a wonderful experience. When the **Double A** opened in the summer of 1995, all of Santa Fe was on the edge of its seat, waiting to see if this multimillion-dollar ship would float. Well, the results are in and the answer's a resounding yes. The decor's spectacular in a Santa Fe–meets–L.A. kind of way (leather chairs, soft lighting), the bar is one of the few dressy places in town for stylish hanging out, and the kitchen delivers on each and every promise, combining new American with southwestern and California/nouveau themes, all with tremendous success. One of the best places in Santa Fe to impress a date, or even your spouse, is **Geronimo**, a Canyon Road spot that's got a lock on the town's "most romantic setting" award. Everything here is seductive, from the lighting to the fabrics and table settings to the curved adobe walls, and especially to the food, a sensual mix of Mediterranean and New Mexican flavors. The bar is memorable—sort of a Georgia O'Keeffe goes to Paris setting, if that makes any sense. **Santacafe**'s uncluttered, timelessly elegant interior communicates a wonderfully romantic, sophisticated feeling, which may be why it's got such a see-and-be-seen thing going—that and the hybrid East-meets-West cuisine. The cool but competent waitstaff memorizes exactly who its regular customers are and exactly what it is that they like… and there's parking.

Hotel restaurants worth checking into… Like most restaurant reviewers, I'm wary of any hotel dining room—

SANTA FE | DINING

after all, how many rubber chicken dinners can a body stand? But there are two places in Santa Fe that completely break anyone's preconceptions, performing culinary miracles every time you walk through their doors. The **Eldorado Hotel**'s Old House restaurant and the **Inn of the Anasazi** (see Accommodations for both) are perfect places to find great food, fabulous ambiance, extensive wine lists, and flawless service. Anasazi's got the edge on ambiance, set as it is in a dramatically designed interior intended to replicate an ancient Native American ruin, but both restaurants run neck-and-neck when it comes to everything else that's important. Old House, while it travels along the nouveau pathway in many of its entrees, shows more appreciation for the tradition of northern New Mexico foods, and has some really great desserts. Anasazi seems perfectly comfortable breaking all the rules, recombining each element with its own signature twist (example: chile-encrusted filet mignon, New Mexican champagnes, Navajo flatbreads, raspberry sorbet), and placing it all in front of you to see if you're up to the challenge. At either place you'll be made to feel like an old friend who has just dropped in after a long stretch away from home, and that's always appreciated when you're visiting.

Artists' and writers' hangouts... With thousands of residents who refer to themselves as artists, or writers, or channelers, or art dealers, Santa Fe also has lots of meeting places and hangouts for the so-called creative crowd. Naturally, the most likely spots are the city's coffeehouses. The **Aztec Cafe** has been around since 1990, from the very first day attracting an eclectic group of local slackers, itinerant pseudo-hippies, bikers (both the motorized and pedaling varieties), college students, and various artists from the visual arts realm, as well as the film people who always seem to be shooting some sort of western nearby. Aztec's also a good place to find local art by artists without gallery representation, and the crew behind the counter knows how to make a great café latte. In-the-know itinerants head here immediately upon arriving in these parts, checking the bulletin boards for roommates and rides to the West Coast. Though it still has a slightly countercultural edge, **Downtown Subscription** draws a better-heeled crowd, mostly thanks to its Canyon

Road—area location, within easy reach of places where artists live and have their studios. There's a great selection of pastries and cakes, as well as hundreds of magazines from across the U.S. and Europe. A couple of dozen outdoor tables are in use year-round, and I can think of no better place to read the *New York Times* on a sunny Sunday morning than in Downtown Sub's rear patio, surrounded by blossoming lilacs. **Old Santa Fe Trail Books & Coffeehouse** pulls in a more mixed crowd of art dealers, idle musicians waiting to be called on stage during open mike night, and laid-back locals who have hung around coffeehouses from Berkeley to Bologna. The cafe here puts together some great salads and sandwiches, there's a bar pouring alcohol as well as caffeine, the seats are comfortable to the point where you might doze off, and the ambiance is oh-so-hip and casual. In the downtown area, **Galisteo News** was the favorite local artists' spot until the coffeehouse competition moved in a few years ago; it's still a good place to grab the Sunday papers, but the crowd now is strictly tourists. **Cloud Cliff Bakery** is in the Second Street Studios complex, so artists (as well as many Hollywood types) pour through its doors simply for convenience. Here, though, you get the added attraction of great food served in an arts-loaded setting. Some will argue this point, but for my dollars Cloud Cliff is also the best bakery in town, with European-trained masters running the ovens.

Of course, the creative spirit can't be nurtured by caffeine alone…and more than a few great Santa Fe arts careers have been flushed down the sewers owing to a passion for the bottle. Those who know how to manage their liquor, as well as the ones who can't, gravitate toward **El Farol**, the Canyon Road institution that on weekends attracts groups of Harley riders, thirsty artists who can coax their way into running a tab, and an aggressive singles crowd scoping for flesh. Other artists prefer the confines of the **Pink Adobe**, a place that's been run for more than 50 years by its original proprietress, an accomplished oil painter born and bred in New Orleans. The food here has a certain Creole flair, tempered by the traditions of northern New Mexico, and the results are superb.

Kid pleasers… Some of the best places to take your kids to lunch or dinner are also some of the funnest and cheap-

SANTA FE | DINING

est. If it's lunchtime, think about grabbing a bite at the outdoors Mexican **Jackalope Cafe**, attached to a Cerrillos Road import business that's one of Santa Fe's funkiest spots on the map (see Shopping). There's also **Tortilla Flats**, close by Jackalope, which is open for breakfast, lunch, and dinner. It's friendly and casual enough that you won't feel a bit out of place if some little person starts fussin' and whinin', or if someone spills their iced tea. If you're downtown, the **Burrito Company** is a decent bet for a family lunch or dinner. When your kids get tired of Mexican food, then schlep over to **Pastability** for an inexpensive Italian meal.

Best breakfast... The king of the early morning crowd's hill is **Tecolote Cafe**, a Cerrillos Road standout that usually has a line waiting for tables, despite its south-of-the-Plaza location. Known for its breakfast burritos and fresh-squeezed juices, Tecolote charges more-than-reasonable prices, and its service almost always meets the challenge, even at the crack of dawn. Downtown, the line outside of **Cafe Pasqual's** starts forming around 7:30am, a full hour before Tecolote's, which shows how many early birds like walking from their hotel room to a seat at one of Pasqual's funky, but always interesting, breakfast tables. One of the best ways to go here is to request seating at the community table, a mammoth, 18-seat table in the middle of Pasqual's crowded dining room, where you can start conversations with whoever's seated at your right elbow... kind of like a blind date at a dinner party. **Tia Sophia's** doesn't pack them in quite as tightly as Pasqual's, but you'll usually encounter a line at this downtown cafe as well. Tia's has an outstanding reputation for dynamite breakfast burritos and wickedly hot salsa (if stinging your tongue at the crack of dawn doesn't sound like fun, then be sure to order your chile on the side). I'm partial to the inventive kitchen mastery turned out by **Cloud Cliff Bakery**, a place in the Second Street studio district that serves innovative breakfast numbers as well as the expected standbys. The incredible aroma of fresh-baked bread permeates this place as still-hot rolls are delivered to your table with huge pots of raspberry jam. The same aroma swirls around at the **Santa Fe Baking Company**, a more modern place with a sophisticated, Seattle-esque atmosphere. Local artists and musicians while away their daylight hours here, gulping cappuccinos and lunching on the spot's invariably great sandwiches and pastries. (The fresh-baked breads are sublime.) The crowded patio outside the front door has zero ambiance, but it nonetheless attracts a great crowd, scheming over ways to snag one of the woefully few umbrella-shaded seats. **Harry's Roadhouse** is only 10 minutes from the Plaza, yet it feels totally removed from Santa Fe's summertime tourist crunch, which may be why it attracts its own loyal crowd of breakfast-lovers. Come here for the omelettes, as well as the terraced garden patio that's open during the warmer months.

Where the locals go... Get away from the out-of-town crowd by slipping over to **Fox's Bar & Grill**, a St. Michael's Drive sports bar and burger joint that's actually a fine place to relax over a cold brew. **Dave's Not Here** is another locals' joint, and a low-budget one at that. The grubby ambiance of the place, with its tables crowded close together, probably turns off any visitors who might venture out into this residential neighborhood in the first place, but once you focus on the food everything works out great. **Harry's Roadhouse**, with its hidden location off the Old Las Vegas Highway, attracts locals from Santa Fe and Eldorado but very, very few tourists. That's great for those of us who come here for the homemade soups and fantastic lunch fare. **Healthy Dave's Cafe**, a natural foods joint inside the Design Center, is another place where tourists are scarce. With zip ambiance and a purely local crowd, Healthy Dave's has to focus on what it does best: cranking out fantastic food at reasonable prices. Funked-out **Cafe Oasis** is another place where you won't have to worry about bumping into your friends from back home. It sure doesn't look like what people expect to find in Santa Fe—it's straight out of some time warp, like a little piece of Berkeley from the 1960s.

Where the locals don't go... One place I've never understood is the **Plaza Restaurant**, a downtown cafe that owes its life to the tourist trade. Locals don't come here for two reasons: there's no parking, and the food is nothing special. The Plaza Diner (as we call it) is always filled with tourists, breakfast, lunch, and dinner. Just proves the ancient adage: When it comes to the restaurant biz, location's everything. Same can be said for two other Plaza-area eateries, the **Ore House** and the **French Pastry Shop**. I've stopped in at both for a few meals over the years, but I never notice much of a presence from local residents. One thing the Ore House has going for it is an outdoor patio overlooking the Plaza—this feature alone attracts me on summer nights when I'm in the mood to sip a cold Tecate and watch the evening traffic pass by. The **Burrito Company** is another downtown place where locals won't tread, for two reasons: the crowds of tourists elbowing each other in front of the cash registers, and the mediocre food. The **Casa Sena Fajitas Stand** is another no-no for the local crowd, who realize that if it's fajitas you want, the best thing to do is to head for **Maria's** (see above). After having lived in Seattle for ten years, and knowing what's from Chinese and Thai food, I can do all of you a favor by dismissing all of Santa Fe's Chinese and Thai restaurants from your list. Some of these places are simply awful, while others are awfully unsatisfying. Save this culinary urge for when you get home. On the upscale side of things, **The Compound** on Canyon Road survives by catering to tourists who have been directed there by hotel concierges. This stuffy, sauce-driven old dame still pulls down four-star ratings from some guidebooks, which proves that most out-of-state travel writers don't know what they're doing.

The Index

$$$$	over $35
$$$	$20–$35
$$	$12–$20
$	under $12

Price categories are based on per-person cost for dinner, not including drinks and tip.

Alfalfa's Market. Some local folks prefer the selection here to that at Wild Oats, its main competition. I say both are great.... *Tel 505/986–8667. 500 W. Cordova Rd. $*

Aztec Cafe. Serves the best latte around, in an artistic, creative atmosphere unmatched by any other coffeehouse in town. Small patio outside attracts an incredibly diverse crowd of artists, intellectuals, foreigners, and slackers, mostly under 30.... *Tel 505/983–9464. 317 Aztec St. No credit cards. $*

Bagelmania. Great bagels and unsatisfying food in the setting of a former car dealership. Wednesday is "18 bagels for the price of 12" day.... *Tel 505/982–8900. 420 Catron St. $$*

Baja Taco. A funky drive-through on Cerrillos Road that serves some of the hottest chile in Santa Fe, as well as great enchiladas, tacos, and burritos to go. At happy hour (5:30–6:30 on weekdays), the prices drop 25%.... *Tel 505/438–7198. 2621 Cerrillos Rd. $*

Bobcat Bite. Locals (and a few tourists) line up outside this edge-of-town eatery for some of the best green-chile cheeseburgers in the state. A few small tables, a tiny counter, and that's it, except for awesome food served in huge portions.... *Tel 505/983–5319. Old Las Vegas Highway S. No credit cards. $*

Bull Ring. A favorite hangout for the local business, political, and lobbyist crowd, this downtown steak house lacks atmosphere. The steaks fail to measure up to their stiff prices—what's stiff, however, are the drinks poured in the Bull Ring's bar.... *Tel 505/983–3328. 150 Washington Ave. $$$$*

Burrito Company. Downtown's fast-food entry into the regional-food sweepstakes, Burrito Company will fill your tummy at a fair price, in a setting jammed with tourists.... *Tel 505/982–4453. 111 Washington Ave. No credit cards. $*

Cafe Escalera. One of the best places in town to see and be seen, this chi-chi restaurant packs people in for lunch and dinner. The food has a Mediterranean and southwestern flair, the breads are always great, the service is expert, and the bar mixes a mean martini.... *Tel 505/989–8188. 130 Lincoln Ave. $$$*

Cafe Oasis. The 1960s flourish at this wacked-out restaurant/coffeehouse/summertime-patio hangout. Oasis serves vegetarian and some meat dishes—a few pastas, good pies, wine and beer, and a whole lot of trippy atmosphere.... *Tel 505/983–9599. 526 Galisteo St. No credit cards. $$*

Cafe Pasqual's. Always crowded, always great, this innovative restaurant takes the best of northern New Mexico's culinary traditions, marries them with snippets drawn from across Mexico, and presents it all in a fantastic, funky setting.... *Tel 505/983–9340. 121 Don Gaspar Ave. $$$*

Carlos' Gospel Cafe. Hallelujah for Carlos' egg-salad sandwiches on thick slices of fresh-baked bread. Praise heaven for Carlos' mighty hangover stew, and maybe a pasta salad on the side.... *Tel 505/983–1841. 125 Lincoln Ave. No credit cards. $*

Casa Sena Fajitas Stand. Crammed into a dark corner behind the popular La Casa Sena restaurant, this tourist-friendly spot serves so-so fajitas.... *Tel 505/988–9232. 125 E. Palace Ave. $$*

Celebrations. In a quintessential adobe setting, Celebrations has fireplaces, a small (but loud) patio, good Cajun-accented food, and a casual atmosphere.... *Tel 505/989–8904. 613 Canyon Rd. $$*

Cloud Cliff Bakery. Starting out as a coffee bar attached to a bakery, it has evolved into a fantastic, art-filled restaurant space serving innovative European/southwestern/American cuisine. And there's still an espresso machine. Very big with local artists.... *Tel 505/983–6254. 1805 Second St. $*

The Compound. Expensive, elaborate, and filled with senior citizens, the Compound cruises by on its 25 years of reputation, but does so with a sense of style.... *Tel 505/982–4353. 653 Canyon Rd. $$$$*

Cordelia's. Locals only know about this place from word of mouth. Fantastic regional cooking including all the usual New Mexican specialties.... *Tel 505/988–1303. 1601 Berry Ave. No credit cards. $*

Corn Dance Cafe. Intriguing menu that combines Native American food traditions drawn from tribes across the continent. Somewhat pricy and the portions could be larger, but the quality's there, and the back patio is one of the nicest places in Santa Fe for a summer evening meal.... *Tel 505/ 986–1662. 409 W. Water St. $$$$*

Cowgirl Hall of Fame. One day you'd swear Cowgirl is a barbecue joint, the next it's a bar packed with slackers and cowpoke wannabes (or maybe they're just wanna-pokes). There's a great outdoor patio and a back room offering comedy, cabaret, and music.... *Tel 505/982–2565. 319 S. Guadalupe St. $$*

Coyote Cafe. When chef/owner/entrepreneur Mark Miller arrived in Santa Fe after cutting his chops in the Bay Area, this town was in for the surprise of its culinary life... and it's never been the same since. Everything at Coyote is first-rate, from the Chimayo cocktails to the red chile bread. Not to be missed, even if you can only do it one time.... *Tel 505/983–1615. 132 W. Water St. $$$$*

Coyote Cantina. At this outdoor counterpart to Coyote Cafe (see above), you can eat almost as well as inside the main restaurant, but at a fraction of the price. Great salsas and chips, cold Mexican brews, fast service.... *Tel 505/983– 1615. 132 W. Water St. $$*

Dave's Not Here. Who cares where Dave went—the most important thing about this incredible bargain is the great food at jaw-dropping prices.... *Tel 505/983–7060. 1115 Hickox St. No credit cards. $*

Diego's Cafe. Located in a mall within 10 minutes' walk of the Plaza, Diego's has all the sorts of New Mexican specialties locals love.... *Tel 505/983–5101. De Vargas Center Mall, Paseo de Peralta. $*

Double A. Since opening in mid-1995, the Double A has set a new standard for Santa Fe chic, serving wonderfully cooked dishes reflecting American food traditions. The monied set's current favorite after-dark hangout.... *Tel 505/982–8999. 331 Sandoval St. $$$$*

SANTA FE | DINING

Downtown Subscription. The best coffeehouse in the Canyon Road area, Downtown Sub has a great selection of out-of-town papers, a humongous patio, and pastries from all of Santa Fe's best bakeries.... *Tel 505/983–3085. 376 Garcia St. No credit cards. $*

El Farol. A swingin' bar, and some of the finest tapas this side of Seville. The house wine selection tilts heavily in favor of Spanish vintages, the decor is as authentic Santa Fe as you can find, and live music starts most evenings at 9.... *Tel 505/983–9912. 808 Canyon Rd. $$$*

El Nido. This Tesuque restaurant has a loyal following for straightforward steaks, seafood, and New Mexican special-ties. Too-high prices and uneven service, not to mention food that often misses the mark, make dining at El Nido a crapshoot. If things are right, this place can be wonderful, but.... *Tel 505/988–4340. N.M. Hwy. 591, at Bishops Lodge Rd. $$$*

Encore Provence. Classic French cooking in a lovely setting, but Encore Provence is overpriced and a tad on the pre-cious side. Tables are poorly arranged in a crowded set-ting.... *Tel 505/983–7470. 548 Agua Fria St. $$$$*

Felipe's Tacos. An absolutely authentic touch of Michoacan street food in the clean setting of a Santa Fe shopping-cen-ter restaurant. Fantastic bargain prices for the real thing.... *Tel 505/473–9397. 1711 Llano St. No credit cards. $*

Fox's Bar & Grill. This sports bar has fantastic burgers, cold drafts, lively tunes, and one of the best patios in town for catching sunsets.... *Tel 505/473–3697. 720 St. Michael's Dr. $*

French Pastry Shop. Convenient place to grab a croissant and a cup of coffee when you're downtown by the Plaza.... *Tel 505/983–6697. 100 E. San Francisco St. No credit cards. $*

Galisteo News. Downtown's best coffeehouse and a place to pick up the Sunday *New York Times*.... *Tel 505/984–1316. 201 Galisteo St. $*

Garduno's. This big, brassy restaurant has more of a Tex-Mex slant to its menu than northern New-Mex. Nonetheless, the service is great, the portions enormous, and the kitchen does a decent job. Best happy hour in town.... *Tel 505/ 983–9797. 130 Lincoln Ave. $$*

Geronimo. One of Santa Fe's most cherished "great night out" places. The food blends Mediterranean and southwestern influences, the decor is a perfect blend of New Mexican and southern Mexican elegance, and the bar is one of Santa Fe's best places to fall in love.... *Tel 505/982–1500. 724 Canyon Rd. $$$*

Guadalupe Cafe. Another of the many New Mexico–style restaurants sprinkled around the fringes of downtown, this one attracts large lunch crowds of state government workers.... *Tel 505/982–9762. 422 Old Santa Fe Trail. $$*

Harry's Roadhouse. A favorite with locals who enjoy sitting on the shaded, terraced patio, Harry's has fantastic soups and lunch specials. This is one place that knows how to treat an egg, so expect a crowd at breakfast.... *Tel 505/989–4629. Old Las Vegas Hwy. $$*

Healthy Dave's Cafe. Excellent and very inexpensive vegetarian restaurant inside the cavernous guts of the Design Center. Zero ambiance, moody service, great food at fantastic prices. Lunch only, unfortunately.... *Tel 505/982–4147. 418 Cerrillos Rd. No credit cards. $*

Horseman's Haven. Home of the half-pound burger, this is where real working folks come to tank up on huge portions of enchiladas, burger baskets, fries, and everything else that makes America great.... *Tel 505/471–5420. 6500 Cerrillos Rd. No credit cards. $*

Il Vicino. Fantastic wood-fired pizza just a stone's throw from the Plaza.... *Tel 505/986–8700. 321 W. San Francisco St. $$*

India Palace. Does best what it promises: foods from the land of Ghandi and Gunga Din. A favorite of local residents hankerin' for an escape from Santa Fe flavors.... *Tel 505/986–5859. 227 Don Gaspar Ave. $$*

Jackalope Cafe. Strange and wonderful Mexican place for summer-only patio dining, amid the eclectic madness of a large home-and-garden furnishings store.... *Tel 505/471–8539. 2820 Cerrillos Rd. No credit cards. $*

Josie's Casa de Comida. Popular downtown lunch spot that serves some of the best, simplest local foods found anywhere in Santa Fe. Fabulous pies, renewing posole, and cheap.... *Tel 505/983–5311. 225 E. Marcy St. No credit cards. $*

Julian's. Marvelous setting, attentive service, but a too-cute hand behind the stove, and really not Italian enough to pass muster as a northern Italian restaurant.... *Tel 505/988–2355. 221 Shelby St. $$$*

La Casa Sena. An elegant restaurant in historic Sena Plaza, the Casa Sena combines fine dining with a fabulous setting and a selection of fine art unequaled anywhere in the state.... *Tel 505/988–9323. 125 E. Palace Ave. $$$$*

La Choza. Casual atmosphere, fine local foods, and plentiful parking make this authentic New Mexico–style restaurant a favorite with the local crowd.... *Tel 505/982–0909. 905 Alaird St. AE not accepted. $$*

La Tertulia. Set in what once was a convent for the nearby Santuario de Guadalupe, the sins committed in La Tertulia's kitchen far outweigh its good deeds.... *Tel 505/988–2769. 416 Agua Fria St. $$$*

Maria's New Mexican Kitchen. The best northern New Mexican food in Santa Fe and the very best margaritas in town are served in an old roadhouse that's part adobe bar, part hallway, and part dance hall. Massive burritos, the best fajitas north of El Paso, enormous and fresh guacamole salads, an inspiring and inexpensive wine list, and freshly made tortillas.... *Tel 505/983–7929. 555 W. Cordova Rd. $$*

Natural Cafe. Santa Fe's only restaurant seriously dedicated to the pursuit of vegetarian and vegan foods, although you'll still find chicken and fish entrees on the menu. Specify if you want your food to be spicy. Great patio for summer dining.... *Tel 505/983–1411. 1494 Cerrillos Rd. AE not accepted. $$*

Old Mexico Grill. Though set in a shopping mall, this place does justice to the entire concept of Mexican food.... *Tel 505/473–0338. 2434 Cerrillos Rd. $$*

Old Santa Fe Trail Books & Coffeehouse. Great salads, soups, and sandwiches in a bookstore/cafe that's no mere snack bar—it's got a full bar, live music, two patios.... *Tel 505/988–8878. 613 Old Santa Fe Trail. $$*

On Water. A historic hotel's dining room is home for this innovative, western-meets-southwestern-meets-American restaurant. Wood-paneled bar and tiny outdoor courtyard are romantic spots.... *Tel 505/982–8787. 210 Don Gaspar Ave. $$$*

Ore House. The best thing to do here is grab a table on the second-story porch overlooking the Plaza and watch the wacky world pass by. Order a Tecate and nachos, and that's lunch.... *Tel 505/983–8687. 50 Lincoln Ave. $$$*

The Palace. A favorite with the downtown business crowd as well as certain well-heeled Texas oil millionaires. Sit in the see-and-be-seen bar, rather than one of the red leather booths at the back of the restaurant; in summer, ask to sit on the lovely courtyard patio.... *Tel 505/982–9891. 142 W. Palace Ave. $$$*

The Pantry. Looks like just another joint from the outside, but inside there's mom behind the stove and some of the best northern New Mexico cooking you'll ever experience.... *Tel 505/982–0179. 1820 Cerrillos Rd. No credit cards. $*

Pastability. Bizarrely situated inside a cavernous mini-mall within 5 minutes' walking distance of the Plaza, this tiny northern Italian spot may be Santa Fe's best Italian restaurant. Amazingly low prices, always high-quality food, casually hip service, and a well-chosen wine list.... *Tel 505/988–2856. 418 Cerrillos Rd. No credit cards. $*

Paul's. Classic European cuisine successfully blends with an appreciation for northern New Mexico's food traditions. Unpretentious, art-filled setting with great music on the sound system, close to the Plaza.... *Tel 505/982–8738. 72 W. Marcy St. AE not accepted. $$$*

SANTA FE | DINING

Pink Adobe. Longtime hangout of the funniest and most enjoyable crowd in town. The limited wine list is loaded with affordable surprises, and the multi-room dining area has a personality to fit anyone's mood. Superb, flavorful food.... *Tel 505/983–7712. 406 Old Santa Fe Trail. $$$*

Plaza Restaurant. Known for being the closest thing Santa Fe has to a Greek restaurant, the Plaza is always filled with tourists who come here for the place's location right on the (you guessed it) Plaza.... *Tel 505/982–1664. 54 Lincoln Ave. $$*

Poulet Patate. Spit-roasted chicken and lamb, Provençal style. Lots of herbed preparations, good house wines, pleasant atmosphere, and many tourists due to its downtown location.... *Tel 505/820–2929. 106 N. Guadalupe St. $$*

Pranzo. This two-story northern Italian restaurant stays open until 11pm, making it one of Santa Fe's all-too-few late-night alternatives. The food here is always nicely prepared, if a little short on inventiveness. There's a good pizza oven, great bread placed on the tables, and a loud, jovial atmosphere.... *Tel 505/984–2645. 540 Montezuma St. $$$*

Roque's Carnitas. Roque hauls his carnitas stand to sunnier climes once the snow starts flying. But oh, what a treat you've got in store if Roque's firin' up his mouth-watering street food.... *No telephone. Corner of Washington and Palace Aves. Summers only. $*

San Francisco Street Bar & Grill. Open 'til 11pm and serving an armful of microbrews, this downtown joint has the sort of casual air of a neighborhood bar, even if there really isn't any neighborhood nearby.... *Tel 505/982–2044. 114 W. San Francisco St. AE not accepted. $*

Santa Fe Baking Company. Artsy, metropolitan-style coffeehouse and cafe in a modern setting on Cordova Road. Great baked items, fast service, strong coffee, and a tiny but popular patio.... *Tel 505/988–4292. 504 W. Cordova Rd. AE not accepted. $$*

Santacafe. An elegant restaurant located in historic, gorgeous surroundings, Santacafe serves innovative Asian/southwestern/nouvelle fare. A great place to see and be seen, it also has one of the city's most romantic courtyards, eye-popping interior design, and designer food to match its steep prices.... *Tel 505/984–1788. 231 Washington Ave. $$$$*

The Shed. This legendary local restaurant has wonderfully funky, yet elegant and historic surroundings. The atmosphere is pure Santa Fe, but in an authentic, 1940s sort of way, and food is sublime.... *Tel 505/982–9030. 113 1/2 E. Palace Ave. No credit cards. $*

Tecolote Cafe. The meal of the day here is breakfast, and since this large restaurant can accommodate a crowd, drive here if the crowd at Cafe Pasqual's (see above) stretches halfway to Española.... *Tel 505/988–1362. 1203 Cerrillos Rd. $$*

Tia Sophia's. One of the best places in town to enjoy a local wake-up specialty known as a breakfast burrito, this warm and friendly cafe draws both locals and tourists. Great chile and sopapillas.... *Tel 505/983–9880. 210 W. San Francisco St. No credit cards. $*

Tiny's. Fine steaks and superb northern New Mexico dishes at bargain prices are a big hit with the Santa Fe political crowd (this is the state capital, after all); at night a bunch of musicians whoops it up onstage in the tiny bar. If you see a smiling guy playing accordion, that's Tiny himself.... *Tel 505/ 983–9817. 1015 Pen Road Shopping Center. $$*

Tomasita's. Both local folks and tourists flock to Tomasita's for outstanding northern New Mexico food, including Santa Fe's best enchiladas and sopapillas. Because there's always a wait you'll be asked to sit in the bar and down a few margaritas, along with a hundred or so other folks crammed in waiting for tables. Service is attentive, if sometimes a bit hurried.... *Tel 505/983–5721. 500 S. Guadalupe St. AE not accepted. $$*

Tommy's Bar & Grill. This yupscale downtown bar is known for great food and stiff drinks—but beware, it turns into a young and restless hot spot on weekend nights.... *Tel 505/989– 4407. 208 Galisteo St. $*

Tortilla Flats. Not much to look at from the outside, this Cerrillos Road joint serves first-rate regional foods at good

SANTA FE | DINING

prices. Always filled with families.... *Tel 505/471–8685. 3139 Cerrillos Rd. AE not accepted. $$*

Upper Crust Pizza. Located in an old adobe right on the Old Santa Fe Trail, Upper Crust has a front porch that's a great place to eat pizza and watch the world cruise past.... *Tel 505/983–4140. 329 Old Santa Fe Trail. No credit cards. $*

Whistling Moon Cafe. Innovative slant on Mediterranean foods, with some southwestern touches. Crowded tables, convivial crowd, and the best service in town.... *Tel 505/ 983–3093. 402 N. Guadalupe St. No credit cards. $$*

Wild Oats Market. Since adding hot food entrees and a sushi bar to its enormous salad bar and first-rate sandwich counter, Wild Oats has become one of Santa Fe's best, and cheapest, places to grab a fast meal that's good for you (and cheap!).... *Tel 505/983–5333. 1090 S. St. Francis Dr. $*

Woolworth's. Everyone goes here for one reason: the Frito pies. Order one, stroll over to the Plaza, eat the mess with a plastic spoon, and congratulate yourself for having done the right thing.... *Tel 505/982–1062. 58 E. San Francisco St. $*

Zia Diner. A diner in name only, Zia's stakes its claim to diner status with a menu full of homestyle entrees with veggies and mashed spuds. The bar is a surprisingly lively hangout at times. The breads served all come from Zia's own adjacent bakery, which does a breathtaking job with apple pies.... *Tel 505/988–7008. 326 S. Guadalupe St. $$*

Downtown Santa Fe Dining

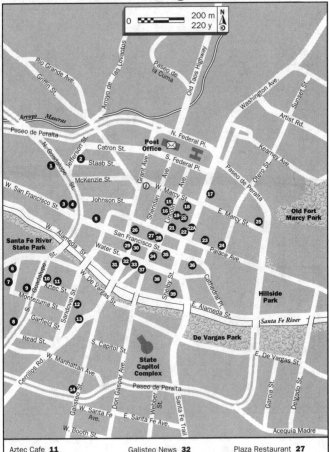

Aztec Cafe **11**	Galisteo News **32**	Plaza Restaurant **27**
Bagelmania **2**	Garduno's **15**	Poulet Patate **4**
Bull Ring **20**	Healthy Dave's Cafe **13**	Pranzo **7**
Burrito Company **21**	Il Vicino **5**	Roque's Carnitas **22A**
Cafe Escalera **16**	India Palace **38**	San Francisco Street Bar
Cafe Oasis **14**	Josie's Casa de Comida **25**	& Grill **30**
Cafe Pasqual's **34**	Julian's **39**	Santacafe **17**
Carlos' Gospel Cafe **19**	La Casa Sena **22**	The Shed **23**
Casa Sena Fajitas Stand **24**	La Tertulia **6**	Tia Sophia's **29**
Corn Dance Cafe **3**	On Water **37**	Tomasita's **8**
Coyote Cafe/Coyote Cantina **33**	Ore House **28**	Tommy's Bar & Grill **31**
Cowgirl Hall of Fame **10**	The Palace **26**	Whistling Moon Cafe **1**
Double A **12**	Pastability **13**	Woolworth's **35**
French Pastry Shop **36**	Paul's **18**	Zia Diner **9**

Greater Santa Fe Dining

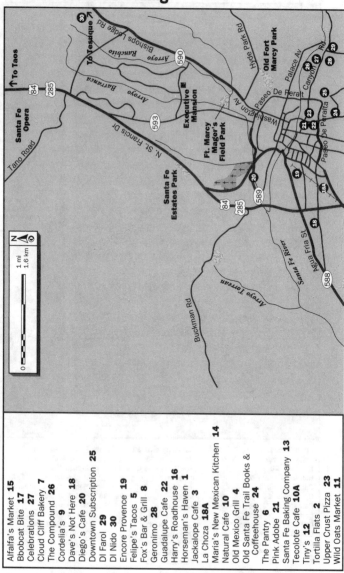

Alfalfa's Market **15**
Bbobcat Bite **17**
Celebrations **27**
Cloud Cliff Bakery **7**
The Compound **26**
Cordelia's **9**
Dave's Not Here **18**
Diego's Cafe **20**
Downtown Subscription **25**
DI Farol **29**
DI Nido **30**
Encore Provence **19**
Felipe's Tacos **5**
Fox's Bar & Grill **8**
Geronimo **28**
Guadalupe Cafe **22**
Harry's Roadhouse **16**
Horseman's Haven **1**
Jackalope Cafe **3**
La Choza **18A**
Maria's New Mexican Kitchen **14**
Natural Cafe **10**
Old Mexico Grill **4**
Old Santa Fe Trail Books &
  Coffeehouse **24**
The Pantry **6**
Pink Adobe **21**
Santa Fe Baking Company **13**
Tecolote Cafe **10A**
Tiny's **12**
Tortilla Flats **2**
Upper Crust Pizza **23**
Wild Oats Market **11**

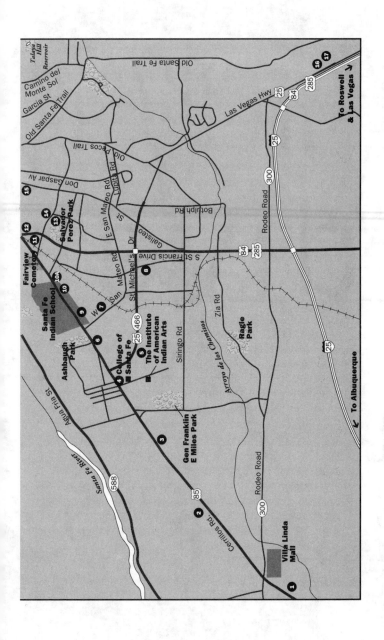

3
sions

Santa Fe is a
seductively laid-
back alternative to
the real world—
dangerous unless
you've pulled a
load of self-

motivation into your psyche (you'll never find it *after* you get here). Things may or may not (but probably won't) get done on time; if people show up 20 minutes late for a meeting, they're still considered to be on time. Stopping in the post office to chat with a friend for 15 minutes is simply considered good manners, and it's not unusual for people driving down the street in opposite directions to stop their cars in the middle of the road and shoot the breeze for a few minutes while holding up traffic.

So take a tip from us locals and try, during your stay in Santa Fe, to forget your normal need to follow life's fast track. Leave your watch at home, have a margarita before noon, take a long nap before dinner. Let this funky corner of the Southwest work a little bit of its magic into your frontal lobes. It'll all make for a more enjoyable stay, and maybe even make Santa Fe's weirdness seem a bit more logical.

Getting Your Bearings

If you stand on the Plaza in downtown Santa Fe and look at the Sangre de Cristo Mountains towering over the older parts of the city, your natural inclination is to point at the mountains and feel absolutely certain that it's true north. Even people who have lived here all their lives will point at the mountains and tell you that they're north. Well, you're all dead wrong. Listen up, you mapless turistas—if you stand on the Santa Fe Plaza and face the Sangre de Cristos you're facing EAST! This explains why the summer sunsets behind the Eldorado Hotel on the other end of downtown are not mysteriously fading into the south. From the Plaza, true north is in the direction of the Palace of the Governors, the state historical museum. The Santa Fe River cuts across downtown, east to west, just south of the Plaza.

From the Plaza you can walk to anything worth visiting downtown, on Canyon Road (a 10-minute walk heading east), or in the Guadalupe district (a slightly shorter walk heading southwest). If you're in the mood for an especially invigorating two-mile ramble, you can even walk from the Plaza to the museums on the upper reaches of Old Santa Fe Trail, which will take you anywhere from 30 to 45 minutes. Keep in mind that the latter half of this southeasterly jaunt is a steady uphill climb. Several minivan tour operators can take you to the museums from the Plaza for a few bucks; look for the van boarding area on the Plaza's northwest corner in front of the New Mexico Museum of Fine Arts.

The main highway into Santa Fe is Interstate 25, which runs north–south through much of the Rocky Mountain region. From the Albuquerque airport (which is where almost all of Santa Fe's visitors arrive and depart), we're an hour's drive north on I–25. When you get off I–25, it's another 5 miles into downtown along Cerrillos Road, your typical godawful strip of fast-food shacks, shopping areas, inexpensive hotels, and used-car dealers. Cerrillos Road eventually leads you into the older parts of town, changing its name to Sandoval Street when it hits Paseo de Peralta.

If you're planning on driving around town during your visit, keep in mind that there's no rhyme or reason to Santa Fe's street grid or its numbering system. It's not at all uncommon for streets to change names from one block to the next, nor is it unusual to see home and business addresses numbered out of sequence and with designations such as "45" or "22A" (which should tip you off that the place is down an alley or at the end of a dirt lane). The best way to handle the city's completely wacko way of messing up street names and addresses is to buy a comprehensive, up-to-date Santa Fe street map as soon as you hit the airport, or from a bookstore in your hometown before you leave.

The Lowdown

Must-sees for first-time visitors from Peoria...

It's not the "town square," it's the **Plaza**. After all, we're in a part of the U.S. that once was ruled by bureaucrats in Mexico City (and you thought the dolts in D.C. were incompetent!). As in other small towns, the Plaza was once Santa Fe's center of social and business activity. Not too many years ago, there were drugstores, shoe shops, department stores, town drunks, and food markets in downtown Santa Fe. Today, businesses and other people have been run off by unconscionable rent increases and the triumph of a 20-year trend that has turned downtown into a shopping mall for tourists. The Plaza, however, remains a refuge of sorts, and even if old folks don't come here to relax and socialize with their friends, it's still a relief to enter its tree-shaded lawns and crossing pathways, to get an idea of what the heart of Santa Fe must have once represented. On the Plaza are dozens of wrought-iron benches and a water fountain. In the middle stands a blank obelisk that's supposed to commemorate either Union soldiers who died in northern New Mexico during the Civil War (the official version) or the Hispanic and Anglo settlers who died in hundreds of years of battles with the Southwest's Native Americans (the original but now un-p.c. version). From the middle of the Plaza you can turn north and face the front portal of the **Palace of the Governors**, the state's original capitol, which dates back to Spanish colonial times; today it's our historical museum. Turn east, south, and west and you'll be confronted with about two dozen overpriced stores and art galleries. One place you may want to visit early in your stay is the **Santa Fe Convention and Visitors Bureau information booth** underneath the portal of the bank building on the Plaza's south side. Staffed in the warmer months by volunteers, the booth is loaded with brochures, maps, and copies of the city visitors' guide.

One sight in the downtown area you don't want to miss is the historic structure on Palace Avenue known as **Sena Plaza**. Once home to Dona Isabel and Don Jose Sena, this former hacienda includes a shaded courtyard and central fountain as well as a long, low portal running nearly 100 yards along Palace Avenue. Stores and restaurants fill nearly every cubbyhole in Sena Plaza; at one time it even housed the administrative offices of the Manhattan Project, that collection of scientists and soldiers, who, in the mid-1940s, cooked up the first atomic bomb. One of the best restaurants in town for authentic local food, The Shed (see Dining), is in Sena Plaza; lunch there should be another must-do on your itinerary. A second great place to walk to in the downtown area is the **New Mexico Capitol Building**, across the river on Old Santa Fe Trail. Known hereabouts as the Roundhouse (because, you guessed it, it's actually round), it's supposed to resemble a Native American ceremonial kiva, though its bastardized design really looks more like a tall stack of pancakes served up by an intergalactic Denny's. If the legislature's not in session, you won't run much of a risk of being run over by a drunk-driving state legislator (sadly, the court records prove it, year in and year out). The capitol's grounds are worth seeing, if for nothing else than their great collection of sculpture and public works of art by New Mexican artists. These rotating displays are courtesy of the **Governor's Gallery**, an actual art gallery open to the public in the fourth-floor lobby of the offices of the governor. Some of the shows here are inspired attempts to bring the state's diverse arts scene into focus, while other exhibitions pander to special interest constituencies.

A short walk eastward from the Plaza leads you to **Canyon Road**, a must-see on anyone's Santa Fe itinerary simply because it holds the city's largest concentration of art galleries. Once the kind of lazy, unpaved street where struggling artists kept the front rooms of their homes open to the public, Canyon Road is today a high-powered gallery district—artists from across the nation would kill for an opportunity to have their works displayed and sold here. Will Rogers once took a ramble up Canyon Road and declared that it must have been designed by a drunk riding backward on a jackass, which gives you an idea of how absurdly winding this old cow path is. Canyon Road has a couple of places where you can stop in for a drink or a meal—El Farol is a good bet (see Nightlife and Entertainment), as is Geronimo or Celebrations (see Dining)—and dozens of places sell paintings, jewelry, photography, Indian rugs,

Georgia on my mind

By the time Georgia O'Keeffe died on March 6, 1986, her status as one of America's greatest artists was in the bag, her iconographic images of the Southwest—whether calla lillies, cow skulls, sparse landscapes, or pelvises—etched into the nation's collective arts consciousness. Santa Fe wasn't her home, though she spent some time living here and in Taos; it was Abiquiu, a village about an hour north of Santa Fe, where she lived in an adobe home on a hill overlooking the Chama River Valley (phone 505/685-4539 in advance for a guided tour). Sometimes it seems like half the older artists in New Mexico have a story about hanging out with Georgia at Abiquiu. You can also visit Ghost Ranch, about 20 miles up the road from Abiquiu, where she spent several summers (tel 505/685-4333). The New Mexico Museum of Fine Arts in Santa Fe maintains a collection of O'Keeffe paintings, but none of her most important works. For those you'll have to wait until late 1996 when the O'Keeffe Museum, a branch of the Museum of New Mexico, opens at 217 Johnson Street, displaying not only MNM's O'Keeffes but also major works bought and borrowed from collectors and dealers around the country.

SANTA FE | DIVERSIONS

sculpture, Native American artifacts, and ersatz cowgirl clothing. My best advice is to take as long as you possibly can to shop around, not just to compare prices but also to find what you really like. Only when you see something that truly speaks to your inner eye, your emotional self, should you even start considering price.

You'll know you're really in the Southwest when you see... The **Santuario de Nuestra Señora de Guadalupe**, parts of which date back to the late 18th century, is a mission church on the edge of downtown at the near end of the Guadalupe Street shopping district. Typically New Mexican on its inside, the Santuario isn't fancy, isn't filled with stained glass or gilded treasures, and probably won't take your breath away when you walk through its front doors. And that's what makes it so beautiful in the eyes of local residents, who still worship here. Its dark, adobe-walled interior and ornate altar give an authentic feel for the emphasis this region's Hispanic Catholic settlers placed on their religion. Imagine what sacrifices it must have taken for poor farmers and store owners to raise the church's construction funds! As you walk out the Santuario's front door and look eastward across the Santa Fe River and toward the Sangre de Cristo Mountains, try to picture what this place must have looked like just 40 years ago, before hotels and paved streets changed its character forever.

One other place every visitor should see is a lovely street known as **Acequia Madre** (literally, the mother ditch), which runs parallel to Canyon Road one block east. This street winds along beside the aqueduct original-ly built by Spanish settlers to transport mountain waters into the agricultural lands that once flanked downtown Santa Fe. While you won't find any art galleries or restau-rants, you will find adobe walls and the types of random-ly designed homes that drew so many appreciative eyes toward Santa Fe's design style a couple of decades ago. With the exception of a few newer residences, there's nothing canned about Acequia Madre or its several side streets. A leisurely stroll along the dirt path that serves as its sidewalk takes you past dozens of charming, Santa Fe–authentic places. Overdesigned developments such as Quail Run and Las Campañas pretend they strive toward this look and feel, but they fall woefully short.

The Native American thing... A local entrepreneur I know runs her own web site marketing Santa Fe artists and food products, and she tells me that most of the queries she gets are about Native American art and artists. I'm not surprised. When you come into contact with Native Americans in Santa Fe, you're coming into contact with a predominantly successful group of artists, teachers, businesspeople, civil servants, whatever—the cream of the crop, drawn here by Santa Fe's special opportunities for Native Americans. Some of the older Indian folks you may meet here will have problems understanding the dialects and speeds at which Anglos speak, but the younger Native Americans are products of modern America— schools, television, malls, concerts, and all the rest. They're often exceedingly family-oriented people, trying to balance lives in the contemporary world with lives in their culture's traditional and spiritual worlds.

One of the easiest ways to get a handle on Native American culture is to visit Santa Fe's three great museums of Native American art. Downtown's **Institute of American Indian Arts Museum** (IAIA) is a great place to start, because it includes as much work from contemporary Native American artists as it does work from traditional

Burn him!

The weekend after Labor Day, all hell breaks loose with **Fiestas de Santa Fe**, a wild and sometimes scary weekend of street celebrations. Fiestas kicks off with the annual burning of Zozobra, a gigantic puppet that's supposed to be a repository for all of Santa Fe's cares, concerns, and traumas. (Oh, if only it were that easy to blow away all our hang-ups and neuroses.) Tens of thousands of New Mexicans from Albuquerque to Taos pour into Santa Fe to stand shoulder-to-shoulder in Fort Marcy Park and witness the 50-foot-tall Zozobra's annual rite of destruction, often in the drizzling rain (September's our wet season). Costumed dancers carrying torches run madly up and down a hillside from which mighty Zozobra glowers down at the multitudes, his motorized head twisting and arms flailing, an eerie growl emanating from deep within. Then a chief dancer appears and finally lights Zozobra's long white robes. Fireworks stashed inside the effigy blow Zozobra to kingdom come—or at least into another dimension, from which he'll reappear next year to purge our civic soul again.

SANTA FE | DIVERSIONS

Indian artists. IAIA's galleries display art by some of the nation's most energetic, political, and emotionally power-ful creative voices, in regularly changing exhibitions year-round. The sculpture garden out back of the IAIA is ded-icated to the memory of Allan Houser, a tremendously influential Native American sculptor who paved the way for today's generation of Native American sculptors. You can spend hours at the IAIA Museum, all of which will be well invested. The privately supported **Wheelwright Museum of the American Indian** and the **Museum of Indian Arts and Culture** (MIAC) are a mile or so from the Plaza, on a hillside overlooking much of Santa Fe's southern and western fringes. While both museums are well worth visiting, both tend to be rather sedate places, and most of their exhibits are much less interesting and inspired than those at the IAIA Museum. MIAC tends to focus on traditional Native American arts—ceramic pottery, woven basketry, rugs, clothing, and jewelry. The Wheelwright's galleries, on the other hand, occasionally have strong exhibitions of paintings and sculpture by fan-tastic younger artists, including some of the same out-spoken voices who raise artistic hell at IAIA downtown.

A number of commercial art galleries around Santa Fe represent contemporary and traditional Native American artists, and there are even a few galleries owned by Native American artists. Foremost of these is painter/sculptor Dan Namingha's **Niman Fine Arts**, the city's finest one-artist gallery and a testament to one of America's greatest living artists, period. Jeweler Ray Tracey's **Ray Tracey Gallery** is one of the best in a city that attracts intense competition for jewelry sales; his Palace Avenue gallery exhibits work by some of the Southwest's most popular painters and sculptors. On Canyon Road, sculptor/painter Estelle Loretto's **Gentle Spirit Gallery** also represents various Native American artists; Loretto's own sculpture makes it truly worth the visit. Downtown galleries specializing in Native American artifacts include **Joshua Baer and Co.** (known for antique Navajo rugs), **Channing Gallery**, **Rainbow Man**, and **Dewey Galleries**; elsewhere in town, nearly every gallery and jewelry store has at least one—if not several—Native American artist represented.

One of the more interesting culture stops in any visit to Santa Fe is the downtown portal (porch) of the **Palace**

of the Governors museum on the Plaza. Here, in a Santa Fe tradition that's been carried on for hundreds of years, a few dozen Native American jewelers and craftspeople sell work created by them or their immediate family members. This open-air marketplace looks like a haggler's haven; actually, it's a decidedly straightforward place where vendors almost always refuse to budge on their prices. There's lots of silver jewelry (with and without turquoise or semiprecious stones), small Indian pots representing the ceramics traditions of different pueblos, beadwork, sand paintings, drums, and occasionally even horno (adobe oven) bread. It's interesting to keep in mind that most of these vendors are doing quite well sitting on that cold sidewalk, day in and day out. A friend of mine who occasionally sells there tells me that a few of the Native American vendors pull in as much as $80,000 a year after taxes. Try doing *that* in front of your home town's history museum.

The Hispanic thing... One of the most interesting things you can delve into while visiting Santa Fe is the region's Hispanic culture. Not as commercialized as Santa Fe's Native American culture, it's different from other North American Hispanic experiences, neither Cuban nor Puerto Rican nor Chicano. One of the best places to start is at the **Palace of the Governors**, the state historical museum on the north side of the Plaza. The old state capitol building, it goes way back to the Spanish colonial days; there are rooms dedicated to ancient colonialist documents and weaponry, desks of long-departed colonialist bureaucrats, and Hispanic works of art spanning four centuries. Another Santa Fe institution, the **Museum of International Folk Art**, has a Hispanic heritage wing that rotates high-quality exhibitions of everything from carnival costumes from the northeast coast of Brazil to the work of traditional New Mexican *santeros*—Hispanic artisans who create saintly three-dimensional *bultos* and painted wood *retablos*, inspired by religious themes. It's just too bad there isn't a Santa Fe arts center dedicated to exhibiting contemporary works of art by the state's Hispanic painters, sculptors, jewelers, and ceramicists.

Depending on what time of year you arrive, there are two fantastic community celebrations of Hispanic culture that you can amble into. The first, and most serious, of these is the **Spanish Market** (tel 505/983–4038 or 505/ 988–1878), a celebration of traditional and contemporary Hispanic arts and artists that takes place in and around the downtown Plaza over a weekend in late July. Everyone who is anyone in New Mexico's appealing world of Hispanic arts takes part in Spanish Market, whether the artist is a contemporary printmaker creating landscapes or a traditional wood-carver or weaver crafting unique and intricate religious carvings and tapestries. There's also a children's section that's a real sleeper for anyone looking for a low-priced way to collect Hispanic art, as well as demonstrations of Hispanic performing arts—flamenco dancing, folk music, and the hybrid *matachines* dancing, which combines elements of both Native American and Hispanic cultures. The other great festival of Hispanic heritage, and one that's heavily weighed toward the lunatic end of the spectrum, is the **Fiestas de Santa Fe** (tel 505/988–7575), a wild week-long affair that starts the weekend immediately following Labor Day, in early September. Like Mardi Gras, a historical pageant, and a harvest festival all rolled up into one and spiced with a strong dose of Fourth of July, it's one of the few times when Santa Fe's downtown is turned back over to its Hispanic residents. It's been taking place, in one form or another, since the early 1700s, which makes it the oldest continually celebrated community festival in the nation, at least according to the Fiesta council. The main stuff is on the Plaza, but some events take place at Fort Marcy Park, the Santa Fe Community Theatre, Sweeney Center, and St. Francis Cathedral.

Of course, you may not have planned a visit during one of these two Hispanic cultural festivals, in which case you'll need an alternative way to get an intoxicating whiff of our local flavor. Walk through the historic district known as **Barrio de Analco**, located southeast of the Plaza and south of the river, on a couple of blocks of De Vargas Street between Paseo de Peralta and Don Gaspar Street. Though it's no longer exclusively home to families with names such as Baca and Griego, this historic and funky part of town has several historic homes, sensually curvaceous adobe walls, and towering cottonwood trees. Art galleries are sprinkled here and there, and there are a few shops selling clothes and historic artifacts in the neighborhood. The Barrio de Analco may not look like much from the windows of a passing car, but I promise you that if you get out of the car, walk along De Vargas Street, and let the place's spirit seep into you, its charm will eventually hit you right between the eyes.

Enough with the charm—what do today's Hispanic youth do in their spare hours? To find out, just catch the **low-rider cruising** that takes place almost year-round on weekend nights in and around the Plaza. Carfuls of dudes and babes, not just from Santa Fe but also from small towns all over northern New Mexico, drive down Alameda Street and Palace Avenue, check each other out (and, of course, their cars), and try to do what kids everywhere do: get paired up with a member of the opposite sex. Kids who aren't car-bound congregate in front of the ice-cream shop at the southwest corner of the Plaza, playing guitars, acting cool, and showing off the clothes they just bought at the mall. Walk along the sidewalks or sit on one of the Plaza benches and the parade of low-slung Chevys and monster trucks will pass you by, searching for weekend dream destinies.

Art in the streets... Summer in Santa Fe, like summer in any tourist town, is the perfect time for outdoor art festivals, most of which take place around the Plaza. One of the most popular events is the annual **Santa Fe Indian Market** (tel 505/983–5220), an event that's now in its 75th year. Indian Market draws nearly 100,000 visitors to town for three days of art shows, gallery exhibitions, dance performances, and food booths selling Indian fry bread. Taking place on the third weekend in August, Indian Market is acknowledged as the height of Santa Fe's busy summer season, and if you're smart you'll make your hotel reservations a year in advance. It's a time when galleries put their best foot forward and when the best-financed art buyers flood into town to spend massive amounts of cash on everything from $100 opera tickets to $10,000 concha belts. Native America's most accomplished artists also flood into town, entering their best pieces in a highly competitive prize contest the day prior to the market's Saturday opening. Artists' sales booths, which number nearly 300 strong, are spread around the downtown streets and even near the shopping mall, selling jewelry, basketry, weaving, paintings, sculpture, beadwork, and any other art form associated with native

SANTA FE | DIVERSIONS

America. Santa Feans break out their favorite Native American–made necklaces, bracelets, and earrings to wear with cowboy boots, broomstick skirts, Stetson hats, and a whole lot of southwestern style. One of my favorite things is to arrive downtown as early as possible on Saturday morning, which usually means around 6am, to watch the artists madly polishing, arranging, gulping coffee, and socializing. By the time the market opens at 7am, the Plaza is filled with thousands of frenzied art buyers, running from one booth to another, snapping up everything in sight and creating absolute mayhem. After I tire of the sight of so much money changing hands so quickly in exchange for so much art, I head over to the food booths on Palace Avenue to snag a cup of hot chocolate and an Indian fry bread, sprinkling powdered sugar on the hot bread and sitting down somewhere on the sidewalk nearby to watch the craziness of yet another year's market take hold of Santa Fe.

Spanish Market, the other major Plaza art festival of the summer, takes place at the end of July each year. Not as wildly commercial as Indian Market, it's a major celebration of contemporary and traditional Hispanic arts and craftsmanship. Each year Spanish Market draws larger and larger crowds into Santa Fe for a weekend of artists' sales booths, traditional food, dance performances, and even flamenco music. The festival is divided into the Traditional Spanish Market (tel 505/983–4038), which takes place directly on the Plaza and whose artists create pieces strongly influenced by the historic trends of Spanish art (heavy on the Catholicism); and the Contemporary Spanish Market (tel 505/988–1878), whose artists congregate on Lincoln Avenue adjacent to the Plaza to sell work ranging from fine jewelry to watercolor landscapes of northern New Mexico to bronze sculpture. Myself, I've started to make a couple of art purchases at Spanish Market each year—not just because I'm convinced it's still being sold at bargain prices (which it is), but also because I feel that the market's artists have a special talent for capturing elements of the New Mexico experience. Spanish Market also holds a winter holiday market each year at the La Fonda hotel ballroom, an event not nearly as large as the summer market, but still a great time and place to purchase reasonably priced, artistically fine gift items.

A number of weekend outdoor art and craft fairs take place in and around the Plaza area during the summer months, often mundane affairs with no special focus. The **Santa Fe Artists' League** shows feature anywhere from a dozen to a few dozen exhibiting artists and take place in downtown's Cathedral Park (next to St. Francis Cathedral) and in the parking lot of First National Bank on the west side of the Plaza. There's an exhibition of one type or another every weekend from May through October. The **Santa Fe Council for the Arts** (tel 505/ 988–1878) organizes several large arts and crafts fairs on the Plaza each summer, on weekends such as July Fourth, Labor Day, Memorial Day, and a couple of other times each year. What's more interesting, though, are the Council's twice-annual Santa Fe open studio tours, weekends during which several dozen artists, scattered across the Santa Fe landscape, open their doors for visitors to come sip iced tea, wander through their home studios, and check out their (usually) bargain-priced art. Dates vary each year, as do the dates of the Plaza arts and craft fairs, so call for precise schedule information. **Photo Santa Fe** (tel 505/937–5482) is another art festival to keep in mind, taking place indoors at Sweeney Center over a weekend in late July (usually the weekend preceding Spanish Market). Since it draws photography dealers and collectors from across the nation, the city's photography galleries stage their best one-artist exhibitions to coincide with Photo Santa Fe, as well as lectures and demonstrations by their featured artists. One other important art festival to keep in mind isn't really a festival, but is rather an ongoing exhibition of contemporary art known as **Site Santa Fe**. This very forward-looking entity is a privately funded, top-notch effort to bring nationally and internationally known "name" artists into Santa Fe for lectures, performances, site-specific art installations, and gallery exhibitions. Housed in what once was a beer warehouse, it is now the state's largest indoor art exhibition space, in the Guadalupe district railyards a 10-minute walk from the Plaza—a place absolutely devoid of anything even passingly familiar with southwestern adobe style. It is, in a way, the perfect place to find works of art by contemporary art-world forces such as Bruce Nauman, Ann Hamilton, Jenny Holzer, Barbara Bloom, Rebecca Horn, Gerald McMaster, and Andres Serrano (to name

SANTA FE | DIVERSIONS

just a few of the artists who were exhibited in Site Santa Fe's opening show).

Gallery hopping: near the Plaza... Two parts of Santa Fe have the most concentrated gallery districts: the downtown Plaza area and Canyon Road. Downtown galleries worth a visit include the **Riva Yares Gallery**, which is best known for its roster of contemporary Mexican, South American, and Native American artists. The Yares space is dramatically modern, designed by an Italian architect and well suited to large sculptural and painted works. It's expensive, at times quite daring, and a must-see stop on your itinerary. Nearby, **Horwitch LewAllen Gallery**, known for contemporary American and Native American art, is another large, modern space, with a broad representation of predominantly high-priced textile arts, sculpture, ceramics, and paintings. The staff is very willing to talk your ear off about any arcane (or obvious, for that matter) artistic point. **Kent Galleries** is the city's most prominent showcase of fine crafts and home furnishings—a great place to find that $7,000 rocking chair you've been dreaming about, or to get your fill of more affordable functional ceramics and paintings by local artists. Don't overlook Kent's jewelry cases, which are also filled with great local and regional work. **Garland Gallery** represents most of the state's best contemporary glass masters, as well as some truly notable glass artists from places such as Seattle; Penland, NC; and Corning, NY.

Joshua Baer, **Channing Gallery**, **Rainbow Man**, and **Dewey Galleries** are the downtown's best places to find Native American artifacts, though most sell some work by contemporary artists as well. These four artifacts galleries tend to be quite expensive and can at times treat the under-attired as if they're hobos, but their standards are high and their well-heeled clientele is loyal. Joshua Baer also has primitive art from around the globe, while Dewey's big on southwestern landscapes and Channing and Rainbow Man are into Americana. At Rainbow Man you'll find the widest selection of prices, as well as a Coke machine filled with glass bottles of the Real Thing.

Peyton-Wright Gallery represents some of the region's hottest younger artists, including Darren Vigil Grey and Deborah MacNaughton. Peyton-Wright's pricing tends to keep most works of art moderately affordable, so this is a place quite popular with collectors. The gallery's occasional exhibitions of oddball objects such as European watches and pre-Columbian textiles are well conceived and shouldn't be missed. **Contemporary Southwest Gallery** is best known for its roster of enthusiastic, individualistic regional artists such as sculptor Bill Worrell and painters Andrew Peters and Frank Howell. The gallery is one of Santa Fe's friendliest as well as one of its most readily affordable, and the art can at times be captivating, though it tends to stay within the southwestern vernacular. **Joe Wade Gallery** is the home of the highly collectable Roger Williams, one of the state's most elegant interpreters of the southwestern landscape, as well as several other artists working in regional and old West themes. The Plaza area's newest and splashiest art space is the **Waxlander-Khadoure Gallery**, home to the widely popular watercolor landscapes of artist/owner Phyllis Kapp. Her work, which is affordable, energetic, emotional, and individualistic, is also used for tapestry designs. If you arrive while Phyllis is on one of her frequent visits, you'll meet one of Santa Fe's warmest and most enthusiastic art-scene personalities. The state's best folk/outsider art space is **Leslie Muth Gallery**, a couple of blocks from the Plaza. Leslie scours the South and Southwest for the kinds of artists who paint portraits on flattened beer cans or fashion an animal sculpture from rusted piles of junk. A lot of the stuff here is very affordable, and Leslie herself is a mile-a-minute talker who likes her customers, her artists, her life, and her pets.

Finally, don't even think of leaving Santa Fe without taking a look inside the **New Mexico Museum of Fine Arts** (MFA), the massive, pueblo-like structure on the northwest corner of the Plaza. Home to a great collection of Georgia O'Keeffe paintings, a number of which are always on display, as well as changing exhibits running the gamut from contemporary to cowboy, the MFA is a great place to get a perspective on how this region's art fits into what's happening elsewhere in the art world.

Gallery hopping: along Canyon Road... The Canyon Road area has a wealth of great art galleries, starting with **Nedra Matteucci's Fenn Galleries**, an incredibly beautiful adobe mansion at the corner of Acequia Madre and

Paseo de Peralta. The gallery is filled with paintings by deceased artists from the original Santa Fe and Taos art colonies of the 1930s, '40s, and '50s, much of it outrageously priced yet highly popular with wealthy collectors and museums. There's a fantastic jewelry room as well as an old bank vault filled with historic artifacts, an outdoor sculpture garden around a lush pond (look for sculpture by Glenna Goodacre, creator of the Vietnam Women's Memorial), and a few back galleries that show work by some of the Southwest's most popular living artists. Another not-to-be-missed space is the **Gerald Peters Gallery** on Camino del Monte Sol, a rambling adobe home that's known for its mind-boggling exhibitions of works by Georgia O'Keeffe, William Wegman, founders of the Santa Fe and Taos artists colonies, and many other great, exciting artists.

Lower Canyon Road has the **Meyer Gallery**, a friendly and affordable center for southwestern regional landscapes such as the elegant work of Colorado painter William Hook, while the nearby **Munson Gallery** is an artists' stable more national in scope, with slightly more expensive and more dramatically contemporary paintings. Across the street from these two art spaces is **Dreamtime Gallery**, specializing in Australian Aboriginal art (who says we Santa Feans are provincial?). Just up the road a few yards, **Copeland-Rutherford Fine Art** is one of Santa Fe's most unusual galleries. Friendly, funky, affordable, unpretentious, and authentic, Copeland-Rutherford represents a wide range of contemporary artists from all ethnic backgrounds and all walks of life; it adjoins (of all things) a Tibetan coffeehouse, and is set in a spacious compound with a spectacular sculpture garden in the middle of its parking lot. Copeland-Rutherford also stages Santa Fe's most popular poetry slams and an occasional late-night party with rock bands and general nuttiness.

Slightly farther up the street, in a section referred to as middle Canyon Road, the **Cline Gallery** is noted for somewhat expensive but great-quality work by established national and regional artists. There is also another **Waxlander Gallery** with many different artists than the ones at its Plaza location, and the **Martha Keats Gallery**, which has uniformly great displays of art at reasonable prices (some of it regional, some totally contemporary). Nearby, in one of the road's most attractive buildings, is

Edith Lambert Gallery, owned by one of the city's most opinionated and most respected voices in Santa Fe's arts scene. Edith chooses artists—often female artists—who offer something a bit special; sometimes you may find the work off-putting, sometimes you may find it irresistible, but at all times your mind will slip into gear and engage with what you see on this gallery's walls. **Houshang's Gallery**, home to a number of southwestern regionalist painters, is a great place to find a canvas depicting an adobe home surrounded by an adobe wall surrounded by hollyhocks, etc.

Farther up the road is **Turner-Carroll Gallery**, one of Santa Fe's most interesting contemporary art spaces, exhibiting a top-notch roster of artists from the region as well as across the U.S. and Europe. The gallery may be small, but it is friendly and unpretentious, keeps its prices affordable, and always chooses art that you're not likely to find in other Santa Fe galleries. The nearby **Downey Gallery** is owned by one of the town's more unusual artists, Dennis Downey—not only a great landscape painter but also one of Santa Fe's busiest dentists. His dental offices, I can testify, are filled with art by some of this state's most notable painters, too. If by chance you get a toothache on your visit southwestward, keep in mind that in Santa Fe you can actually have a professional artist/dentist work on your mouth!

Technicolor skies and purple mountainsides...

The spectacular light show that trumpets the arrival of nearly every Santa Fe evening is one of the main reasons why so many great landscape painters moved southwestward in the 1920s and '30s. Our crystal-clear skies, enormous expanses of mesas, mountains, and highlands, and the region's southerly orientation on the continent combine all the right elements for stunning and colorful sunsets. The best places to watch the spectacle unfold are outdoor bar patios, which of course limits your sunset watching to the warmer months. The rooftop lounge on the southwest corner of **La Fonda** hotel (see Accommodations) is a fantastic place for clear, unobstructed views of the skies above. The outdoor cantina at **Coyote Cafe** (see Dining) has a more limited view, but it compensates with an interesting crowd gathered here in early evening. **Cowgirl Hall of Fame** (see Dining) on Guadalupe Street has a southwest-facing patio—it doesn't give you much of a view except of the sky above, but the brews are cheap and the shit-kicker music on the sound system is downright inspirational. As for places you can reach on foot, the oval running track at **St. John's College**, a 25-minute walk from the Plaza, has a heart-stopping view of the entire landscape to the south and west, while the **Cross of the Martyrs** hilltop shrine downtown (something about monks massacred by Indians) has a superb overlook of the Plaza district and a partially obstructed view of the setting sun.

Where to meet someone... The absolute best place and time to strike up a conversation with the Santa Fe person of your dreams is on Friday evening at the art gallery opening reception scene. But if you can't make it to a gallery on Friday, there are a few good alternatives. **Downtown Subscription** is a Canyon Road area coffeehouse and magazine stand with a dozen tables inside and a dozen or so tables outside. It is one of Santa Fe's great daytime gathering places for people with time on their hands; some may be artists, some may be vacationing stockbrokers, some may be retired Hollywood types, but almost all are good for a chat. Another similar arrangement exists at **Old Santa Fe Trail Books & Coffeehouse**, except that you'll find a full bar and restaurant to go along with your magazines and novels, as well as live evening entertainment for a small cover charge. **The Ark Bookstore**, a new age bookstore and metaphysical equipment shop (you know, camping stuff for the world beyond), is the best place in town to meet that starry-eyed shaman you've been dreaming about, while the city's two largest natural supermarkets, **Alfalfa's** and **Wild Oats**, both have sit-down cafes and a funky clientele. Folks may or may not be into talking to you, it sorta depends upon where they're at with their therapy, if you know what I mean. Many, many affinity-group meetings are held all over town, night after night, addressing everything from sex addiction to intergalactic spiritualism; a complete listing of these meetings is published in the Sunday edition of the Santa Fe *New Mexican*.

Aches, pains, and pampering... Around this amusing town, people take their relaxation quite seriously, which is probably why Santa Fe has two schools teaching massage, one teaching acupuncture, and another teaching holistic healing. Alternatives to standard health care, anything from chiropractic to past-life regression, aren't just accepted here—they're the norm. When Santa Fe residents want to relax they head up Hyde Park Road a few miles to one of the most unusual places on the Southwest's map, a Japanese-style spa called **10,000 Waves**. The Waves, as it's known locally, is a breathtakingly scenic facility with outdoor hot tubs, indoor massage tables, roaring fireplaces, and a full range of body treatments by professional masseuses, skin therapists, and herbal health consultants. Tubs are not segregated by sex and can be either private or public, with the private ones costing a bit more but absolutely worth it. You shower in a single-sex locker room, wrap yourself in a cotton kimono, slide into a pair of rubber flip-flops, and enter a world of complete, totally irresponsible relaxation. A trip to Santa Fe isn't complete until you try the Waves, especially during our snowy and cold winter. Another spa experience that takes longer to reach (an hour's drive) is at **Ojo Caliente**, north of Española. Its slightly funky, 1930s-style atmosphere is more traditional than the Waves, with separate facilities for men and women (except for the outdoor swimming pool). The attendants at Ojo wrap you in a muslin sheet after you emerge from soaking in one of the naturally heated pools; you lie on a massage table for a half hour and are treated to the most restful downtime you could imagine. One of Ojo's attractions is the variety of water piped into its outdoor drinking fountain—supposedly, by tapping into different parts of the underlying rock, the spa can pipe in drinkable water with high concentrations of iron, lithium, and calcium, all part of what you get with your admission fee.

Then there's massage—that's professional massage by professionally trained masseuses (as opposed to sleazy "massage," wink, wink). There are more than 50 masseuses listed in the Santa Fe Yellow Pages, and dozens more around town who prefer to work through word-of-mouth recommendation. You can even sit down and get a 15-minute at either of the town's two largest natural foods supermarkets, **Alfalfa's** and **Wild Oats**. For a recommendation on a masseuse, ask the concierge or front-desk clerk at your hotel, or try the Yellow Pages or **Network Chiropractic Center** (tel 505/989–9373, 826 Camino del

Monte Rey). A surprising number of Santa Fe hotels maintain massage rooms for their guests, and have on-call arrangements with one or more of the city's massage businesses. The hotel can probably recommend an acupuncturist, too; one of the most popular is **Daniel Bruce** (tel 505/988–5106, 1301 St. Francis Drive, Suite C). Another option is **Concepts Day Spa and Salon**, which offers a full range of hair treatments, manicure, massage, steam bath...the works! **Sterling Silver Salon** does similar work, without the hair styling, as well as body wraps from seaweed to paraffin. Irma Lasky Skin Care is a type of therapy practiced at the **Alternative Skin Care Salon**, which promotes itself as being "no fluff and for the serious client."

New Age vibes... Start by checking out the bulletin boards at the downtown library or at any of the city's four natural food markets. Filled with flyers announcing appearances by healing deities, internationally famous psychics, mediums channeling all sorts of beings and spiritual forms, traveling musicians, and lectures, the bulletin boards at **The Marketplace** and **Wild Oats** (see Shopping) on St. Francis Drive give probably the best overview of Santa Fe's huge New Age scene. New Age interests are so widespread in Santa Fe, there's even a locally published monthly newspaper, *The Sun*, specializing in interviews and feature articles about New Age practices and practitioners. *The Sun* carries advertisements for everything under the New Age sun, from bookstores and music shops to cranial massage and sweat lodge builders. The chief New Age bookstore in town is **The Ark**, while the best of what can be called New Age art is exhibited at **Moondance Gallery** on Canyon Road. One of the best places in town to get a psychic reading is at **Adevina!**, a south-of-the-border coffeehouse in the Guadalupe district that keeps two psychics, Mari Red Moon and Saben, on hand for spur-of-the-moment readings. Channeler **Bart Emerson Lee** is one of Santa Fe's best-known mediums for his work with the entity Oryon; his groups usually meet weekly at the Bodhi Tree Refuge (tel 505/820–6152 for private consultations). Animal psychics and pet psychics are also very popular in Santa Fe, with **Judy Meyer** (tel 505/820–PETS) and **Melissa Weiner** (tel 505/988–2054) being two of the best-known.

Catholicism's legacy... One of the most popular ways to get a sense of the city's historic foundations is to visit downtown Santa Fe's magnificent collection of adobe churches, such as the **Santuario de Nuestra Señora de Guadalupe**, the **San Miguel Chapel** (which lays claim to being the oldest church in the country), and **Cristo Rey Church** on upper Canyon Road. What you want to watch for in these adobe structures are the *reredos* (altar screens), which are filled with exquisite paintings, carvings, and wood inlay. Two other downtown churches, built in the more traditional Gothic style, are also worth visiting. The city's largest, **St. Francis Cathedral**, towers over the Plaza's east side, even though it's a block away; it looks subdued from the outside, but it is breathtaking inside. The **Loretto Chapel**, a jewel of a church adjacent to the Inn at Loretto, is the site of worship of the "miraculous staircase," a freestanding, winding stairway with no visible means of support. Performances by Santa Fe chamber music groups and choral societies are set here year-round.

Glimpses of the past... There's no place in town that better captures a sense of what the old, pre-tourist Santa Fe must have been like than the historic exhibition rooms in the **Palace of the Governors**. They're filled with everything from relics of the World War II warship *USS New Mexico* to Civil War weaponry, Spanish colonialist documents, suits of armor, works of art spanning four centuries, and Wild West memorabilia galore. You can watch a turn-of-the-century print shop in action, get close up to the religious-inspired creations of New Mexico's *santeros*, and on odd days throughout the summer even see a Wild West–style mountain-man encampment. The Frontier Experience room is another jackpot, with exhibits ranging from Billy the Kid's handguns to frontier sheriffs' badges, stagecoaches, Pony Express saddlebags, buffalo-soldier uniforms, and Comanche leather clothing. But one of the best reasons for coming here is just to walk inside the building's 24-inch-thick adobe walls, to amble along its ancient pine-planked floors, to duck your head as you enter 300-year-old doorways, and to wander into the museum's garden courtyard. **El Rancho de las Golondrinas** (Ranch of the Swallows), located south of Santa Fe along I-25, is a restored Spanish hacienda and working farm/ranch that's more than 250 years old. Throughout the summer and into the fall it presents historically oriented weekend arts, crafts, harvest, and cultural heritage festivals. This is also a great place to bring children, since Las Golondrinas offers hands-on demonstrations of everything from apple cider making to wool shearing, chile ristra stringing to adobe brick making, and folk dancing.

Another great dose of the past greets you the moment you step into the lobby of **La Fonda** hotel (see Accommodations), a high-ceilinged reminder of what touring the Southwest must have been like in the 1920s, when the hotel was expanded into much of its present form. **Sena Plaza**, despite being filled with retail shops and restaurants, retains much of its historic charm and architecture. Not so ancient, yet truly funky in a 1960s sort of way, is the collection of stores cubbyholed into **Santa Fe Village**, an eclectically built shopping mall just a block off the Plaza on Don Gaspar Avenue. It's a great place to find resale clothing and home knick-knacks. For a look at what home life was once like in Santa Fe, visit the gardens and adobe hacienda grounds known as **El Zaguan**, a complex on lower Canyon Road where local artists have been painting the early-blooming floral landscape for decades. People can even rent apartments in this historic residence complex. El Zaguan is maintained by a private foundation that keeps the place open without charge year-round.

Kid-pleasers... Santa Fe isn't the best place to visit when you're towing along a child (or two or three)—kids don't tend to be into the high-end shopping and gallery-hopping that are The City Different's chief pleasures. Still, there are a number of places geared toward entertaining as well as educating youngsters. The **Santa Fe Children's Museum** is a modern facility with hands-on scientific experiments and exhibits, art classes and demonstrations, family programs, and occasional performances by musicians and theater troupes. A great way to occupy nearly a full day is the **Santa Fe Southern** train trip to nearby Lamy, which departs from downtown Santa Fe's old rail depot in mid-morning and returns late that same afternoon. The train operates three times weekly; on Friday evenings there's a starlight ride that gets back into town at 11pm. They only serve food on the Friday night run, so you've got to remember to bring your own lunch. The weekend programs at **El Rancho de las Golondrinas** are always oriented toward families, with lots of hands-on activities inspired by the Southwest's pioneer days. The **Museum of Indian Arts and Culture** has in its Girard Wing an enormous collection of miniature ethnic costumes, figures, and folk toys. For an instant dose of Wild West culture, swing past the **Palace of the Governors** for a look at the Frontier Experience room, loaded with artifacts from New Mexico's vaquero and cowboy past—from Spanish colonial times right up to the late 1800s, when Billy the Kid himself walked Santa Fe's streets. During the summer months, the **Wheelwright Museum of the American Indian** presents free evening storytelling programs for kids, with local personalities weaving tall tales in front of a 15-foot-high buckskin tepee.

Bizarre bazaars... Trader Jack's Flea Market, a few miles outside of Santa Fe adjacent to the Santa Fe Opera, is an ideal low-rent counterpart to the opera's highbrow digs, keeping everyone's egos in check. Open generally from April to late November on Friday, Saturday, and Sunday, it's a great place to find most of the same jewelry, clothing, and funky home accessories sold at downtown Santa Fe stores, except at half the price. But besides straightforward vendors, you'll find a few traditional herb and medicinals vendors, Africans selling rugs, Mexicans selling used tools, masseuses, normal folks having garage sales, hat tycoons, etc., etc.—a perfect microcosm of Santa Fe, only cheaper. Another summer and fall favorite is the **Santa Fe Farmers' Market**, which takes over the parking lot of Sanbusco Center every Tuesday and Saturday morning from June through late October, with vendors selling the usual farmers' market fare, along with local goodies such as homemade salsa and jalapeño peppers. I especially like the Crawford farms garlic booth; the man who sells ears of corn out of a flatbed truck; Ken, the honey guy from Star G farms; Elizabeth Berry, the tomato and bean goddess of Abiquiu; and the Hispanic men who fresh-roast chile peppers from early September through mid-October.

Pleasing the southwestern palate... Okay, so you want to return home and impress your friends with more than just stories about the great food you ate in Santa Fe's restaurants—you actually want to show off new kitchen tricks. Haven't you always wanted to learn how to fix the perfect roasted-pineapple salsa? The **Santa Fe School of Cooking**, located on the top floor of downtown's Plaza Mercado, runs a year-round program of classes designed to teach beginners everything from how to make a breakfast burrito to how to prepare a southwestern-style Thanksgiving dinner. The classes, which usually start in mid-morning and include lunch, cost $25 and up and feature established local chefs and cookbook authors. Another great resource for cooking classes, though not necessarily Southwest-oriented, are the town's two largest natural foods markets, **Wild Oats** and **Alfalfa's**. Both have demonstration kitchens in their stores, where a wide range of year-round classes cover things like grilling organic meats, using natural grains, and brewing natural teas. You'll need to contact the markets' service counters to get a schedule of which classes are being offered during your visit.

Calling all rail buffs... You don't have to worry about attacks from Indian raiding parties or masked banditos blazing away with six-shooters, but taking a train ride in this part of the West is still a great adventure. **Santa Fe Southern** operates year-round from the Guadalupe district's train depot, running a few converted passenger cars behind a diesel locomotive along a rail spur that terminates in Lamy, a two-hour ride south. The train leaves at 10:30am and returns at 4pm; in summer there's also an evening train ride on Fridays that has bar service. Bring along a picnic lunch and anything other than cold drinks, which are sold on the train. If you want more of a Wild West train experience, drive two hours northwest of Santa Fe to the mountain town of Chama, New Mexico, and board the **Cumbres & Toltec Railroad** narrow-gauge train. This old-time coal-fired steam train chugs across a mountain pass and into the small Colorado town of Antonito, skirting a breathtakingly steep river gorge much of the way. One word of advice: If you sit outside for any length of time on this day-long trip, be prepared to be covered with a layer of coal dust, thrown skyward by the locomotive's trusty furnace.

Work out the kinks in your legs... If you would rather not investigate Santa Fe on your own, check out any of a half-dozen or so tour operators that guide visitors along the town's curving streets and historic sites.

They just may help you to uncover some architectural or shopping gems you'd ordinarily overlook. Some tours meet on the Plaza, others in hotel lobbies, but all last nearly three hours. The guides really do try to make their tours interesting, with the emphasis being on things historical, romantic, and mysterious. **Afoot in Santa Fe**, **Aboot/About Santa Fe**, and **Santa Fe Detours** are some of the more established walking tour companies, with not much difference among them. Each offers tours in foreign languages such as French, Japanese, German, Italian, and Spanish (which really isn't a foreign language in Santa Fe), and each charges in the $10-per-person range. One of the funkier and funnier walking tours available is the **Aspook/About Ghosts** tour that leaves from the Eldorado Hotel lobby at 8pm during summer. The tour leader, usually an out-of-work actor or actress, dresses up like a Halloween spirit and leads you through a maze of back alleys, murder sites, ghost-sighting sites, and other parts of Santa Fe's past that the city's visitors' bureau would rather you not know about.

Road-tripping... To northern New Mexico, Santa Fe is the "big city," which is another way of saying that we're surrounded by small villages—villages that are generally quite far apart from each other. Driving out of Santa Fe in any direction (except south to Albuquerque or west to Los Alamos) takes you directly into rural areas that are predominantly Hispanic or Native American. Some of them aren't especially keen on being visited by tourists, but a few routes are very well traveled—finding restaurants, art galleries, and gas stations is no problem. One half-day trip leads south of Santa Fe into the former mining community of **Madrid** (pronounced MAD-rid). A half hour's drive down State Road 14 brings you to this picturesque collection of art galleries, clothing shops, and restaurants. There's even a museum exhibiting old mining equipment and a sometimes-biker bar, the **Mine Shaft Tavern**, that has live entertainment on weekends. A calendar of music festivals takes place at Madrid's 1930s-era ball field—some weekends it may be blues festivals, others it may be classical or even folk music, but whatever it is the events are casual, inexpensive, and definitely family-oriented. Check the Pasatiempo section in Friday's *New Mexican* to see if a summer ballpark show's scheduled while you're in town.

Los Alamos is another option for a day trip, but aside from visiting the **Bradbury Science Museum**'s exhibits of atomic bomb memorabilia and high-tech weaponry (your billions of tax dollars at work, folks), there's not much to see or do in Los Alamos. For all intents and purposes, this town looks and feels more like a military base in North Dakota than it does a mountain town in the Southwest. Los Alamos is, however, close to **Bandelier National Monument** (see Getting Outside) and may be a good stopping-off place to load up on picnic goodies or fast food before you hit the cliff dwellings.

They're not apartment buildings, they're Native American pueblos... Santa Fe is located in the region of the Eight Northern Pueblos (pueblos are Indian homelands, which people in other parts of the nation refer to as reservations). The **Eight Northern Pueblos Council** (tel 505/852–4265) publishes a comprehensive visitors' guide to the region's Native American pueblos and coordinates a summer arts and crafts show that changes locales each year, from one pueblo to another. Visiting these nearby tribal lands is one of the best ways to look at real life in native America. As for which pueblo to visit, that's a matter of deciding how far you want to drive, whether or not there are public ceremonies being held on the days you intend to visit, and the types of Native American artwork you're most interested in purchasing. The pueblos most noted for their pottery and jewelry (and the ones with the most retail shops) are **San Ildefonso**, **Santa Clara**, and **Taos**. Santa Clara and San Ildefonso are close to each other, both about a 45-minute drive northwest of Santa Fe. Santa Clara is the most entrepreneurial of all the Northern Pueblos, selling pottery renowned for its attention to detail and finish, with many open studios and artists selling from their homes. It also operates guided tours of the pueblo and of the Puye Cliff Dwellings. San Ildefonso is most famous for the black-fired pots made by seminal pueblo artist Maria Martinez. Twice as distant from Santa Fe, Taos Pueblo, in addition to its art, is probably best known for its handmade drums, ceremonial dances, and architectural beauty. **Tesuque** is the closest to town, just a 15-minute drive from the Plaza, and has a casino; **Nambe** is a good place for a picnic beside its lake and waterfall; small **Picuris** has a little museum; **Pojoaque** has a casino; and **San Juan**, the farthest out of these five, about a 35-minute drive north of town, has the adjacent **Tewa Indian Restaurant**, a great place to load up on high-calorie specialties such as fry bread and green-chile stew. All of these latter five have gift shops, and while they aren't as well known for out-standing artwork, you'll still find great jewelry, beadwork, pottery, etc.

The Eight Northern Pueblos, however, aren't the only ones in the area. **Cochiti Pueblo**, a 30-minute drive south of Santa Fe, is a great place to find high-quality sterling silver jewelry as well as ceramic pots, ceramic dolls (called storytellers), and painted handmade drums. Cochiti is a friendly place with a few gift shops and a his-toric old church on its central plaza. (Most of the pueblos have large Catholic churches in their central areas, a result of the Christianization forced upon Native Americans hundreds of years ago by Spanish priests.) Farther from town (a two-hour drive) is **Acoma Pueblo**, which is also known as Sky City because of its location on top of a sheer, towering mesa. Acoma's claim to artistic fame is the intensely detailed nature of the decorations painted on its artisans' pots, patterns so geometrically intricate they can practically give you a migraine if you try following them too closely.

Each pueblo allows visitors to differing degrees. Keep in mind that each is a self-governing nation with its own police force, government structure, courts, and character. For you, the visitor, this means two very important things: First, you can get nabbed for speeding on the roads cutting across pueblo lands by radar-loving tribal cops; and second, you need to find out from each pueblo's visitors' center the days when and the places where you may visit. Each pueblo sets its own rules as to whether or not you may take photographs or pull out a sketchbook or record your visit on a videocam. Some don't allow photography, video shooting, or sketching of any sort at any time; others allow limited artists' access and photography for a daily fee. One of the biggest mis-takes visitors make at a pueblo is to ignore the rules, which will make the pueblo residents and pueblo author-ities angry. You could be booted off the pueblo if you act like an idiot, and nobody around here will feel the least bit sorry for you if you do.

Most pueblos have gift shops or small art galleries that are open to visitors, and most pueblos also allow visitors to observe their occasional ceremonial dances, which celebrate things important to Native American spiritual life such as agriculture, wildlife, and even Christmas. Remember that pueblo dance ceremonies are religious observances and are quite sacred—just as you maintain dignity in synagogues or churches back home, so must you also refrain from pointing, talking loudly, walking around, or otherwise acting like a boor during tribal ceremonies. To find out the schedule for pueblo ceremonies and whether visitors are allowed, call the pueblo's visitors' office or ask for a pueblo visitors' guide from the state visitors' bureau.

Santa Fe's first tourists... The Anasazi Indian culture disappeared from New Mexico nearly 1,000 years ago, leaving behind their cliff dwellings, kivas (ceremonial houses), and lodges. You can hike several nearby ruin sites, including the Anasazi cliff dwellings at **Bandelier National Monument** outside Los Alamos (see Getting Outside), to get a taste of how the early human inhabitants of this part of the Southwest lived. The nearby cliff dwellings at Puye are on **Santa Clara Pueblo** lands; they're open to visitors for $5 a person. While not as ancient as the Anasazi ruins at Bandelier, Puye is nonetheless quite spectacular and haunting in its abandoned beauty. At **Pecos National Historic Park**, a short drive northeast of Santa Fe, for $2 a person you can take self-guided tours of a partially restored Spanish mission church built adjacent to a restored Anasazi kiva, as well as visit a small historical center and gift shop. There's also a state-run historical center, **El Rancho de las Golondrinas**, a Hispanic frontier village dedicated to demonstrating and exhibiting what western life was truly like in Santa Fe's past—a history predating more common images of cowboys, cavalry soldiers, and frontier fur trappers by hundreds of years.

Churches and chalupas on the high road to Taos... It'll take you at least six hours at a moderately leisurely pace to drive the **high road to Taos**, a twisting, back-country set of roads that leads you from Santa Fe into Taos through some of northern New Mexico's most beautiful and most culturally authentic small villages. The High Road to Taos actually starts on the outskirts of Española, a small city half an hour's drive north of Santa Fe. If you wanted to get to Taos as quickly as possible you would drive along U.S. Highway 84/285, a road taking you up through the Rio Grande gorge after cutting through the middle of Española. But to get onto the High Road, veer off Highway 84/285 at Pojoaque and drive onto State Road 503, which takes you 5 miles onto **Nambe Pueblo** and eventually into **Chimayo**, which is 35 miles from Santa Fe. This historic village is known hereabouts as the "Lourdes of the Southwest," primarily because of its Easter week religious pilgrimage, with thousands of faithful hiking into Chimayo from all across the state. Once there, they congregate at the Santuario de Nuestro Señor de Esquipulas, a place most of the state refers to as the **Santuario de Chimayo**. This historic adobe church's anteroom draws hundreds of Christians seeking special blessings for everything from foot ailments to cancer, and troubled marriages to good grades in elementary school; dipping their fingers into a round hole in the anteroom's floor, they scoop up some "holy dirt" that's been blessed by the Chimayo parish priests, which is thought by some to have special healing powers. The Santuario's anteroom is filled with talismans representing people's hopes and dreams, like the tiny tin *milagros* (usually depicting legs, hearts, arms, etc.) you see sold in religious shops and hammered onto folk art from across the Spanish-speaking world. Wooden canes, faded photographs of Hispanic women, rosaries, shoes, crutches, you wouldn't believe it unless you've seen it. A visit to the Santuario de Chimayo is like taking a trip to another land, another place in time. Chimayo is also home to a good restaurant known for its great enchiladas, the **Rancho de Chimayo**, and a renowned tortilla shop, **Leona's of Chimayo**, known for its thick, flavored flour and wholewheat tortillas. Leona's is across the parking lot from the Santuario, and I always enjoy buying a dozen fresh, warm tortillas as I'm heading back out of Chimayo, to munch as I continue on my way to Taos. Chimayo is also famous for being the home of some of the Southwest's most accomplished textile artisans, most of whom create woven tapestries in the traditional Hispanic pattern known as Rio Grande–style or Chimayo-style weaving. **Ortega's**

Weaving Shop, which you'll pass on your way back out of town heading toward Taos, is one of the most famous of these, a great place to find everything from woven rugs to handmade crafts to Chimayo baseball caps. If Andrew Ortega's adjacent cafe is open, stop in to have an iced tea underneath the cooling cottonwood trees.

Continuing on the High Road, you leave Chimayo and drive onto State Road 76, heading past the wood-carving mecca of **Cordova**, where many local artisans sell their art from their homes (just look for signs posted in some front yards), and go 10 miles into the high mountain town of **Truchas**, which is best known as the place where Robert Redford shot *The Milagro Beanfield War*. Truchas has a good cafe and several very worthwhile art galleries, some selling local art, some selling work by artists from elsewhere in the state, and one even selling mostly contemporary art. Continuing north on State Road 76 about 20 miles, you'll eventually enter the village of Penasco, which has another good cafe, but you should probably hold onto your appetite until the road winds 20 miles or so farther north, leading you back onto the main route, State Road 68, at the southern end of **Taos**. Once there, find your way into **Eske's Brewpub**, order a fresh draft and a burger, sit out by the picnic tables if the weather's suitable, and take a few deep breaths of Taos' 8,000-foot-high mountain air. You'll probably also want to visit **Taos Pueblo**, which provided much of the inspiration behind New Mexico's 1930s-era revival of the pueblo architectural style that's now so prevalent throughout Santa Fe. The Taos Plaza is worth a brief visit, but I find its proliferation of T-shirt shops and stores selling tourist trinkets depressingly familiar. A better bet for a Taos walk is to stroll eastward on Kit Carson Road, a route that will take you past several of the community's better art galleries as well as the **Cafe Tazza**, a fantastic coffee shop and inexpensive restaurant. There are two outstanding art museums in Taos, the **Harwood Foundation Museum** and the **Millicent Rogers Museum**. You'll need a car to get to the Millicent Rogers, but both of these places are widely acknowledged for their collections. The Harwood, housed in an old historic house, focuses on works by founders of the Taos art colony and the community's contemporary artists; the Millicent Rogers exhibits traditional Hispanic and

Native American art as well as occasional shows of more contemporary works.

Coming back into Santa Fe you'll have two great routes to choose from. The first, and most direct, is to head south on State Road 68 and wind back down the Rio Grande Gorge, passing the white-water rafting center of Pilar, the tiny artists' community of Dixon, and the riverside brewpub and smokehouse at **Embudo Station**, a place serving some wickedly good beer called Red Chile Ristra and the best barbecue sandwiches this side of the Texas border. Eventually, State Road 68 hooks up with U.S. 84/285 in Española and takes you straight into Santa Fe. The alternate route, and one that will add at least an hour onto your trip, is to head north of Taos on State Road 68 until you come to the flashing red light that's the intersection of 68 and U.S. Highway 64. Turn west onto 64 and drive 10 miles to the spectacular bridge overlook of the Rio Grande Gorge. After stopping here for a half hour or so to oooh and aaah at the view, go west 20 miles on 64 until it intersects at another flashing light with U.S. 285, turn south on 285, and follow it 40 miles all the way into Española. This route takes you through **Ojo Caliente**, the town noted for its hot springs and old-fashioned spa. It's a great place to stop for another couple of hours and soak in a naturally heated mineral spring or take a swim in the outdoor pool.

Slots, craps, and blackjack... Since mid-1994, Indian gambling palaces have been popping out of the New Mexico landscape like boletus mushrooms on an early autumn morning. The state's largest gambling hall is right on the outskirts of Santa Fe at the Tesuque Indian Pueblo's **Camel Rock Casino**. Hundreds of slot machines, craps tables, roulette wheels, giant buffets, and bars that stay open until the dawn's early light (pueblos are excepted from state liquor laws) are what you get when you pass through Camel Rock's southwest-style doors. If for no other reason, you should drop by the casinos at least briefly for some of the best people-watching in the region. I mean, where else could you see the entire spectrum of New Mexico's melting pot of Native American, Hispanic, Anglo, and cowboy cultures, all peacefully sitting side by side, hooking their hopes and dreams on the roll of the dice? Nearby, in Pojoaque, the Pojoaque Pueblo's **Cities of**

Gold Casino is another heterogeneous gambling palace—not quite on the grand scale of Camel Rock Casino, but still loaded with all the gambling and whoopee-making bells and whistles. Who knows, maybe you'll win back the cost of your Santa Fe vacation with one pull of a slot machine handle!

The Index

Aboot/About Santa Fe. Walking tours of downtown and Canyon Road area, as well as guided out-of-town walking trips.... *Tel 505/988–2774. Departs from Eldorado Hotel and Hotel St. Francis. Year-round. Admission charged.*

Acoma Pueblo. Composed of an old village atop a steep mesa and a newer village that's considerably more accessible, Acoma offers guided tours of its ancient site. Several shops and artists are always selling the pueblo's famed pottery.... *Tel 505/252–1139. 50 miles west of Albuquerque off I-40. Call ahead to determine when visiting hours and public ceremonies are scheduled. Fees charged for tours and photography.*

Adevina! One of the town's favorite places to hang out, find inexpensive gifts, meet friends over coffee, get psychic readings, shop for clothes, etc. In other words, what Santa Fe once was all about.... *Tel 505/983–8799. 333 Montezuma St. Closed Sun.*

Afoot in Santa Fe. Walking tours of downtown and Canyon Road areas.... *Tel 505/983–3701. Departs from the Inn at Loretto parking lot. Operates Mar–Nov. Admission charged.*

Alfalfa's Market. Natural-food market and deli/coffeeshop.... *Tel 505/986–8667. 500 W. Cordova Rd. Open 8am–10pm daily.*

Alternative Skin Care Salon. Specific Irma Lasky therapies for problem skin, as well as facials.... *Tel 505/983–3824. 712 Calle Grillo. By appointment.*

The Ark Bookstore. Widest selection of New Age literature in the Southwest, as well as accoutrements to carry you into the next dimension.... *Tel 505/988–3709. 133 Romero St. Open Mon–Sat 10–6.*

Aspook/About Ghosts. Evening walking tours with an emphasis on the macabre.... *Tel 505/988–2774. Departs from Eldorado Hotel. Operates Memorial Day–Labor Day. Admission charged.*

Bradbury Science Museum. Atomic bomb exhibits and other end-of-the-world surprises cooked up by the government agents and mad scientists living in Los Alamos.... *Tel 505/667–4444. 15th and Central sts., Los Alamos. Open Tues–Fri 9–5, Sat–Mon 1–5. Admission free.*

Cafe Tazza. Taos' most popular hangout for the caffeine-addicted and a great place to check out the local bulletin boards.... *Tel 505/758–8706. 122 E. Kit Carson Rd. Open Mon–Thur 8–5, Fri–Sat 8am–10pm.*

Camel Rock Casino. Indian reservation–style gambling hall.... *Tel 800/GO–CAMEL. 10 miles north of the Plaza on U.S. 285. Open 24 hours daily.*

Channing Gallery. Specialists in antique Americana and Native American historical artifacts.... *Tel 505/988–1078. 53 Old Santa Fe Trail. Open Mon–Sat 10–5.*

Cities of Gold Casino. Indian reservation–style gambling hall.... *Tel 505/455–3313. 20 miles north of the Plaza on U.S. 285. Open 24 hours daily.*

Cline Gallery. Exhibits strong work by national artists and some regional artists, both contemporary and traditional imagery.... *Tel 505/982–5238. 526 Canyon Rd. Open Mon–Sat 10–5.*

Cochiti Pueblo. Located close to a lake and the state's premier 18-hole golf course, Cochiti Pueblo is home to some of the Southwest's most skilled artists, known for their drums, storyteller ceramic figures, pottery, and jewelry.... *Tel 505/465–*

2244. Located 25 miles south of the Plaza on N.M. Hwy 22. Call ahead to determine when visiting hours and public ceremonies are scheduled. No fees. Cameras not allowed.

Concepts Day Spa and Salon. Everything from nails to massage, haircuts, and facials.... *Tel 505/988–3840. 500 Montezuma St. Open Mon–Sat 9–6 and by appointment.*

Contemporary Southwest Gallery. As its name implies, the work here reflects a regional sensibility, with artists so highly skilled that they almost always transcend regional limitations.... *Tel 505/986–0440. 123 W. Palace Ave. Open Mon–Sat 10–5.*

Copeland-Rutherford Fine Art. Eclectic space exhibits work primarily from New Mexican artists of individualistic contemporary vision. Also stages poetry slams and other community gatherings.... *Tel 505/983–1588. 403 Canyon Rd. Open Mon–Sat 10–5.*

Cristo Rey Church. One of the region's finest examples of pueblo-revival architecture. Has a beautiful altar.... *Tel 505/983–8528. 1120 Canyon Rd. Open 7–7 daily. Donations accepted.*

Cross of the Martyrs. Hilltop shrine dedicated to Franciscan monks killed by Native Americans during the Pueblo Revolt of 1680.... *No phone. Off Paseo de Peralta between Otero St. and Hillside Ave. Open year-round.*

Cumbres & Toltec Railroad. This seasonal narrow-gauge train travels across a high mountain pass straddling New Mexico and Colorado.... *Tel 505/756–2151. In Chama, a 90-minute drive north of Santa Fe on U.S. 64. Open Memorial Day–mid-Oct. Admission charged.*

Dewey Galleries. Native American artifacts as well as paintings by some of the Southwest's best-known artists.... *Tel 505/982–8632 or 6244. 76 E. San Francisco St. Open 10–5, Mon–Fri.*

Downey Gallery. Landscapes from Europe and the Southwest as well as fine furnishings and some figurative paintings.... *Tel 505/982–6701. 820 Canyon Rd. Open Mon–Sat 10–5.*

Downtown Subscription. The most comprehensive selection of magazines and newspapers in Santa Fe, sold in a contemporary coffeehouse atmosphere.... *Tel 505/983–3085. 376 Garcia St. Open 7–6 daily.*

Dreamtime Gallery. Aboriginal art from Australia's traditional and contemporary native artists.... *Tel 505/986–0344. 223 Canyon Rd. Open Mon–Sat 10–5.*

Edith Lambert Gallery. A national roster of primarily female artists working with individualistic, highly personal themes.... *Tel 505/984–2783. 707 Canyon Rd. Open Mon–Sat 10–5.*

El Rancho de las Golondrinas. Historical center housed in a centuries-old hacienda south of town. Water mill, blacksmith shop, sheep, and harvest celebrations.... *Tel 505/471–2261. 15 miles south of the Plaza at exit 276 on I-25. Open Wed–Sun 10–4. Closed Nov–Mar. Admission charged.*

El Zaguan. A historic garden and building located halfway up Canyon Road. The building's private, except for its entrance into the garden.... *No phone. 545 Canyon Rd. Open daily 9–5. Admission free.*

Embudo Station. Brewpub, smokehouse, and wonderful restaurant along the cottonwood-shaded banks of the Rio Grande.... *Tel 505/852–4707. On N.M. Hwy 68 between the towns of Velarde and Pilar. Open 10–6 daily. Closed Dec–Apr.*

Eske's Brewpub. Friendly neighborhood tavern with great home-brewed beers and sandwiches.... *Tel 505/758–1517. In parking lot, behind bicycle shop, off Paseo del Pueblo Sur in Taos. Open noon–11 daily.*

Garland Gallery. Dedicated to exhibiting glass art, Garland Gallery may not represent the art-glass world's biggest names, but it does exhibit fabulous work by highly skilled glass artists from across the U.S.... *Tel 505/984–1555. 66 W. Marcy St. Open Mon–Sat 10–5.*

Gentle Spirit Gallery. The only gallery in Santa Fe owned by a female Native American artist, Estelle Loretto, it specializes in work by Indian artists from the Southwest as well as Loretto's own sculpture and lithographs.... *Tel 505/989–4793. 708 Canyon Rd. (in Gypsy Alley). Open Mon–Sat 10–5.*

Gerald Peters Gallery. The only gallery in Santa Fe capable of mounting exhibitions of work by Georgia O'Keeffe.... *Tel 505/988–8961. 439 Camino del Monte Sol. Open Mon–Sat 9–5.*

Governor's Gallery. Actually part of the spacious lobby area in the suite of offices housing the governor and his staff, this gallery space is administered by a branch of the state museum department. Always worth a visit.... *Tel 505/ 827–3000. Fourth floor of state capitol, Paseo de Peralta and Old Santa Fe Trail. Open weekdays 9–5 except for state and federal holidays.*

Harwood Foundation Museum. Art by leading Taos artists of the 20th century, as well as Hispanic artwork by New Mexican artists.... *Tel 505/758–9826. 238 Ledoux St., Taos. Open Mon–Fri 12–5, Sat 10–4. Donations requested.*

Horwitch LewAllen Gallery. One of the most dynamic art spaces in Santa Fe, this gallery is dedicated to contemporary art by painters, sculptors, and craftspeople from across the U.S.... *Tel 505/988–8997. 129 W. Palace Ave. Open Mon–Sat 10–5.*

Houshang's Gallery. Southwestern regionalism and some rather funky contemporary art.... *Tel 505/988–3322. 713 Canyon Rd. Open Mon–Sat 10–5.*

Institute of American Indian Arts Museum. A definitive exhibition facility for Native American arts and crafts, both traditional and contemporary. Outdoor sculpture park regularly exhibits startlingly fresh, exciting three-dimensional work by major talents.... *Tel 505/988–6211. 108 Cathedral Place. Open Mon–Sat 10–5, Sun 12–5, Closed Mon. Admission charged.*

Joe Wade Gallery. Small, underrated art space representing some middlin' artists, others as good as anything you can find in Santa Fe. Affordable, as well.... *Tel 505/988–2727. 102 E. Water St. Open Mon–Sat 10–5.*

Joshua Baer and Co. An outstanding showcase of valuable Native American artifacts.... *Tel 505/988–8944. 116 Palace Ave. Open Mon–Sat 10–5.*

Kent Galleries. The city's premier showcase for contemporary fine crafts, Kent Galleries also exhibits jewelry, weavings, and paintings by local artists.... *Tel 505/988–1001. 130 Lincoln Ave.*

Leona's of Chimayo. Tortilla makers supreme.... *Tel 505/ 351–4660. Located at the edge of the parking lot for Santuario de Chimayo, on N.M. Hwy 76 in Chimayo. Open Mon–Fri 10–5.*

Leslie Muth Gallery. Outsider and primitive art from across the U.S., but especially strong on artists from Texas and New Mexico.... *Tel 505/989–4620. 225 E. De Vargas St. Open Mon–Fri 10–5.*

Loretto Chapel. Small, beautiful house of worship.... *Tel 505/988–5531. 211 Old Santa Fe Trail. Open 9–5 daily. Admission charged.*

Martha Keats Gallery. Great selection of contemporary paintings, curious crafts, and stunning photography.... *Tel 505/982–6686. 644 Canyon Rd. Open Mon–Sat 10–5.*

Meyer Gallery. Strongest in realism by southwestern regionalist painters.... *Tel 505/983–1434. 225 Canyon Rd. Open Mon–Sat 10–5.*

Millicent Rogers Museum. Outstanding collection of Native American and Hispanic art.... *Tel 505/758–2462. 4 miles north of Taos on N.M. Hwy 522. Open 9–5 daily. Closed major holidays. Admission charged.*

Mine Shaft Tavern. Harley Davidsons, college students, tourists, and aging hippies make this hamburger joint/bar one of the best places in the state for a few hours of people-watching.... *Tel 505/473–0743. On N.M. Hwy 14, in Madrid. Open 11–11 daily.*

Moondance Gallery. Canyon Road's only New Age art gallery, Moondance represents some surprisingly skilled artists working in imagery you may find inspirational and enlightening.... *Tel 505/982–3421. 233 Canyon Rd. Open Mon–Sat 10–5.*

Munson Gallery. Good group of contemporary artists from the Southwest and elsewhere.... *Tel 505/983–1657. 225 Canyon Rd. Open Mon–Sat 10–5.*

Museum of Indian Arts and Culture. Exhibits historical arts and crafts of Native American cultures, with a special focus on southwestern tribes. Astounding displays of pottery, clothing, and basketry in spacious galleries.... *Tel 505/827–6344. 710 Camino Lejo. Open 10–5 daily, Jan–Feb. Closed Mon and major holidays. Admission charged.*

Museum of International Folk Art. Brimming with folk arts and crafts from overseas, treasures galore from New Mexico's Hispanic past and present, nationally prominent collections of Latin American and Mexican folk art, and a definitive collection of historic textiles. One of Santa Fe's best art galleries is the museum's gift shop.... *Tel 505/827–6350. 706 Camino Lejo. Open 10–5 daily. Closed Mon (pending funding) and major holidays. Admission charged.*

Nambe Pueblo. Not a particularly artsy place, Nambe Pueblo is best known for its lake, waterfall, and picnic grounds.... *Tel 505/455–2036. 15 miles north of the Plaza on N.M. Hwy 503. Call ahead to determine when visiting hours and public ceremonies are scheduled. Fees charged for activities, photography, and sketching.*

Nedra Matteucci's Fenn Galleries. Great art by founders of the original Santa Fe and Taos art colonies; antique Native American jewelry and sculpture by several prominent Southwest realists.... *Tel 505/982–4631. 1075 Paseo de Peralta. Open Mon–Sat 10–5.*

New Mexico Capitol Building. A.k.a. The Roundhouse. A bizarre round structure housing the state's legislative body.... *Tel 505/827–3000. Corner of Paseo de Peralta and Old Santa Fe Trail. Open weekdays 9–5 except state and federal holidays. Admission and tours free.*

New Mexico Museum of Fine Arts. Housed in a massive, pueblo-revival-style building at the northwest corner of the Plaza, the Fine Arts Museum has a collection of Georgia O'Keeffe's paintings as well as work by master artists of the original Santa Fe and Taos art colonies. The contemporary art wing stages some of Santa Fe's most innovative group exhibitions.... *Tel 505/827–4455. 107 E. Palace Ave. Open 10–5. Closed Mon Jan–Jun and closed major holidays. Admission charged.*

Niman Fine Arts. Exclusively exhibiting the work of Hopi painter/sculptor Dan Namingha.... *Tel 505/988–5091. 125 Lincoln Ave. Open Mon–Sat 10–5.*

Ojo Caliente. Remnant of another era, this authentically New Mexican spa is the sort of place people have been visiting for decades in search of "healing waters."... *Tel 505/583–2233. 35 miles north of the Plaza on U.S. Hwy 285. Closed on major holidays. Reservations recommended. Admission charged.*

Old Santa Fe Trail Books & Coffeehouse. Funky building, eclectic crowd, interesting bar, wonderful selection of books, erratic cafe, espresso, couches, outdoor patio...in other words, priceless!... *Tel 505/988–8878. 613 Old Santa Fe Trail. Open Mon–Thur 9am–10pm, Fri–Sat 9am–midnight.*

Ortega's Weaving Shop. Elegant tapestries, rugs, shawls, and interior accessories made by one of New Mexico's most famous artistic families. Lots of local art displayed on the shop's walls.... *Tel 505/351–4215. On N.M. Hwy 76 in Chimayo. Open Mon–Sat 10–5.*

Palace of the Governors. The state's historical museum and original capitol building dates back to Spanish colonial times and was once used as a headquarters for Confederate troops who temporarily won custody of The City Different. Viva Santa Fe, y'all!... *Tel 505/827–6476. 914 Palace Ave. Open daily 10–5, Closed Mon and major holidays. Admission charged.*

Pecos National Historic Park. Ancient civilization ruins.... *Tel 505/757–6414. 28 miles east of the Plaza in Pecos, NM. Open 8–5 daily except major holidays. Admission charged.*

Peyton-Wright Gallery. Small, affordable gallery specializing in younger contemporary artists from the Southwest, but some out-of-region artists also.... *Tel 505/989–9888. 131 Nusbaum St. Open Mon–Sat 10–5.*

Picuris Pueblo. Smallest of the Eight Northern Pueblos, Picuris has a restaurant and discount tobacco shop as well as stocked fishing ponds and a picnic area. There's also the small Picuris Pueblo Museum.... *Tel 505/587–2957. 25 miles north of Española on N.M. Hwy 75. Call ahead to determine when visiting hours and public ceremonies are scheduled. Fees charged for admission, activities, photography, and sketching.*

Pojoaque Pueblo. Businesspeople to the core, Pojoaque Pueblo's members operate a huge casino, a somewhat smaller visitors' center, a restaurant, and a shopping mall. Not much to look at besides the tourist-oriented attractions.... *Tel 505/455–2278. On U.S. Hwy 285, about 13 miles north of the Plaza. A few fees apply.*

Rainbow Man. Displays a wide range of Native American art, Americana, and western memorabilia.... *Tel 505/982–8706. 107 E. Palace Ave. Open Mon–Sat 9–5 and Sun 10–5.*

Rancho de Chimayo. Best restaurant on the high road to Taos. Famous for its chile.... *Tel 505/351–4444. N.M. Hwy 520 in Chimayo. Open noon–9 daily in summer. Closed Mon in winter.*

Ray Tracey Gallery. Painting, sculpture, and jewelry by southwestern artists, as well as outstanding fine jewelry by Ray Tracey.... *Tel 505/989–3430. 135 W. Palace Ave. Open Mon–Sat 10–5.*

Riva Yares Gallery. Contemporary art from Mexico, Latin America, Europe, and the U.S. One of Santa Fe's must-see galleries.... *Tel 505/984–0330. 123 Grant Ave. Open Tue–Sat 10–5, By appointment Mon and Sun.*

San Ildefonso Pueblo. The most outstanding pottery artists come from this pueblo. Several art galleries as well as a stocked trout pond.... *Tel 505/455–3549. 15 miles north* *of the Plaza on N.M. Hwy 502. Call ahead to determine when visiting hours and public ceremonies are scheduled. Fees for entry, photography, and sketching.*

San Juan Pueblo. Northern Pueblo best known for its arts and crafts shop and adjacent Tewa Indian Restaurant.... *Tel 505/852–4400. 25 miles north of the Plaza on U.S. Hwy 70. Call ahead to determine when visiting hours and public ceremonies are scheduled. Fees charged for photography.*

San Miguel Chapel. Said to be the oldest church in the U.S., it's an architectural treasure loaded with art work dating back centuries.... *Tel 505/983–3974. 401 Old Santa Fe Trail. Open Mon–Sat 9–4 (10–4 in winter), Sun 1:30–4. Donations requested.*

Santa Clara Pueblo. Northern Pueblo noted for its pottery; there is also a large lake for fishing, swimming, and boating.... *Tel 505/753–7326. 25 miles north of the Plaza on N.M. Hwy 30. Call ahead to determine when visiting hours and public ceremonies are scheduled. Fees charged for lake access, cliff dwellings visits, photography, and sketching.*

Santa Fe Children's Museum. Hands-on place to learn about science, art, technology, and human relations.... *Tel 505/989–8359. 1050 Old Pecos Trail. Open 10–5, Wed–Sun in summer, Thur–Sun in winter. Closed major holidays. Admission charged.*

Santa Fe Detours. Walking tours of downtown and Canyon Road areas.... *Tel 505/983–6565. Departs from La Fonda hotel lobby. Operates Mar–Oct. Admission charged.*

Santa Fe Farmers' Market. The usual goodies from small farms, including some southwestern specialties.... *No telephone. 500 Montezuma St. Open Tues–Sat mornings, June–Oct.*

Santa Fe School of Cooking. Downtown cooking school teaches you how to do everything from making your own tortillas to stuffing a chile relleno.... *Tel 505/983–4511. 116 W. San Francisco St. Open year-round. Fees charged for classes.*

Santa Fe Southern. Train rides to nearby town of Lamy.... *Tel 505/989–8600. 410 S. Guadalupe St. Trains operate Tues,*

Thur, Sat, year-round, leaving at 10:30am. Also offers summer evening trains. Admission charged.

Santa Fe Village. Eclectic shops, cafes, and second-hand stores in downtown's last un-gussied-up spot.... *No phone. 227 Don Gaspar Ave. Open 9–6 daily.*

Santuario de Chimayo. A sacred shrine to the Southwest's Catholic faithful, this small-town adobe church attracts pilgrims year-round, but especially during Easter week.... *No phone. In Chimayo, 30 miles north of Santa Fe on N.M. Hwy 520. Open 9–4 daily. Donations accepted.*

Santuario de Nuestra Señora de Guadalupe. Still used by local parishioners, this centuries-old house of worship is also home to art exhibitions, classical music concerts, and a flood of spring weddings.... *Tel 505/988–2027. 100 Guadalupe St. Open 9–4 Mon–Sat May–Oct; Mon–Fri rest of year. Admission free (donations accepted).*

Sena Plaza. This two-story former hacienda retains much of its historical charm and visual appeal, though these days its rooms are filled primarily with commercial shops, law offices, and restaurants.... *No phone. 125–137 E. Palace Ave.*

Site Santa Fe. Contemporary art installations, lectures by national contemporary art authorities, internationally focused exhibitions by some of the art world's most prominent names in cutting-edge art.... *Tel 505/989–1199. 1606 Paseo de Peralta. Open Mon–Sat 10–5. Admission charged.*

Sterling Silver Salon. Facials, hair treatments, pedicures, pampering.... *Tel 505/984–3223. 402 Don Gaspar Ave. By appointment. Closed Sun.*

St. Francis Cathedral. Large downtown Catholic cathedral.... *Tel 505/982–5619. 131 Cathedral Place. Open 6–6 daily. Donations accepted.*

St. John's College. Private university nestled into the foothills of the Sangre de Cristo Mountains. Great place to watch sunsets.... *Tel 505/984–6000. 1160 Camino de la Cruz Blanca.*

Taos Pueblo. An architectural masterpiece, this is the pueblo most closely associated with the pueblo-revival building style. Not an especially friendly or outgoing place, Taos Pueblo is just used to having visitors, all the time.... *Tel 505/758–9593. 2 miles north of Taos on N.M. Hwy 68. Call ahead to determine when visiting hours and public ceremonies are scheduled. Fees charged for admission, photography, and sketching.*

10,000 Waves. Japanese-style spa in the Sangre de Cristo Mountains. Kimonos, cedar soaps, massage, hot tubs.... *Tel 505/988–1047. 2 miles from the Plaza on Hyde Park Rd. Open 10–10 weekdays, 10–11 weekends. Reservations required. Charges for treatments: anywhere from $20 to $75.*

Tesuque Pueblo. Closest to Santa Fe, this pueblo is becoming better known for its mega-casino action than for its arts and crafts, which is probably just as well.... *Tel 505/983–2667. 9 miles north of the Plaza on U.S. Hwy 285. Call ahead to determine when visiting hours are scheduled as well as public ceremonies. Fees for photography, when permitted.*

Trader Jack's Flea Market. Everything under the open sky— the same stuff found in more expensive downtown shops as well as stuff found only here.... *No phone. Located on U.S. Hwy 285, 5 miles north of the Plaza. Open Thur–Sun, Easter–Thanksgiving.*

Turner-Carroll Gallery. Innovative selection of artists representing national and international schools of creative thought.... *Tel 505/986–9800. 725 Canyon Rd. Open Mon–Sat 10–5.*

Waxlander-Khadoure Gallery. Fantastic watercolors by Phyllis Kapp as well as sculpture and fine glass art by several other artists. The downstairs rug and Middle Eastern furniture shop look like things lifted from a Moroccan souk.... *Tel 505/984–2202, 74 E. San Francisco St. Tel 505/984–2202, 622 Canyon Rd. Open Mon–Sat 10–6.*

Wheelwright Museum of the American Indian. Sometimes dull, sometimes exciting, and always worth a visit, this privately funded institution has lately made great

SANTA FE | DIVERSIONS

strides toward becoming a national-caliber exhibition space for contemporary Native American painting, sculpture, jewelry, and ceramics. Also has summer programs with storytelling for kids.... *Tel 505/982–4636. 704 Camino Lejo. Open Mon–Sat 10–5, Sun 1–5. Admission free (donations requested).*

Wild Oats Market. Natural food market, deli, sushi bar, and the best bulletin boards in town.... *Tel 505/983–5333. 1090 St. Francis Dr. Open daily 8am–11pm.*

Downtown Santa Fe Diversions

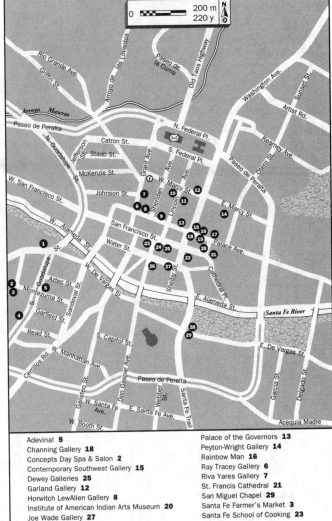

Adevina! **5**

Channing Gallery **18**

Concepts Day Spa & Salon **2**

Contemporary Southwest Gallery **15**

Dewey Galleries **25**

Garland Gallery **12**

Horwitch LewAllen Gallery **8**

Institute of American Indian Arts Museum **20**

Joe Wade Gallery **27**

Joshua Baer & Co. **19**

Kent Galleries **10**

Leslie Muth Gallery **28**

Loretto Chapel **22**

New Mexico Museum of Fine Arts **9**

Niman Fine Arts **11**

Palace of the Governors **13**

Peyton-Wright Gallery **14**

Rainbow Man **16**

Ray Tracey Gallery **6**

Riva Yares Gallery **7**

St. Francis Cathedral **21**

San Miguel Chapel **29**

Santa Fe Farmer's Market **3**

Santa Fe School of Cooking **23**

Santa Fe Southern **4**

Sante Fe Village **26**

Santuario de Nuestra Señora de Guadalupe **1**

Sena Plaza **17**

Waxlander Khadoure Gallery **24**

134

Greater Santa Fe Diversions

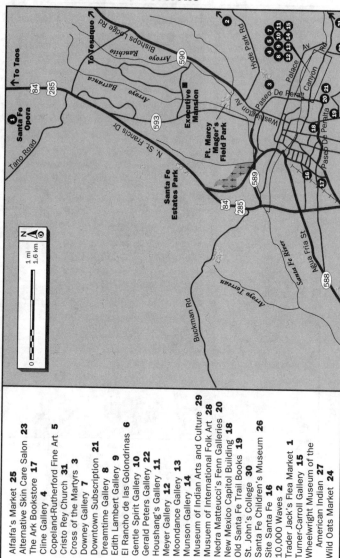

Alfalfa's Market **25**
Alternative Skin Care Salon **23**
The Ark Bookstore **17**
Cline Gallery **4**
Copeland-Rutherford Fine Art **5**
Cristo Rey Church **31**
Cross of the Martyrs **3**
Downey Gallery **7**
Downtown Subscription **21**
Dreamtime Gallery **8**
Edith Lambert Gallery **9**
El Rancho de las Golondrinas **6**
Gentle Spirit Gallery **10**
Gerald Peters Gallery **22**
Houshang's Gallery **11**
Meyer Gallery **12**
Moondance Gallery **13**
Munson Gallery **14**
Museum of Indian Arts and Culture **29**
Museum of International Folk Art **28**
Nedra Matteucci's Fenn Galleries **20**
New Mexico Capitol Building **18**
Old Santa Fe Trail Books **19**
St. John's College **30**
Santa Fe Children's Museum **26**
Site Santa Fe **16**
10,000 Waves **2**
Trader Jack's Flea Market **1**
Turner-Carroll Gallery **15**
Wheelwright Museum of the
American Indian **27**
Wild Oats Market **24**

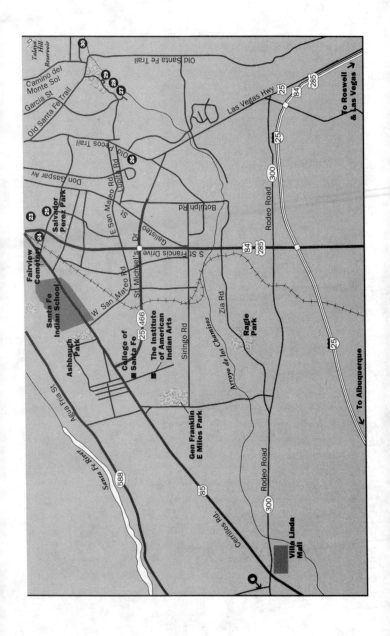

getting

4
outside

For starters, chuck
out all your
notions about the
landscape around
Santa Fe as a
saguaro-and-
rattlesnake-filled

corner of the Sonoran Desert. Sure, it's dry enough most times of the year to make your ears ring (if you don't drink enough water, that is), but we're in what's known as the high desert. If you want the low desert—the Wile E. Coyote vs. Roadrunner type of desert—you'll have to hightail it down to the southern reaches of New Mexico and Arizona.

Our high desert's main geologic feature is the southern edge of the Rocky Mountains, which in this part of the West are referred to as the Sangre de Cristos (yes, that's the Blood of Christ Mountains to all you big-city heathen). The spine of this incredibly scenic wonder stretches from just outside Salida, Colorado, south to the Sandia Crest in mid-state New Mexico, the mountain formation that's Albuquerque's eastern border. The highest point in the Sangres is Wheeler Peak (13,616 feet), northwest of Taos, but the mountains framing Santa Fe are nearly as tall, with Santa Fe Baldy at 12,622 feet and Truchas Peak to the north at 13,102 feet. Nature has graced the town itself with a 7,000-foot elevation, which is damn high for a city of 55,000 or so.

Because of the Sangres, most outdoor recreation around here involves the mountainous mazes contained within the massive Pecos Wilderness area and the adjoining Santa Fe National Forest. There are loads of great trails for everything from day hikes to mountain-bike treks, open from late spring through early November; during the winter months, these same paths turn into cross-country ski trails and snowshoe trails. Year-round, there's usually some sort of organized activity or competition on weekends in the Sangres, from ski races in winter to mountain-bike treks in summer and mushroom picking in the early autumn. To find out what's taking place while you're visiting, the best place to check is the Thursday edition of *The New Mexican*, Santa Fe's daily newspaper, which publishes its "Outdoors" section on that day.

Every sport and outdoors activity in northern New Mexico has its proper season—there are some things you just don't want to try when the weather's going to be uncooperative. In early spring, river rafting, for example, can be frigid, given both the icy snowmelt that feeds our raftable rivers and the frequent cloud cover and windstorms blasting into our area from the Colorado end of the Rockies. What looks like a warm and sunny day on a May morning can, by noon, have all the charm of a February snowstorm—the type that ices daffodils and forces flabbergasted visitors to shell out hundreds of dollars on gloves, down jackets, and thermal undies. Even dur-

everything from largemouth bass to kokanee salmon. If you want to try casting a line close to town, there's the Pecos River, about a 40-minute drive northeast of Santa Fe on I-25 at the Pecos exit. Get a license first at the state's **Department of Game and Fish** (tel 505/827–7911, 408 Galisteo St.), located at the state capitol complex just a few blocks from the Plaza. Here, there's a display case with maps of lakes and streams from one end of the state to the other, as well as some helpful staff who can let you in on which sort of fish are showing up in which waters. Licenses are also available at outdoors stores around town and at some country stores and bait shops closer to lakes.

On Native American–owned lands you won't need a state fishing permit, but you'll have to pay the tribal or pueblo government office a few dollars for a day fee. Pueblos such as Nambe and Picuris (see Diversions) administer fishing areas within short drives from Santa Fe, and others have stocked lakes. Call the **Eight Northern Pueblos** office (tel 505/852–4265) for a complete tourism guide to fishing opportunities and tribal ceremonies at the area's Indian pueblos.

Guided fishing excursions and the region's best stock of gear for the serious angler are the forte of **High Desert Angler** (tel 505/988–7688, 435 S. Guadalupe St.), a fishing shop in the city's Guadalupe neighborhood. The **Santa Fe Fly Fishing School** (call 505/986–3913) arranges gear rentals as well as private instruction and guided day trips, and they even throw in a free lunch when you're out there in the wilderness, casting away for the trout of your dreams.

Thrill-seeking on a wild river... In this part of the Southwest the Rio Grande is a fast-flowing and surprisingly clean river that, year in and year out, delivers some of the West's best white-water rafting thrills. And it's been discovered, big-time. Each year, more and more river-running companies slide their inflatable rafts into the Rio Grande, making more and more seats available for day-long, half-day, and even overnight rafting trips through the river's spectacular canyons and rapids. Shorter trips cost less than $50, while the day trips are generally somewhere between $75 and $100, depending on which month of summer you choose and whether or not your trip is scheduled for a weekend. Each river-rafting company throws in a lunch with all their trips; you bring however much beer or soda you think you'll need to get you through the day (the rafts are equipped with coolers). On some days the Rio Grande can seem as crowded as a shopping mall parking lot during Christmas week, so if crowds aren't your thing, go on a mid-week trip. Otherwise expect to ride in a full boat that at times will have to wait in line to run the tougher rapids stretches.

The most popular Rio Grande stretch (and the most challenging) is the section referred to as the **Taos Box**, a steep-walled canyon that's rated as one of the West's more difficult series of rapids. Sixteen miles long and about a six-hour trip (with lunch), running the Taos Box is a yearly tradition with some thrill-seekers, which tells you just how dependably fast and furious this river runs during the height of white-water season (roughly, mid-June to mid-July). The **Lower Race Course** is another popular, if less action-packed, slice of the Rio Grande's turbulent waters. Trips on the Race Course, which is much more accessible than the Taos Box, are less expensive and briefer.

Another river that's run from mid-spring through late August is the **Chama River**, a wider and considerably flatter river than the Rio Grande. The attraction here, though, is the scenery: The Chama flows through the heart of what's known as Georgia O'Keeffe Country, which is actually the rural community of Abiquiu, about an hour's drive north and west of Santa Fe.

If you're here in spring or early summer and plan on running a New Mexican river, keep in mind that no matter how warm (or even hot) it gets each day, the water in our rivers is still going to be damn cold—they're fed by snowmelt off the high slopes of the southern Rockies. It's not until midsummer that you can dip your foot into the Rio Grande for any stretch of time without getting blue toes. It's a good idea to have a wet suit on hand.

Several new white-water rafting operators seem to start operating in northern New Mexico each year; some of the more established ones are **Kokopelli Rafting** (tel 505/983–3734, 513 W. Cordova Rd.), **Far Flung Adventures** (tel 505/984–1684, in Taos), and **New Wave Rafting** (tel 505/984–1444).

Windsurfing, sailing, waterskiing, and canoeing... Rivers, yeah...but lakes in New Mexico? Land-locked as we are and without much water coming our way through rainfall, it's no surprise that the Land of Enchantment is dead last when it comes to the amount of surface water within state borders. Which explains why most of us head to the beach wherever and whenever we can plan a vacation. The lakes in northern New Mexico tend to be remote and relatively undeveloped in comparison to, say, Elephant Butte Lake in southern New Mexico. There aren't many boats being towed behind pickups in our part of the state; the few that there are tend to end up at one of four lakes within driving distance of town. **Cochiti Lake** (tel 505/465–0307), about a 40-minute drive south of town, is the closest one to Santa Fe. It's a better place for sailing and canoeing than for powerboating, as speeds on this no-wake lake are limited by the Army Corps of Engineers to 10 miles per hour or so. Still, the boat ramps are free and this is a great spot to haul your sailboard in and out of the water for a few hours of windsurfing. There's no decent swimming area—if you've got your heart set on swimming and sunbathing, bring a beach chair to keep your butt off the shore's rocky dirt, and wear water sandals to keep your feet from being ripped up by smashed beer bottles. **Abiquiu Lake** (tel 505/685–4371, one hour northwest of town on US 84), also administered by the Army Corps of Engineers, is the largest lake in northern New Mexico, and most waterskiers head here for the lake's several miles of undeveloped shoreline and rural beauty. The boat ramps are free but there aren't any services such as gas stations or concessions, so bring everything you'll need including ice and a map of how to get home. **El Vado Lake** (tel 505/827–7465, New Mexico State Parks and Recreation Division) is another waterskiers' and powerboaters' favored spot, about a two-hour drive northwest of Santa Fe near the resort village of Chama. It's even got a concession renting canoes and pontoon boats (**Stone House Lodge**, tel 505/588–7274). **Storrie Lake** (tel 505/827–7465), another lake administered by the state's parks department, is the most popular with windsurfers, sailors, and anyone looking for a beach-like environment with concessions and picnic areas; it's fairly shallow, so its water gets warmish in summer. Storrie is about a 90-minute drive from Santa Fe, north of Las Vegas.

Par for the course... In the past few years, it seems as if every half-cracked real-estate scam artist west of St. Louis has at one time or another dropped into Santa Fe, announcing plans to build a mega-resort complete with an 18-hole golf course designed by some aging golfer who years ago was somebody people reading the sports pages paid attention to. A lot of press kits get put together by one of our city's minuscule ad agencies, a few reporters get taken out to a fancy restaurant by the developer, and some office space gets rented out and turned into the development's nerve center. Then, the tamales hit the fan. Local environmental groups start screaming bloody murder about our already-raped countryside, state officials start wondering where the developer will find enough water to keep 36 greens and fairways in decent condition, and longtime residents of Santa Fe start wailing about yet another nail being driven into the adobe coffin of their once-rural and peaceful city. News coverage starts turning, threats are fired back and forth, and as sure as the sun sets in the west, that back-slapping real-estate tycoon has quietly packed his bags and headed off to (you name it) Scottsdale, Sun Valley, Jackson Hole, or Cabo San Lucas.

But every once in a while, someone with that magic combination of patience, political muscle, and deep, deep pockets steps up to the plate and hits a homer, which is exactly what the developers of **Las Campanas** (tel 505/ 995–3500, Tano Rd.) did a few years back when they announced their plans for yet another golf course/real-estate development. All the local naysayers took their best swings at the Las Campanas plans, but in the end the developers had the last laugh. Today, Las Campanas is a successful development where wealthy, out-of-state white folks tool around in overpriced Range Rovers, live in overpriced stucco (it only looks like adobe) homes filled with bad art, and compliment each other on how smart they were to find their share of life's rainbow on a dismal prairie five miles outside Santa Fe. By mid-1996, Las Campanas' golf course should have expanded to its full 36 holes, as planned. It's a decent course, but by no means the most challenging one in the area. Unless you know one of the people who actually call Las Campanas home, the chances of your getting onto the course to play a round or two are nil. Those rules may change one day (after Las Campanas hits a financial wall), but for now you're faced with two options: Sneak past the security guards after 5pm, or swallow your self-respect and try to buddy up to one of the resort's residents.

Quail Run (tel 505/986–2255, 3101 Old Pecos Trail) is another private golf course built around a real-estate development, but its nine holes are even less challenging than Las Campanas'. Priority for getting onto Quail Run's course goes first to its residents, club members, and their guests, but if there are free tee times, out-of-town visitors can pay a $25 greens fee (which includes a free cart) and play a round of nine. Funny thing here is that residents of Santa Fe can't pay that same $25 to play the course...we're shut out unless we know someone who lives there. Fortunately, there are three local golf courses that have their heads screwed on right. The most challenging of these, **Cochiti Lake** (tel 505/465–2239, N.M. Hwy. 16), is rated as the state's best course and easily tops Las Campanas in length and difficulty. It takes a true golfer and not some coddled sissy to get out and match Cochiti's grueling layout. Framing Cochiti's 18-hole, par-72 monster is a mind-boggling backdrop of sheer red cliffs and treacherous canyons. The greens fees here are an incredible bargain at $17 on weekdays and $19 on weekends for 18 holes, and the restaurant even serves green chile cheeseburgers (as opposed to the wimpy salads at you-know-where). **Santa Fe Country Club** (tel 505/471–0601, Airport Rd.) is another 18-hole, par-72 course; what sets this older course apart from its competitors are the towering trees flanking its monstrous fairways. Unlike Las Campanas (which besides being nearly flat is about as vegetated as Yul Brenner's head), Santa Fe Country Club is the closest thing in this area to the type of wooded expanse that's common in Colorado and the Pacific Northwest. Weekday greens fees are $18 for locals and $37.50 for non-residents who want to play 18 holes. (On weekends the price for non-residents stays the same, but it goes up to $27.50 for locals.) **Los Alamos Golf Course** (tel 505/662–8139, 4250 Diamond Dr., Los Alamos), a city-owned, par-71 18-holer nestled underneath the Jemez Mountains, is a bit shorter than Santa Fe's other two public courses, but it's got fantastic scenery and ridiculously low greens fees—$12 on weekdays and $15 on weekends. Being so close to The Bomb's birthplace at Los Alamos, who knows? Maybe it even glows in the dark for night golf. If you came to New Mexico looking to sharpen your golf game, give the **Santa Fe Golf Practice and Teaching Center** (tel 505/474–4680, 4680 Wagon Rd.) a call. Buckets of practice balls are $5 each, and you can use them either on the driving range or putting green. They've also got a computerized swing analyzer that pinpoints soft spots in your technique.

The tennis racket... Tennis courts are fairly easy to find in Santa Fe, with the city's parks department maintaining nearly three dozen outdoor courts at **Fort Marcy** (409 Washington Ave.), **Ortiz** (160 Camino de las Crucitas), **Larragoite** (corner of Agua Fria and Cristobal Colon), **Martinez** (2240 Carlos Rey), and **Salvador Perez** (610 Alto Vista) parks. Most of them are well maintained and some are illuminated at night, but the courts at Fort Marcy are generally considered to be the best. The **City of Santa Fe Recreation Department** (tel 505/438–1480) can update you on whether there are any classes or tournaments scheduled, but outside of those two instances, all public courts in the city are free of charge and are available on a first-come, first-served basis. **Bishop's Lodge** (tel 505/983–6377, Bishop's Lodge Rd.), **El Gancho** (tel 505/988–5000, Las Vegas Hwy.) and the **Santa Fe Country Club** (tel 505/471–3378, Airport Rd.) have indoor courts and allow non-members and non-guests to use them for a fee, but the best tennis facilities in town are the courts at **Sangre de Cristo Racquet Club** (tel 505/983–7978, 1755 Camino Corrales), which is a members-only operation.

Back in the saddle... What's a trip to the West without saddle sores? If your idea of fun in Santa Fe includes at least one experience atop the beast that Spanish colonialists used to subdue this region's native population, there's plenty of opportunity. Prices range from $20 an hour on up, depending on when you want to ride and how much experience you've got under your saddle. Most places offer hourly rides and a few can put together an overnight pack trip or fishing trip running anywhere from a few days to a couple of weeks in length. The mountainous trails and sprawling mesas of northern New Mexico are ideal for horseback riding, and besides, its a great way to get your head into the mind-set of those rough-ridin' gals and dudes of the Wild West era. One other great reason for riding is that it's peaceful... incredibly peaceful and quiet when you're out on a New Mexico mesa, staring off 50 miles into the distance at a purplish range of mountains, with just the sound of rustling wind and your horse's breathing to listen to.

Bishop's Lodge (tel 505/983–6377, Bishop's Lodge Rd.) is a multipurpose resort with hotel rooms, lush gardens, a swimming pool, and riding stables...to name a few of its offerings. The stables here are open for parts of the spring and fall as well as the entire summer, with experienced wranglers taking riders out onto the lodge's 1,000 or so acres of hilly splendor adjoining the Santa Fe National Forest. Call ahead to make a reservation and find out about specific times rides are being offered. There are usually two rides daily, one in the morning and another in the afternoon, each lasting around 90 minutes and costing $35 per person for hotel guests and $45 for others, and you need a reservation. **Rancho Encantado** (tel 505/982–3537, State Rd. 22) is a hotel resort that has boarding facilities for its guests and for horse owners who use its stables year-round. The wranglers here have a few horses available for trail rides, but the only folks allowed to sign up for a ride into the Tesuque countryside have to be staying here as guests. Rides here last an hour to an hour and a half and are offered four times daily during the summer. Hotel guests pay $35 and guests' guests pay $45, and you need to make a reservation. **Galisteo Inn** (tel 505/466–4000), in Galisteo, a Hispanic village 20 miles south of the Plaza, has adjoining stables that are independently run, but can arrange for the inn's guests to take guided rides out into the extraordinarily scenic Galisteo Basin. Single riders can take escorted trips for $35 an hour, while groups of three or more are charged $25 per person, with additional riding time costing only $10 per person for each half-hour. Reservations are required. **Round Barn Stables** (tel 505/583–2233, in Ojo Caliente), about an hour's drive north of town, offers two-hour rides for $30 per person, as well as overnight trips into northern New Mexico's national forest areas. They can also put together barn dances, barbecues, and birthday parties for kids, but you'll need to make special arrangements with Ernie. **Broken Saddle Riding Company** (tel 505/470–0074, in Cerrillos), a few miles south of town, offers two-hour rides into the old mining areas above the town of Cerrillos and into the Devil's Basin area for $47 per person. Reservations are required and no riders under age 12 are permitted.

Scoping the feathered friends... New Mexico's Rio Grande river valley is known as the bosque, a Spanish term meaning woodlands. What that means for bird-watchers is that some of North America's busiest migratory flyways are concentrated on a direct, north–south configuration from one end of the state to the other. During a few weeks each spring and autumn, wildlife refuges along the Rio Grande are filled with migrating sandhill cranes, swans, and geese (to name a few species), all of whom are on their way between their summer nesting grounds in Canada and their wintering grounds in central Mexico. The largest of these wildlife refuges is the **Bosque del Apache** (tel 505/835–1828), an hour's drive south of Albuquerque, an enormous resting ground for migratory birds and a place attracting tens of thousands of birders on day trips along the refuge's many miles of marked trails and roads. In Santa Fe itself, while you're not going to find much by way of migratory wildlife refuges, there is a wonderful gem in the **Randall Davey Audubon Center** (tel 505/983–4609) at the upper end of Canyon Road. Once the home and estate of Randall Davey, an influential artist, the center is also an environmental education center, wildlife refuge, and the regional headquarters of the **National Audubon Society**. Easy trails wind throughout the center's grounds, which are home to many of the plant and wildlife species native to the region.

Southwestern schussing... I've got this friend in Seattle who laughs each time I tell her about the fantastic skiing in this part of the country. "Come on, John, give me a break...who's ever heard of such a dumb thing," she'll keep repeating, no matter how many times I try to pitch my story about the treasure that's New Mexico's winter. But I'm here to tell each of you that it's all true and if you don't believe me just try coming out here any time between Thanksgiving and Easter. What you'll find will forever change your mind about outdoors life in the southern Rockies (not to mention how it will prove once and for all that, yes, it really does snow in Santa Fe). It's not unusual for there to be anywhere from 10 to 15 feet of base on New Mexico's high-altitude slopes, and yearly total snowfall depths of nearly 300 inches are the norm.

Our northern New Mexico winters can be awfully cold, and while places further south of Santa Fe can have winters ranging from Albuquerque's coolness to Las Cruces' whispers of a slight chill, what happens up here in the state's northern reaches would make an Eskimo feel at home. Our combination of proximity to the mountains and the city's 7,000-foot elevation make snowfalls of anywhere from a couple of inches to nearly a couple of feet in depth no strangers to Santa Fe. But thank the Creator for giving us skiing! Not only is this town so close to the slopes that you can buzz up to the ski area and be storming down the mountain in less than a half-hour's drive from the Plaza, but we're also in the vicinity of several ski areas that are as challenging as any you can find in the Rocky Mountain states.

Many of the ski areas in this corner of the nation have their lodges built at 9,000 or so feet in elevation, which means that the lifts themselves drop you off atop ridges and bowls that can be as high as 12,000 feet. At these sorts of heights you're going to experience a type of oxygen deprivation more common to mountain climbers than to skiers, so if you're not in good physical shape be prepared for a lot of huffin' and puffin' during your first day on the slopes. And the other thing you've got to worry about is dehydration. Sure, that snow holds lots of moisture...but just because you're skiing atop it doesn't mean your body isn't sweating away, trying to get rid of it. It's a dry, dry world out here in the high desert of the Southwest, and if you don't drink lots of water you're playing with real physical danger.

For general information on what's happening with the weather, ski and road conditions, prices, and crowds at ski areas around the state, the two phone numbers to keep posted are those for **New Mexico Snophone** (tel 505/984–0606) and **Ski New Mexico** (tel 505/982–5300). From one end of the state to the other, these two information services can plug you into the best ski conditions and any New Mexico ski area.

From **Santa Fe Ski Area**'s (tel 505/982–4429) 12,000-foot summit, you can stare out across a phenomenally large chunk of central and northern New Mexico. From these heights, the city's just a short drive away, but from the skier's point of view it may as well be in the next dimension, because once you're up there you seem to forget about everything else going on in the world. Five lifts, including a high-speed quad chair and a triple chair, pull skiers to the top of the mountain from 9am to 4pm daily, sending them down a 1,650-foot vertical drop for $35 daily (or $20 for a half-day ticket). There's a fully super-vised children's day-care center with a kid's ski program and snow play programs for non-skiing tots, as well as a snowboarder's half-pipe, a great mid-mountain bar and grill, and a huge rental shop in the base lodge. All this place needs is a sushi bar! The runs are mainly interme-diate and advanced intermediate, with some expert ter-rain. Lift lines are almost always a matter of waiting only a minute or two, and there's usually a few times each month when mother nature dumps a foot or so (some-times a heck of a lot more) of fluffy powder overnight, making this a must-do for any serious Santa Fe skiers the following morning. The one thing you need to keep in mind here is that parking's somewhat limited, so if you want to park your car close to the base lodge, try to arrive by 8:30 (or 11:30 if you're planning a half-day) or you may be forced to park at one of the shuttle lots.

Pajarito Mountain (pronounced PA-ha-REE-toe) (tel 505/662–5725) is slightly less than an hour's drive distant in the national forest lands outside Los Alamos, and while there isn't a bar or day care, what there is hap-pens to be magnificently uncrowded, efficiently operated, and inexpensive. Not much of a beginner's area, Pajarito is best considered as a day trip for skiers who don't want to make the trek to Taos or the ski areas in nearby south-ern Colorado. The tricks to keep in mind at Pajarito are that it's only open to the public three days a week (week-ends and Wednesdays) and that there's no snowmaking. The area has four chairlifts, a 1,241-foot vertical drop, some of the lowest lift ticket prices in the state, and 40 trails that are almost always free of other skiers.

Taos Ski Valley (tel 505/776–2291) is the state's monster ski area. With 72 downhill trails, 10 chairlifts, a few bars, cafes, ski rental shops, and boutiques, it's little wonder Taos is considered to be the equal of any ski area in the West. The terrain here is steep and challenging, with a few parts left for beginners and intermediates, but most of the mountain is geared toward the kind of skiers who know how to handle themselves in all kinds of con-ditions. The vertical drop at Taos is a phenomenal 2,612 feet, spread out across several snow bowls and back-country areas… all of which means that crowds can be spread out across a tremendous amount of territory and you'll never come away feeling like a sardine on the slopes. The lift prices tend to match those at other major ski resorts in the Rockies, so you're going to pay more to ski at Taos, but you'll find out that it's worth every penny.

Cross-country skiers will find some of New Mexico's best ski-touring trails in the Santa Fe National Forest lands. Right off Hyde Park Road (which leads up to the ski area) are the trails into **Back Canyon** campground, **Aspen Vista**, and **Windsor Trails**. Maps of these trails are available through the **Santa Fe National Forest** ranger station (tel 505/988–6940). Another option is **Enchanted Forest** (tel 505/754–2374) cross-country area, located about a two-hour drive from Santa Fe in Red River and featuring 600 acres of groomed trails, warming huts, and picnic tables. The area rents equipment and charges $10 for a day ticket to use the trails.

There are a number of places around Santa Fe that rent both downhill and cross-country skis, boots, poles, and whatnot. **Alpine Sports** (tel 505/983–5155, 121 Sandoval St.) is probably the most popular with visitors, mainly because its building is right downtown near the major hotels. **Ski Tech Rentals** (tel 505/983–5512, 905 S. St. Francis Dr.) is the most competitively priced rental shop in the area. **Base Camp** (tel 505/982–9707, 121 W. San Francisco St.) specializes in snowboard rentals. The ski rental shop at the **Santa Fe Ski Area** (tel 505/982–4429) has everything you'll need for a day on the slopes but is more expensive than the downtown rental shops.

ping

5

It's numero uno,
the big winner, el
slam-dunko of all
Santa Fe action.
By a long shot,
shopping is the
favorite thing for

first-timers, second-time visitors, and incessant visitors. A recent article in the University of Colorado's *Journal of Travel Research* quantified it, but those of us who live here don't need hard data. Just ask people why they visit Santa Fe or keep coming back, and you'll quickly find out that "it's the shopping, stupid!"

Oh yeah, undoubtedly a large number of visitors tell their friends, family, and envious co-workers that what keeps them coming back is Santa Fe's a) natural beauty, b) amazing art, c) great restaurants, or d) New Age energy. But then check out the sterling silver and lapis bracelet dangling from his wrist, or the 10-pound concha belt cinched around her waist, or the pair of Nambeware candlesticks decorating their dining room table. You'll know what really draws them to Santa Fe.

Hey, our economy *depends* on people coming here to spend money on the creative stuff that's crafted, painted, soldered, woven, carved, or hauled into Santa Fe by our local artists and entrepreneurs. Consider us a classy, New Age/artsy version of Wal-Mart—but don't expect too many bargains.

What to Buy

On my first day in Santa Fe (a long story, but let's just say I'm on my eighth year of a one-day visit) I wanted to buy three things: a sterling silver bracelet made by a Native American, an R.C. Gorman poster, and a chiles rellenos dinner. While my taste in art has changed dramatically, I still savor fresh rellenos and I still get compliments for the timelessly stylish bracelet I bought for $55 that day from an Indian vendor underneath the Palace of the Governors portal.

Of course, if you run around buying everything that grabs your eye, you'll wind up making nobody happier than the Salvation Army store shoppers who end up owning your ill-considered Santa Fe purchases. So, here's Rule Number One of the savvy shopper's guide to Santa Fe: Take Your Time! Don't even think about pulling out your credit cards until you've taken an entire morning and half the afternoon to look around, compare prices, and figure out what it is that you really, really like. If you're here for the weekend, wait to make your purchases until Sunday, when nearly everything in town stays open (Monday is the preferred day off during winter months).

Now, there are some things available in Santa Fe that you can find much cheaper closer to home: cowboy boots, western clothing, outdoor gear, winter coats, vintage clothing, fine jewelry, picture frames, sunglasses, home accessories, furniture, and imported rugs. I don't know why, but this stuff costs more here than if you buy it in Albuquerque or Atlanta. It may have something to do with the national mainstreaming of southwestern and western design motifs that took place just a few years ago. Unfortunately, our local prices stay ridiculously high because plenty of tourists are naive enough to pay inflated prices on things they could easily buy at home.

Which leads me to Rule Number Two of the savvy shopper's guide to Santa Fe: Don't But it Here if You Can Buy it Somewhere Else! Without fail, you will save yourself some cash and avoid back strain from lugging your treasures from Santa Fe back home.

So what sorts of things *can* you find here that would be difficult or impossible to find back home? Start by understanding the concept of "one of a kind." Basically, this means anything that an artist or craftsperson creates that is unique, but I'll fudge that definition and include limited editions as well. Original works of art, especially paintings, sculptural ceramics, hand-woven rugs and baskets, some jewelry, some clothing, and some furniture fits into the one-of-a-kind and limited-edition niche. Of course, wherever you live, there are probably people creating one-of-a-kind objects and art. But my general principle is: Whenever any work of art speaks directly to your soul, buy it. If you can afford it, buy it and feel grateful for the opportunity.

Outside the realm of works of original/limited-edition art and fine craft, there's a treasure trove of fine art, clothing, and design objects available in Santa Fe stores. If you're into a cowboy or cowgirl look, we've got lots of it. If you're into a casual, 1990s stylish look, we've got it. If your tastes run urban and contemporary, we may not have as much of it here as you could find in San Francisco or Boston, but there's still enough to make you happy. This goes for clothing, furniture, jewelry, shoes, art, and objects for the home.

Target Zones

Basically, the city's divided into three prime shopping areas: Canyon Road, the Plaza, and the Guadalupe district. The downtown Plaza area is loaded with restaurants, hotels, clothing stores, jewelry boutiques, museums, and art galleries, concentrated in an area four blocks wide and five blocks long, all radiating outward from the Plaza in a crosshatched pattern. Canyon Road is only a short walk from the Plaza, but has a completely different feeling. The number of shops and art galleries there have led to the road's being called "The Art and Soul of Santa Fe" (a dumb saying, but one we're stuck with). They're all stretched along what amounts to six loosely construed blocks of the road, with a limited amount of spillover onto adjacent side streets such as Garcia Street, Delgado Street, and Camino del Monte Sol. The Guadalupe district is also a short walk from the Plaza, across the Santa Fe River, slightly southwest of downtown. A few years ago, this was considered a low-rent commercial area, and parking here is much easier than it is downtown. The combination of easy parking and cheap rent has attracted office-supply stores, furniture stores, real-estate offices, affordable clothing stores, framing shops, art galleries, and coffeehouses, all clustered together in an area four blocks long and four blocks wide.

There's lots of the same sorts of stuff in many of these stores, a trend toward duplication that you'll quickly notice. But for smart shoppers willing to sort through the blur of touristy shops, quirky shops, and authentically funky stores, there are still lots of treasures to be found—you've just got to hustle around Santa Fe's three shopping districts to find them.

How to Get a Good Deal

You're going to find the best prices in the Guadalupe district, a place where store owners have to appeal as much to local shoppers as they do to tourists. A few stores on Marcy Street in the downtown area keep prices reasonable, including some national retail stores that have reduced-price racks toward the back of their sales floors. As for the rest of downtown and all of Canyon Road, forget about finding anything at a decent price unless you arrive during the middle of a sale.

You can, however, sometimes play a form of "I-wanna-discount-or-else" with local art gallery and jewelry store owners. If you're into this sort of psychodrama, my best advice is to take the soft-sell approach. Forget about trotting out your pushy, know-everything, super-confident inner self. Business people around here want to sell, but they won't tolerate a lot of attitude and are happy to show you the door if you push the wrong button.

One good way to save yourself some substantial bucks on expensive purchases of art, clothing, or anything else is to have whatever you buy shipped to your home address. Provided you live outside New Mexico, shipping things home instead of walking out the door with them allows you to legally sidestep the state's 6.25 percent sales tax. Most galleries and store owners will even throw in the shipping at no cost, if you ask nicely. I have a few friends in the shipping and crating business around town, and they can tell you that most of the art sold in Santa Fe winds up getting crated and delivered to buyers' doors by UPS or FedEx.

One mistake you should avoid making involves the Native American vendors who sell underneath the Palace of the Governors portal and occasionally at tables set up outside some of the downtown retail stores (the Indians pay the store owner anywhere from $10 to $30 for the privilege). It is not just bad manners, but downright stupid to treat these people as if they dole out discounts to everyone and anyone who happens down the street. For the most part, these vendors price their jewelry, pottery, and other fine crafts quite fairly. If you don't like their prices, then poke your head into one of the many shops around the Plaza that have tourist-magnet signs hanging in their windows advertising "50% OFF." What you'll find in there is stuff that's been marked up 400 percent in the first place, so when you pay their supposedly discounted price, all you're doing is buying (mostly) junk at twice its normal price.

Of course, we do have our share of factory outlet stores, just to let you know that American retailing trends don't completely pass us by. South of town, the **Santa Fe Factory Stores** (tel 505/474–4000, 8380 Cerrillos Rd., at I-25) are loaded with stuff you shouldn't want to buy, but their Joan & David, Jockey, and Johnson & Murphy shops do present some possibilities.

When Santa Feans shop for clothes and household goods, they don't go downtown by the Plaza, that's for sure. Santa Fe's sprawling **Villa Linda Mall** (corner of Cerrillos and Rodeo Rds.) has stores selling many of the same things you find downtown, but at vastly reduced prices. And then there's Albuquerque, a city with several large shopping malls. The outlet malls along I–25 as you drive between Albuquerque and Santa Fe are well worth checking out, and if it's high style at a deep discount that rings your shopping bell, drive four hours northwest to the Colorado town of Durango. The Ralph Lauren factory store in Durango is the best anywhere, with huge selections of clothes, furnishings, and bedding at enormous discounts. In other words, if it's bargains you want, you'll have to do some digging.

Hours of Business

Art galleries usually open at 10am and close at 5pm. During summer months, some close on Sundays but most stay open seven days a week. During the November–April "slow season," some galleries stay open every day, but most close at least one day—either Sunday or Monday—and some close both days. Retail stores are a somewhat different story. Most open at 8 or 9am, with closing times from 5 to 6pm. Some downtown stores will stay open later during summer months.

Sales Tax

The Santa Fe sales tax is 6.25 percent.; in Albuquerque it's 5.8 percent, while in Taos it's 6.3 percent. As noted above, you don't have to pay this tax if your purchases are shipped to your home address, providing your home address is out of state.

The Lowdown

Shopping bags to show off... The only one that really counts around here is the glossy yellow paper bag with handles that's used by the **Coyote Cocina**, the kitchen accessories and gourmet food shop underneath the famous and chic Coyote Cafe (see Dining). The bag's got a silhouetted, flute-playing coyote dancing on a red background decorated with yellow stars and geometric turquoise doodads. I saw one of these last year at Orly airport, carried by a Frenchwoman who radiated a rather unique, Parisian-meets-Southwestern sense of esprit. If that endorsement's not enough, what is?

Wacky, original, almost unique, and affordable... Funsters, frolickers, interior decorators, and the assorted other toaster-brains who make the world worth living in have a real surprise in store when they set foot in **Jackalope**, the most unusual eight acres of shopping madness this side of Ciudad Juarez. Located on the lower stretches of Cerrillos Road, Jackalope looks slightly unusual from the outside, and just gets weirder and weirder the farther you work your way into the depths of the place. Fortunately, in the case of Jackalope, weird is also wonderful. Owned by Darby McQuade (a man who, were he around a few millennia ago, would have given Noah a run for his money), Jackalope should have as its motto "I want three container-loads in each color." The stuff you'll find here ranges from wrought-iron ice-cream shop chairs straight from an Ecuadoran blacksmith's shop, to row upon row of Italian terra-cotta flowerpots, to Pakistani home furnishings, to Oaxacan textiles. There's a huge outdoor yard with stuff stacked inside tents, outside tents, and everywhere imaginable. Three large buildings are crammed with furniture, folk art, a nursery, imported rugs, an aviary, tin mirrors, tableware, a guy selling ice cream, a mariachi band, Mexican wood carvers, and even (I'm not kidding) a prairie dog refuge. Everybody who comes to visit me gets taken to Jackalope on their first day in Santa Fe, and invariably they beg me to take them back for one last shopping trip right before they leave for the airport. It's that kind of place, and it's so inexpensive you'll end up buying too many things and still not burning a hole in your credit card.

Another great place you shouldn't leave Santa Fe without setting foot in at least once is **Adevina!**, a Guadalupe district shop that's a little bit coffeehouse, a little bit art gallery, a little bit clothing boutique, a little bit import shop, and a whole lot of fun. Owned by a one-time Hollywood camerawoman, it might have a few dozen Elvis buddahs stacked next to a tray filled with Cambodian jewelry boxes one day, and will be sold out of both by tomorrow. Locals know that if you see something great at Adevina!, buy it immediately because two things are certain: the price is great and it won't last long. This shop has a motto—"Local art for the locally paid"—which is kind of a nice concept. There actually is a lot of stuff here made by local folks, including refrigerator magnets, shrines to the Virgin de Guadalupe, unique clothes, affordable and well-made jewelry, greeting cards, and votive candles. If you want to find some unique objects that testify to your great taste and your sharp eye for originality, make Adevina! one of your first day's stops.

The small but exquisite gift shop at the **Museum of International Folk Art** has a limited selection of objects, but what they do carry is fairly priced, imported from a long ways away, and characteristic of the fine craftsmanship and folk traditions of their makers. There always seems to be lots of Third-World toys, carved figurines, metal cars, and other things kids are fond of playing with, as well as affordable jewelry and tableware from around the world.

Designer flash for mucho cash... If you haven't figured it out already, let me be the one who tells you: Santa Fe is expensive! But if money's no object, then you may want to take a look at some of these pricy clothing palaces, all of which are around the Plaza area. For women's clothing, **Jane Smith** is the place to go for that full-blown Dallas look, while **Simply Santa Fe** has a wide range of designs, including several from Europeans who are American-influenced. **Char of Santa Fe** shows off the hip, modern look of its designer/owner, while **French Rags** showcases Brenda French's elegant, patterned woven wear. Men will have a slightly harder time finding what they're in need of, but **Spirit** is a great place to outfit yourself with a casual/hip urban look, while **Ripplestein's** has a strong accessories collection as well as a few designer threads. **James Reid** is the classiest place in town to find designer belts and sophisticated sterling silver buckle sets, while **Jane Smith** (again) is strictly for guys wanting an updated, drugstore cowboy look.

Designer flair with cash to spare... Okay, so you want to find something that'll put you into a snazzy, Santa Fe sorta look, but you want to do it without breaking the bank. For women, three downtown boutiques— **Dust in the Wind**, **Chico's**, and **Blue Fish**—sell some expensive designer stuff. **Susan K's** and **Crazy Fox** are a bit more mainstream, while **Pinkoyote** specializes in the snazzy contemporary cowgirl look, and **Origins** purveys a wild Third-World market look, anything from harem girl to Victorian. In the Guadalupe district, **Bodhi Bazaar** and **Adevina!** usually have some funky, unique items. On Canyon Road, **La Bodega** goes for the Third-World look, too, while **Judy's** is more mainstream. Each of these stores has something you absolutely cannot leave Santa Fe without, from locally designed clothes to affordable, imported shoes.

For guys the pickin's are slimmer. Occasionally, I'll find something at a great price at the **Bodhi Bazaar** (especially their discount racks), a good place for American-designed fashions; **Uli's Boutique** goes more for European styles, but even their regular prices are decent. The very preppy Pendleton shop (a.k.a. **Dewey & Sons Trading**) has a few things worth looking at. I usually like some of the things at pretentious **Santa Fe Dry Goods**, but the prices on their yuppie/outdoorsy clothes are so ridiculously high that I find the place better for getting ideas rather than items.

For shoes, the best places in town are **Goler Shoes**, a fashion shoe shop with the latest in women's designs, and **Street Feet**, which has a lot of snazzy things for women without being too far into the hipness thing. **On Your Feet** is a better all-around choice, though, because it sells hiking boots and Birkenstocks as well as dress-up shoes for men and women; its sock department is Santa Fe's best, hands down.

Duds for ridin' the range, Rover... If you want a pair of western boots that you can wear without gasping every time you spot a puddle of water or a muddy sidewalk, try looking at the selection at **Santa Fe Boot Co.** or at **Santa Fe Western Mercantile**, both of which stock your Tony Lamas, your Nokonas, your Double H boots. Santa Fe Boot Co. tends to be my favorite, just because it's family-owned and has been around for ages. If you're going to buy boots, you should also buy a great belt with a nice sterling silver buckle set. Watch out for belts that look nice but have cheap, plated pewter buckles. The best place in town to find a top-quality belt along with a silver buckle at a great price is **Canyon Trading Post**. These guys import very stylish belts of fantastic quality from their factories in Mexico; they wholesale them to top boutiques and men's stores around the nation, but this is their only retail shop, and the prices are breathtakingly low.

You can't be a cowpoke if ya ain't got a cowboy hat, so git yerself over to **Montecristi Custom Hat Works**, near the Plaza, for the area's best selection for working and retired cowboys and cowgirls. Another place with a strong reputation for quality western hats is **Tree Eagle Trading Co.**, but since both these places tend to be on the expensive side, anyone looking for more style than substance will want to check out **Gina's**; **Pinkoyote** also has some good hats among its women's wear.

As for western threads, the downtown area's **Sanbusco Outfitters** has a lot of nice but expensive duds that look western enough, but are hardly meant to be worn by someone who actually needs to do physical work. Same goes for what's on the racks at **Overland Sheepskin and Outfitters**, also downtown. Nice stuff, but who can afford it? Actual western-wear shops are much less pretentious: No fancy saddles hanging from the ceiling, and the atmosphere is more like a Caldor's that just happens to stock western clothes. If you've never been to one you should take advantage of the opportunity, just to see how the other half shops. **Western Warehouse** has a store near enough to downtown that you can walk over for a peek. What you'll find here is stylish but in a very rural, country-and-western way, and at least the prices won't knock the wind out of your lungs.

Indian jewelry... Let's be honest—Indian jewelry falls into one of two categories. First, there's the inexpensive, mass-produced, glittery junk that's sold from one end of the Southwest to the other, especially in Gallup, Albuquerque, and at any Santa Fe shop that hangs a banner blaring "50% OFF ALL INDIAN JEWELRY." If you shop at one of these places, expect to go home with duplicative, uninteresting trinkets, the kind that tourists have been schlepping out of this part of the nation since the first days of Santa Fe Railroad tourist posters. Sure, it may look great in the store and for the first few days after you buy it, even on the plane going home—but believe me, you'll soon run into someone, somewhere back home, who will not only know the value of what you've purchased, but will also be sporting an original, authentic example of true Native American jewelry craftsmanship, which he or she bought on a recent trip to Santa Fe. From that point on you'll be too humiliated to wear that discounted gewgaw ever again, and it will gather dust in your jewelry case.

When it comes to purchasing jewelry made by Native American artisans, it's much wiser to buy something that's authentic, artistic, and individual. Fortunately, you can still find such jewelry at all price ranges right here in Santa Fe. You've just got to be willing to do a little footwork. As a rule of thumb, don't assume that everything you find in galleries or jewelry shops will be expensive, or that everything you find on a sidewalk vendor's tray is going to be inexpensive. Quite often, the gallery and jewelry store prices for Indian jewelry are very reasonable.

Far and away the best place to find fantastically original Native American jewelry at great prices is from the vendors who flood into town for the Santa Fe Indian Market (see Diversions). But since this is only held during a single weekend in August, the next-best thing to do is check out the dozens of state-licensed vendors selling underneath the portal outside the **Palace of the Governors** (see Diversions), the state's historical museum on the north side of the Plaza. These Native Americans represent most of the state's tribal groups, from Navajo and Zuni to Cochito, San Juan, and Tesuque. You'll find anything from inexpensive earrings to stunning concha belts—the one thing all of it has in common is that each piece is made by either the Indian vendor you're dealing with or by a member of his or her immediate family (that's the state's rule). Besides jewelry, you can also find, depending on which vendors have shown up today, black-fired pottery from San Ildefonso pueblo, baked loaves of horno (adobe oven) bread from Cochiti, sand paintings from Navajo land, necklaces made from nuggets of dried and colored corn, and even contemporary jewelry crafted by recent graduates of the Institute of American Indian Arts' fine jewelry program.

Of course, if you decide to take a day trip out to one of the many Native American pueblos in the Santa Fe region (see Diversions), you can expect to find at least one—and usually several—shops selling jewelry made by pueblo residents, along with fine crafts and original works of art. The prices in these shops are usually very reasonable—not dirt-cheap bargains, mind you, but nonetheless fair and affordable.

Around Santa Fe itself are dozens upon dozens of boutiques, galleries, and jewelry shops selling everything from traditionally styled Indian sterling silver and turquoise jewelry to the contemporary styles of jewelry created by today's generation of university-trained Native American jewelers. Specialists in Indian jewelry downtown include **Dewey Galleries, Ray Tracey Gallery, DW Studio, Packards Indian Trading Co.**, and **Ortega's**, all of which are pretty high-quality; it's a good idea to troll from one to the others, looking for that one piece that you'll fall in love with. Downtown near the Plaza, there's Indian jewelry among a wider range of jewelry at **Spirit of the Earth, Nancy Brown Jewelers,** and the very high-end **Ornament**. Out on Canyon Road, **Edith Lambert Gallery** has some great Indian jewelry along with fine art.

Vintage Native American jewelry is known as "pawn jewelry." Some less-than-scrupulous sellers define this as anything not made in the last two months. But true pawn jewelry refers to objects crafted between 1900 and 1950, and covers a range of sterling silver and turquoise jewelry. Much of it contains elaborate stamped patterns that range from swastikas (don't get upset—it's a traditional ceremonial pattern in some Native American cultures) to sunbursts, stars, and moons. If pawn jewelry interests you, **Arrowsmith's Relics** is dedicated to it; there's also pawn jewelry along with western and Native American artifacts at **Rainbow Man**, **Rio Bravo Trading**, **Morningstar Gallery**, and Canyon Road's **Tiqua Gallery**. Different stores carry different pieces at any one time; comparison shopping is your best idea. **Trinity Antiques**, which deals in general American antiques, carries some good pawn pieces; so does **Nathalie**, a shop where you can put together a whole outfit of contemporary western clothing and accessories.

Other jewelry... Just as visual artists have flocked into Santa Fe to stake their claim to the city's supercharged arts market, so has an entire generation of jewelers come into town and set up shop during the past decade. Their work, which ranges from some fairly striking contemporary designs to the downright whimsical, isn't too hard to find—in fact, there's so much jewelry shown in jewelry stores, shops, and galleries in the downtown area alone, you'll need to take a few shortcuts to avoid falling into a shopper's stupor.

Many Santa Fe jewelers have been strongly influenced by the Southwest's Native American design traditions. While there's some degree of uninventive copying, other jewelers truly improve upon and contemporize what's old. No better place in town exhibits this sort of jewelry than **Ortega's**, a Plaza store that's expensive but in many instances worth it. **Frank Patania** is another Plaza-area jeweler whose influences are in tradition but whose vision stays glued to the horizon.

For truly exquisite jewelry that may or may not echo southwestern influences, check out **Ornament**, an expensive shop that's a magnet for the region's best jewelry designers. This store has a huge following of Hollywood and New York types who drop big bucks whenever they're in Santa Fe. What's sold here tends to be contemporary, usually has precious stones set, inlaid, or incorporated into the piece, and has a big price tag. Downtown's **Nancy Brown Jewelers** and Canyon Road's

Tresa Vorenberg Goldsmiths are two other shops known for pulling in some of the area's best-quality work, while **Luna Felix Goldsmith** has a large national following for designer Felix's ornate baubles, flashy stuff with semi-precious stones and lots of gold.

When it comes to whimsical, nobody does it better than **Richard Lindsay Designs** and **LewAllen & LewAllen Jewelry**. Lindsay's work is wildness itself, influenced by everything from aliens to ski bums to roadkill, but it's superbly crafted, totally ingenious, and always makes for fantastic conversation pieces. LewAllen, a father/daughter shop near the Plaza, pulls in design influences from the real and imagined worlds of its owners. Papa Ross LewAllen's work is often spiritual, totemic, slightly tribal, while daughter Laura's pieces celebrate her zany, outdoorswoman-meets-Spiderman sort of life. Next door to the LewAllens' place is the **Frank Howell Gallery**, home of sculptor, jeweler, and painter Bill Worrell's wacky, shamanic pieces based on the pictographic designs along the banks of the Pecos River. These are unique works of wearable art, and I've spotted people wearing them all over the country.

Funky old stuff... Have we got a flea market for you! **Trader Jack's Flea Market**, which sits just a few miles outside of town adjacent to the opera complex, is one of the funnest and funkiest outdoor flea markets anywhere. African bead traders, Hispanic construction workers selling used tools, local stores doing fast inventory reductions, craftspeople making a few extra bucks selling tables, chairs, and such—it's all out here in row upon row of tidy booths. I always come out here before taking trips back home to visit family, because the flea market is one of the few places in town where you can get authentic Santa Fe stuff at low prices, and if you buy in quantity the vendors will even haggle a little. There's a decent food stand selling breakfast burritos, coffee, and Cokes, as well as a line of porta-potties for the indisposed. Wear a hat so the sun won't get to you, arrive reasonably early, and bring your own shopping bag and lots of small bills. In winter, when the outdoor scene on Taos Highway packs it in, you might want to check out Trader Jack's year-round indoor flea market in a former warehouse in the Guadalupe district, which sells decent furniture, vintage books, some quality import items—a nice enough selection of objects, but it lacks the funkiness of its outdoor big brother.

One of the most popular furniture styles you'll see in Santa Fe homes, retail shops, and hotels is referred to as "Mexican primitive"—basically, roughly used tables, chairs, sideboards, and trasteros (armoires) from south of the border. A great place to find this sort of furniture is **El Paso Import Co.** These folks obligingly haul pieces to el norte from the Mexican interior, paint them, fix them, and ship them to us silly Santa Fe gringos who pay high prices for them. Actually, the prices here aren't unfair, and the quality of the work is usually quite high. Some of what you'll find here is the real antique Mexican thing, while some of it is relatively new and has simply been distressed to look like an antique. But just ask—the salespeople will tell you what's what and why. **La Puerta** is another place that does the vintage furniture import thing, but its focus tends to extend as much to south Asia as it does south of the Rio Grande. This is a great place to find architectural objects from India, for example, or a pair of humongous, hand-carved Mexican church doors.

Funky new home furnishings... Around here, folks are quite enamored of two sorts of interior looks: the typically southwestern look, with patterned fabrics paired with contemporized Spanish colonial furniture designs, and the imported Moroccan souk look that works so well with adobe walls and brick floors. The imported stuff is invariably sold along with kilim-style rugs pulled in from India, Pakistan, Hong Kong, and who knows where. Recent years have witnessed a proliferation of rug shops around Santa Fe, with recently arrived wheeler-dealers locked into an ongoing life-or-death struggle to slit each others' business throats. Feel free to berate them, threaten them, ignore them, or do anything else you can think of to squeeze a better and better deal out of them—you'll just be playing their own game. The better rug and imported furnishings shops in Santa Fe are spread out in all three of the main shopping areas, but be sure to stop in at **Santa Kilim** and **Guadalupe Rug Gallery** in the Guadalupe district, **Khadoure Fine Arts** on Canyon Road, which also carries paintings and sculpture, or **Seret & Sons** in the Plaza area; **Santa Fe Originals** you can visit by appointment. You may also want to stop in to check out **Jackalope**'s furniture building, which stocks hand-carved wood furniture from the same Asian markets, but sells it at substantially lower prices. If you get the chills thinking about haggling with these guys, call **Richard Green**, an importer and furniture sleuth, who will guide you to some of Santa Fe's most secretive furnishings treasures.

Our locally crafted furniture is sometimes referred to as "Taos Style," as opposed to the tired, overused notion of "Santa Fe Style." In any case, it's more or less a stripped-down version of the ornate furniture the Spanish colonials had (remember Don Diego's home in *Zorro*?)—utilitarian enough for rugged frontier lives, but still hand carved to echo the heavy baroque stuff of old Spain. What we've got today is a squared-off, hand-carved look that relies on cushions and suspension for a modicum of comfort (in other words, more stylish than cozy). Some of the area's more established furniture craftspeople have their own retail stores; these include the Guadalupe district's **Collaborations** and **Santa Fe Country Furniture**. Also in the Guadalupe, **Southwest Spanish Craftsmen** sells an ingenious blend of contemporary and Spanish-colonial design. **Taos Furniture** is another excellent source, in the Second Street studio district. **Dell Woodworks** is way out of town by the airport, but it has a great reputation for strong design, good prices, and superb craftsmanship. One of the nation's most prominent craftsmen of the Gustave Stickley school of home furnishings is based in Santa Fe—and if you miss the downtown workshop/showroom of **Randolph Laub Furniture**, you'll be sorry.

For kitchen magicians... For plates, stemware, place mats, napkins, and such, there are two places that you won't want to miss: **Cookworks** has three buildings spread out along Guadalupe Street selling everything imaginable, from the region's premier selection of southwestern cookbooks to a fantastic collection of one-of-a-kind and limited-edition tableware by local ceramicists; and **Gift n' Gourmet**, which is on the east side of the Plaza, has a lot more southwestern theme kitsch on its shelves, yet the selection here is high-quality, and a lot of the lighthearted stuff is great visual fun. Another place you may want to check is the **Chile Shop**, which is close to the Plaza and tends to have a good selection of linens, aprons, and such, all with a theme of guess what.

When it comes to salsas and regional foodstuffs like jams, candies, and spices, the best places to look are **Cookworks**, **Coyote Cocina**, and the **Santa Fe School of Cooking**, where you can also take cooking classes (see Diversions). All are within an easy walk of the Plaza, and each carries enough hot and spicy stuff to completely distress your chile-intolerant pals back home, not to mention make you look like a monument to intestinal fortitude.

Organic shopping scenes... Natural-food markets and health-food stores are serious business in Santa Fe, and we've now got three contenders—two Colorado-based natural-food supermarkets and Santa Fe's own, slightly funky food co-op—slugging it out for the health-conscious community's business. All three places are worth a visit, if for nothing else than to get a glimpse of who lives here and what they do when they're going about their daily lives (I could also send you to my laundromat, but you'll like these markets a whole lot more). Walk the aisles, check out their great pasta sections and herbal remedies shelves, grab a sushi-to-go or a ginseng soda, then take a seat outside the front door and watch the truly local face of Santa Fe go by. The closest one to downtown is the locally born and bred **The Marketplace**, which has a decidedly countercultural feeling. **Wild Oats Community Market** and **Alfalfa's Market**, the two well-financed interlopers, have large stores within walking distance of each other just a short drive from the Plaza. Spend a few minutes reading their great community billboards, which advertise everything from wolf puppies for sale to shared housing for rent.

Book nooks... We're fortunate to have a glut of bookstores in this town, from huge mall superstores to antique and art book dealers to entrepreneur-run shops in each of Santa Fe's main shopping areas. But for local-interest titles that would make great gifts or souvenirs—travel, art, Native American, regional, and historical books focused on the Southwest—there are four stores to zero in on. **Old Santa Fe Trail Books & Coffeehouse** is the most unusual, a cafe and nightspot as much as a fine bookstore. It occupies a former private house with lots of nooks where you can sit for as long as you like, reading through several pages of whatever it is you're thinking of buying. Then walk over to the store's cafe section to grab a latte while you're starting into the book's first chapter (after you've bought it, of course). Downtown, **Collected Works Book Store** has a great staff, a top-notch New Age section, and a fine kids' section; **Parker Books of the West**, which prides itself on a strong fiction department, sells used books as well as new. Just off Canyon Road, **Garcia Street Books** is strongest in art books and travel books. If your tastes run toward the dawning New Age and metaphysical titles, **Ark Books**, in the Guadalupe district, has one of the nation's best selections, ranging from alien travels to Indian spirituality to Venusian sexual practices.

Kid stuff... Bringing home something for the young 'uns isn't nearly as hard to do in Santa Fe as entertaining them is if you bring them with you. Just head for the Guadalupe district. **Capt. Kid Toys** has a great selection of action toys, imported toys, and children's books, including a local travel book, *Kidding Around Santa Fe*, on visiting Santa Fe with kids. The best children's educational toy store is the **Horizons Discovery Store**, which has an incredible selection of astronomical gear, kites, puzzles of all types, science stuff, and creative games. **Pookanoggin** is more of a clothing store than a toy store, yet its selection of stuffed animals and other cuddly things would be right at home in any playroom.

How many days 'til Christmas?... So you're visiting Santa Fe in the middle of a hot spell, or maybe in that glorious autumn stretch we always seem to luck into in mid-October. The very last thing on your mind is Santa Claus, his workaholic elves, and a team of reindeer. But trust me: One of the most unusual (not to mention affordable) shopping experiences you can have while visiting here is to stop in at **The Shop**, which is one of those places where it's jingle-bells time 365 days a year and Santa and his boys never go out of style. There are trees filled with southwestern-themed ornaments ranging from cowpoke to coyote to Pueblo Indian, objects I find are a smash gift hit no matter where or to whom you send presents. A substantially smaller, but in some instances more artistic, collection of holiday ornaments is available at

Susan's Christmas Shop. In both stores you'll find anything Christmas-y imaginable, including twinkling strings of red and green chile pepper lights, one of my personal favorites.

If you really need another T-shirt... We all do it, to one degree or another, so let's be frank about that innermost urge to buy T-shirts: it's pathetic, it sucks, and it's dumb. That said, you're now probably wondering where to line up for a Santa Fe T-shirt of your very own. The good news is that you won't have to go very far to buy a $20 T-shirt with some really cool design that spells S-a-n-t-a F-e. The bad news is that these same shirts are printed up by the tens of thousands, so no matter how hard you've looked for something truly expressive of your own you-ness, the fact is that exactly 5,871 people in Iowa are at this very same moment wearing that identical T-shirt to their weekly lunch at the local Burger King.

Outside of spending a few hundred bucks on a wearable piece of art, the best way to leave Santa Fe with a shirt on your back is to buy one of the tees or sweatshirts printed up by the groups sponsoring the city's annual arts festivals: **Santa Fe Opera** (tel 505/986–5955, Taos Highway), **Indian Market** (tel 505/983–5220, 509 Camino de Los Marquez), **Santa Fe Chamber Music Festival** (tel 505/983–2075, 239 Johnson St.), and **Spanish Market** (tel 505/983–4038, 239 Johnson St.) each create and print an innovative design for these annual summer events. Of course, if you come here outside of the festivals' run dates, you'll have to phone them up and arrange to swing past their offices for a peek at their goodies. But since each group is invariably left with hundreds of extras to tide them through the winter fund-raising season (inducements, I think they call them), there's always a good selection from which to choose. If the Indian Market's organizers, the Southwest Association for Indian Arts, has any shirts left over from the spring pow-wow, run over and grab one without delay.

The Index

Adevina! A little bit of everything (clothes, coffee, and art) and a whole lot of fun.... *Tel 505/983–8799. 333 Montezuma St. Closed Sun.*

Alfalfa's Market. Natural- and health-food co-op. Dig the community bulletin board.... *Tel 505/986–8667. 333 W. Cordova Rd.*

Ark Books. Great selection of New Age and metaphysical books.... *Tel 505/988–3709. 133 Romero St. Closed Sun.*

Arrowsmith's Relics. Indian pawn jewelry, the real vintage stuff from 1900–1950.... *Tel 505/989–7663. 402 Old Santa Fe Trail. Closed Sun.*

Blue Fish. Downtown designer women's clothes.... *Tel 505/986–0827. 220 Shelby St.*

Bodhi Bazaar. The Santa Fe look for guys and gals.... *Tel 505/982–3880. 500 Montezuma St.*

Canyon Trading Post. Best place in town for top-of-the-line belts and buckles.... *Tel 505/988–5015. 670 Canyon Rd.*

Capt. Kid Toys. Great selection of toys kids will actually play with, as well as children's books.... *Tel 505/982–2211. 112 Don Gaspar Ave.*

Char of Santa Fe. Women's-wear designer has her own Santa Fe boutique.... *Tel 505/988–5969. 104 Old Santa Fe Trail.*

Chico's. Snazzy Southwest women's style.... *Tel 505/989–7702. 101 W. Marcy St.*

Chile Shop. Cooking and kitchen store whose theme is those hot, spicy, peppers.... *Tel 505/983–6080. 109 E. Water St.*

Collaborations. Reliable furniture store for the handcrafted Taos style.... *Tel 505/894–3045. 544 S. Guadalupe St. Closed Sun.*

Collected Works Book Store. Well-run general-purpose downtown bookstore.... *Tel 505/988–4226. 208 W. San Francisco St.*

Cookworks. Everything you could possibly want and use—just for your kitchen.... *Tel 505/988–7676. 316 S. Guadalupe St. Closed Sun.*

Coyote Cocina. Gourmet food and kitchen accessories underneath the chic Coyote Cafe.... *Tel 505/982–2454. 132 W. Water St.*

Crazy Fox. Hip women's clothing boutique.... *Tel 505/984–2224. 227 Don Gaspar Ave.*

DW Studio. Traditional and contemporary Native American jewelry.... *Tel 505/984–0265. 815 Early St. Closed Sun.*

Dell Woodworks. Fine quality handcrafted furniture.... *Tel 505/471–3005. 1325 Ruffina Circle. Closed Sun.*

Dewey Galleries. For those who want an exceptional piece of Native American jewelry.... *Tel 505/982–8632. 74 E. San Francisco St. Closed Sun.*

Dewey & Sons Trading. Marvelous menswear, with a preppy slant.... *Tel 505/983–5855. 53 Old Santa Fe Trail.*

Dust in the Wind. Designer clothes, Santa Fe style.... *Tel 505/986–0666. 125 E. Palace Ave.*

Edith Lambert Gallery. Fine arts, including authentic Native American jewelry.... *Tel 505/984–2783. 707 Canyon Rd.*

El Paso Import Co. The "Mexican Primitive" style of furniture.... *Tel 505/982–5698. 418 Cerrillos Rd. Closed Sun.*

Frank Howell Gallery. Home of the shamanic pieces by artist Bill Worrell.... *Tel 505/984–1074. 103 Washington Ave.*

Frank Patania. Traditional southwestern jewelry by a classically trained craftsman.... *Tel 505/983–2155. 119 E. Palace Ave. Closed Sun.*

French Rags. No rags here, just elegant, patterned woven wear for women.... *Tel 505/988–1810. 309 W. San Francisco St. Closed Sun.*

Garcia Street Books. Excellent bookstore just off Canyon Road.... *Tel 505/986–0151. 376 Garcia St.*

Gift n' Gourmet. Lighthearted southwestern-themed kitchen stuff.... *Tel 505/982–5953. 55 Old Santa Fe Trail.*

Gina's. Stylish western hats.... *Tel 505/988–9595. 131 W. Water St.*

Goler Shoes. Fashionable shoe shop for women.... *Tel 505/982–0924. 125 E. Palace Ave.*

Guadalupe Rug Gallery. Imported rugs and furniture.... *Tel 505/988–2181. 314 S. Guadalupe St.*

Horizons Discovery Store. Amazing stock of educational toys and games.... *Tel 505/983–1554. 328 S. Guadalupe St. Closed Sun.*

Jackalope. Eight acres of shopping madness for interior designers and the like.... *Tel 505/471–8539. 2820 Cerrillos Rd.*

James Reid Ltd. Upscale belts and silver buckle sets.... *Tel 505/988–1147. 114 E. Palace Ave.*

Jane Smith Ltd. Men's and women's fashions, very Southwest.... *Tel 505/988–4775. 122 W. San Francisco St.*

Judy's. Wide range of women's clothing.... *Tel 505/988–5746. 714 Canyon Rd.*

Khadoure Fine Arts. Fine furnishings for your adobe abode.... *Tel 505/820–2666. 610 Canyon Rd.*

SANTA FE | SHOPPING

La Bodega. Women's fashions with an exotic whiff of the bazaar.... *Tel 505/982–8043. 667 Canyon Rd. Closed Sun.*

La Puerta. Mexican and Asian objects for the home.... *Tel 505/984–8164. 530 S. Guadalupe St. Closed Sun.*

LewAllen & LewAllen Jewelry. Designs that truly come from the imagination become superbly crafted pieces of jewelry.... *Tel 505/983–2657. 105 E. Palace Ave.*

Luna Felix Goldsmith. A one-artist jewelry store with a national following.... *Tel 505/989–7679. 112 W. San Francisco St. Closed Sun.*

The Marketplace. Countercultural co-op food shop. After you're done shopping, take a seat outside and watch the locals go by.... *Tel 505/984–2852. 627 W. Alameda St.*

Montecristi Custom Hat Works. Best selection of cowboy (and cowgirl) hats in Santa Fe.... *Tel 505/983–9598. 322 McKenzie St. Closed Sun.*

Morningstar Gallery. Native American artifacts, including authentic sterling silver and turquoise pawn jewelry.... *Tel 505/982–8187. 513 Canyon Rd. Closed Sun.*

Museum of International Folk Art. Gift shop carries great Third-World craft items.... *Tel 505/827–6350. 706 Camino Lejo. Closed Mon in winter.*

Nancy Brown Jewelers. Some of the best-made pieces in the area.... *Tel 505/982–2993. 111 Old Santa Fe Trail.*

Nathalie. Contemporary western clothing and accessories.... *Tel 505/982–1021. 503 Canyon Rd. Closed Sun.*

Old Santa Fe Trail Bookstore & Coffeehouse. Browse, enjoy a cup of joe, or sit and read.... *Tel 505/988–8878. 613 Old Santa Fe Trail.*

On Your Feet. Casual designs for men's and women's feet.... *Tel 505/983–3900. 520 Montezuma St. Closed Sun.*

Origins. Eclectic women's styles from around the globe.... *Tel 505/988–2323. 135 W. San Francisco St.*

Ornament. Upscale and modern, this jewelry store has a huge jet-set following.... *Tel 505/983–9399. 209 W. San Francisco St.*

Ortega's. Unique and expensive jewelry store.... *Tel 505/988–1866. 101 W. San Francisco St.*

Overland Sheepskin and Outfitters. Nice western stuff, if you have the bucks.... *Tel 505/983-4727. 217 Galisteo St.*

Packards Indian Trading Co. Native American jewelry store.... *Tel 505/983–9241. 61 Old Santa Fe Trail. Closed Sun.*

Parker Books of the West. Great bookstore, especially for fiction.... *Tel 505/988–1076. 142 W. Palace Ave.*

Pinkoyote. Reasonably priced women's styles, with a western flair.... *Tel 505/984-9911. 315 and 330 Old Santa Fe Trail.*

Pookanoggin. Cute kids' clothing store, stuffed animals too.... *Tel 505/988–3228. 500 Montezuma St. Closed Sun.*

Rainbow Man. Traditional pawn jewelry and western artifacts.... *Tel 505/982–8706. 107 E. Palace Ave.*

Randolph Laub Furniture. Furniture modeled in the 19th-century Arts and Crafts style.... *Tel 505/984–0081. 310 Johnson St. Closed weekends.*

Ray Tracey Gallery. Fine Native American jewelry.... *Tel 505/989–3430. 135 W. Palace Ave.*

Richard Green. Furniture importer and custom furnishings shopping trips.... *Tel 505/982–1167. By appointment.*

Richard Lindsay Designs. Want a great conversation piece of jewelry to take home? You'll find it at this whimsical jewelry shop.... *Tel 505/982–4118. 211 Old Santa Fe Trail.*

Rio Bravo Trading. Traditional Native American and western artifacts.... *Tel 505/982–0230. 411 S. Guadalupe St. Closed Sun.*

Ripplestein's. Mainly accessories for the southwestern gentleman.... *Tel 505/820–1020. 130 W. Water St. Closed Sun.*

Sanbusco Outfitters. Western threads for show, not work.... *Tel 505/988–1664. 550 Montezuma St. Closed Sun.*

Santa Fe Boot Co. The genuine article—to impress the folks back home.... *Tel 505/983–8415. 950 W. Cordova Rd. Closed Sun.*

Santa Fe Country Furniture. Southwestern handcrafted furniture.... *Tel 505/984–1478. 1708 Cerrillos Rd.*

Santa Fe Dry Goods. Expensive menswear shop.... *Tel 505/ 983–8142. 53 Old Santa Fe Trail.*

Santa Fe Factory Stores. Mini-mall of outlet stores, some better than others.... *Tel 505/474–4000. 8380 Cerrillos Rd.*

Santa Fe Originals. Unique rugs designed with southwestern flair.... *Tel 505/471–6030. By appointment.*

Santa Fe School of Cooking. Great selection of regional foodstuffs: jams, candies, and spices.... *Tel 505/983– 4511. 116 W. San Francisco St. Closed Sun.*

Santa Fe Western Mercantile. Boots for men and women.... *Tel 505/471–3655. 6820 Cerrillos Rd.*

Santa Kilim. Fine southwestern furniture and imports.... *Tel 505/986–0340. 401 S. Guadalupe St.*

Seret & Sons. Imported furniture and rugs.... *Tel 505/982– 3214. 149 E. Alameda St.*

The Shop. For those who crave Santa and his elves in June.... *Tel 505/983–4823. 208 W. San Francisco St.*

Simply Santa Fe. Expensive women's wear, from American and European designers.... *Tel 505/988–3100. 72 E. San Francisco St.*

Southwest Spanish Craftsmen. High-quality, hand-carved furniture.... *Tel 505/982–1767. 328 S. Guadalupe St.*

Spirit. The casual urban look for guys.... *Tel 505/982–2677. 109 W. San Francisco St.*

Spirit of the Earth. Jewelry that reflects the Native American spirit.... *Tel 505/988–9558. 211 Old Santa Fe Trail.*

Street Feet. Sharp shoe styles for women.... *Tel 505/984–8181. 221 Galisteo St.*

Susan K's. Classy Santa Fe–wear for ladies.... *Tel 505/989–8226. 229 Johnson St. Closed Sun.*

Susan's Christmas Shop. It looks a lot like Christmas here, all year round. Be sure to pick up a souvenir set of chile pepper lights.... *Tel 505/983–2127. 115 E. Palace Ave.*

Taos Furniture. Spanish-colonial designs of superior quality.... *Tel 505/988–1229. 1807 Second St. Closed weekends.*

Tiqua Gallery. Native American pawn jewelry and artifacts.... *Tel 505/984–8704. 812 Canyon Rd.*

Trader Jack's Flea Market. Fun and funky outdoor market.... *No phone. Taos Highway. Open Thur–Sun, Apr–Oct.*

Tree Eagle Trading Co. Quality western hats.... *Tel 505/986–8770. 115 Old Santa Fe Trail. Closed Sun.*

Tresa Vorenberg Goldsmiths. Some of the best-crafted jewelry in Santa Fe.... *Tel 505/988–7215. 656 Canyon Rd.*

Trinity Antiques. American antiques, including pawn jewelry.... *Tel 505/986–1635. 822 Canyon Rd.*

Uli's Boutique. Stylish threads for guys...*Tel 505/986–0577. 328 S. Guadalupe St. Closed Sun.*

Western Warehouse. Country-and-western duds at reasonable prices.... *Tel 505/982–3388. 149 Paseo de Peralta (in De Vargas Mall).*

Wild Oats Community Market. Natural foods for the health-conscious.... *Tel 505/983–5333. 1090 S. St. Francis Dr.*

night
enterta

6

life &
inment

If you believe
everything you
read, you'd expect
Santa Fe to be
packed with cool
stuff to do after
dark. Well, think

again. Despite all the great travel magazine articles, word-of-mouth recommendations, *New York Times* opera reviews, and national art publications' coverage of what goes on in Santa Fe, this is a community of only 55,000 residents, with limited nightlife. If you're visiting from Spokane or Des Moines, after a weekend here you may think we're packed with concerts, theater, and live music clubs. But if you're coming from New Orleans, Dallas, Minneapolis, or any other city with a legitimate night scene, you may wonder why you bothered packing those dancing shoes.

What we are is a bit, let's say, structured, when it comes to nightlife. As in any other town with a thriving tourist trade, the options here are much greater in high season—during those glorious summer months—than they are the other nine months. But most of those greater options involve classical music, opera, theater, and flamenco. When it comes to nightclubs, juke joints, gay bars, dance halls, piano bars, and neighborhood bars, we rarely support our local club owners and musicians with the same conviction as you'll find in similarly sized places like Burlington, Iowa City, Boulder, or even Albuquerque. But give it a bit of effort and you can have a fairly rewarding time in Santa Fe after dark. The trick is to keep switching venues, and to target the places you need to get to to keep the night interesting. For instance, if I'm planning a full evening's fun I'll make dinner reservations around 6:30, drive to the opera, theater, or concert hall by 8:30 or 9, make a fast swing home for a change of clothes at 11:30, and be on the dance floor of one of Santa Fe's few live music clubs by midnight. Usually, my girlfriend and I won't even know what's hit us until it's time for brunch the next day. The important thing is to scope out the action ahead of time—this is not a city for aimless bar crawling—and keep your expectations within reasonable limits.

Sources

There are a half-dozen or so freebie entertainment, art, and general-interest publications distributed around Santa Fe. Each does a good job of informing its target audience about different events going on in town, but for my money, the best weekly lowdown on the cultural and nightlife scenes is **Pasatiempo**, the Friday entertainment supplement that's inserted into *The New Mexican*, our daily newspaper. *Pasa*, as it's known, is written by a surprisingly astute group of local freelancers who keep up with just about everything in the visual arts, performing arts, and music scenes. During summer's busy season, *Pasa* can run as thick as 80 pages of reviews, previews, interviews, announcements, and calendars, and even during the dead of winter it will usually have 20 or so articles focusing on the local action.

Our free weekly newspaper, *The Reporter*, is published on Wednesdays; its comprehensive calendar listings give you a good jump on the weekend activities. For action on the New Age front—everything from appearances by traveling channelers to workshops in cranial-sacral therapy—there's nothing better than *The Sun*, a monthly freebie loaded with ads, calendar listings, and even some New Age humor (yes, there is such a thing). Both Santa Fe and Albuquerque are covered in the *Crosswinds* free newspaper's calendar listings. Another indispensable freebie publication is *The*, Santa Fe's contemporary arts monthly, which has comprehensive listings of what's going on at galleries in Santa Fe, Taos, and Albuquerque.

The local radio stations are unconcerned with anything other than rock concerts and ladies-night action at Albuquerque bars. If you've got the time, though, check out the flyers posted at dozens of sites around Santa Fe (including the public library downtown)—here's where you'll find announcements of some really offbeat stuff that doesn't even make it into the mainstream publications. My personal favorites: "The biggest, friendliest iguana you've ever seen is still for sale," and "Max the crystal skull is coming to Santa Fe for appointments with his friends."

The Zen of art galleries

Add them all together and you come up with nearly 200 art galleries here in The City Different, a surprising number of them serious art spaces that could hold their own anywhere else in the country. Many gallery owners long for the glory days of 1990, '91, and '92, but all things considered, Santa Fe's gallery scene has been on an upward swing since the early 1980s. Art collectors come here to rub shoulders with their artist pals, pick up a sculpture for that home in the Hamptons, or shop for a fab piece of jewelry for that gorgeous new wife to wear while driving her gorgeous new Range Rover. April through November is prime season, but Friday night opening receptions take place year-round, and gallery hopping on Friday evening is Santa Fe's favorite social activity (map out your strategy through Pasatiempo, a Friday supplement in The New Mexican). Enter the gallery, grab a glass of wine, and start working the crowd. With any luck, by the time you're ready for dinner, you'll have met few dozen local folks and maybe even snagged an invite to an after-reception party.

SANTA FE | NIGHTLIFE & ENTERTAINMENT

Getting Tickets

As a rule of thumb, very little of what takes place around here ever sells out. You can almost always walk up to the door and buy a ticket for that evening's show or performance. On the other hand, if you want *good* seats for a performance or show, you should buy tickets in advance—the local ticket-buying base is big enough that a respectable crowd turns out for most everything that's widely promoted.

All the performing arts and music organizations will take credit card reservations over the phone. Several downtown businesses, including **Galisteo News** (tel 505/984–1316, 210 Galisteo St.), **La Fonda** hotel (tel 505/982–5511, 100 E. San Francisco St.), and **Rare Bear Records** (tel 505/988–3531, 1303 Cerrillos Rd.) sell tickets to different performing arts and music events, but each performing arts and music group cuts independent deals with these businesses, so it's impossible to predict which shows will sell tickets where. June through August, **Santa Fe Opera** has a ticket booth open in the Eldorado Hotel's lobby (309 W. San Francisco St.), while the **Santa Fe Chamber Music Festival** has a ticket booth in the lobby of the New Mexico Museum of Fine Arts (107 E. Palace Ave.). **Santa Fe Stages** has its ticket booth at the Greer Garson Theatre (1600 St. Michaels Dr.), several miles from the Plaza on the campus of the College of Santa Fe.

Liquor Laws

New Mexico is one of the top states for per-capita incidents of drunk-driving arrests, and our liquor laws are a running joke. Drive-up liquor windows are part of the state's peculiar charm, a messy legacy of its Wild West past and an open invitation to the drink-and-drive crowd. Last call at bars, restaurants, and nightclubs is usually at 1:30am, and by 1:35 the lines of cars at some drive-up windows (which close at 2am) stretch halfway down city blocks. Liquor is sold seven days a week. If you want to greet the day with a gin and tonic in your hand, then head out to one of the nearby casinos, where the bars open at the crack of dawn.

The Lowdown

Nightlife

Moonlight strolls... The most romantic (and safest) place to take a moonlit stroll is in the narrow valley flanking the **Santa Fe River** to the immediate east of downtown. As you head away from the Plaza, you'll pass along tree-lined Palace Avenue, where the houses are throwbacks to the city's former Victorianesque architectural style. After nearly a mile, the road jogs south, crosses the river, and links up with Canyon Road, where you turn right (west) and continue back down the road, passing the many art galleries and eventually returning to the downtown area. Another nice evening walk is in the **South Capitol** neighborhood, a district of upper-middle-class residences south of the Plaza area. Walk down Don Gaspar Avenue winding away from the Plaza, continue for a mile or so to East Berger Street, and turn left (east). Follow East Berger until it intersects with Old Santa Fe Trail/Old Pecos Trail (this is where the road splits), where you turn left again (north) and follow Old Santa Fe Trail back into the downtown area, passing the state capitol on your left. Most parts of town are fairly safe (but not foolproof) for couples taking after-dark walks; women walking alone at night, or even in groups of two or three, can expect to be verbally harassed—or even worse—in most parts of town. Forewarned, as they say in the South, is forearmed. And speaking of arms, keep in mind that more than a few people in this part of the country pack guns, or at least keep them concealed underneath the front seats of their vehicles.

Live music... Check out the calendar section of one of Santa Fe's entertainment rags to find out where the music's going to be on the night you want to find some action. For the most part, local bands tend to rotate from one live music joint to another, so the group you see downtown one night will be playing on Canyon Road the next. None of these places are dressy.

    Tommy's Bar & Grill, **Catamount Bar**, and the **Blue Corn Cafe** are the three downtown spots for live rock bands, as well as an occasional blues or jazz act. The crowd at all three places tends to be young and trendy, most especially at Tommy's, where style always substitutes for substance. The crowd at Catamount ranges from mid-20s to mid-30s, including a healthy number of Santa Fe yupsters; it has lots of microbrews on draft, but the bar eats could stand some improvement. The Blue Corn pulls in a somewhat older crowd sprinkled with cast-offs from the other two places; it's sometimes a lively scene on weekends, but more often than not musicians play here to thin crowds. The Blue Corn's bar has dozens of tequilas and a tequila club membership for those hell-bent on trying each one (over time). Weekends are the best times to catch live music at these spots. None of them has a real dance floor, and the action is a lot like what you'd find at bars in a college town, even though the crowd is a bit older. In a much lower key, the **Old Santa Fe Trail Bookstore & Coffeehouse** has a very dark, funky, literary-type bar where local folk musicians play on weekends.

On Canyon Road, there's live music most nights of the week at **El Farol**, with the weekends turned over to rock and blues bands, and weekdays dedicated to folkies, flamenco guitarists, occasional Irish music, and an infrequent cowboy balladeer. The problem with El Farol is that the place gets choked with cigarette smoke and there's no real dance floor. El Farol's crowd is the best in Santa Fe, though, with a wild mix of bikers, artists, tourists, singles of all ages (20s up to 50s), local working folks, and sleazeballs cheating on their spouses. It has great bar food inspired by Spain's venerable tapas, good-looking waitresses, and stiff drinks. In a decent Chinese restaurant right across the street from El Farol, **Club Dr. No**'s weekend bands tend toward R&B stuff, while on weekdays there's a mix of urban DJs and an occasional band trying to break into the local music scene. One reason I like Dr. No is that its comparatively airy interior keeps the place from becoming filled with cig smoke. The crowd here runs all ages, but 30s and early 40s seem to be in the majority.

The one place in Santa Fe booking national touring rock, blues, and new-music acts is **Club Alegria**, about 5 miles south of the Plaza. This club has a split personality: it's a Mexican/Chicano traditional music club on most nights, but some fairly well-known national acts perform one-night gigs here while they're in the region. There's a large dance floor, a well-lit parking lot, lots of tables, and a large bar. The crowd tends to be 30s and older, the spacious room keeps cig smoke to a minimum, and everyone is fairly friendly and well-mannered.

If you're in the mood to check out an older, local crowd of working folks, head for **Tiny's**, about a three-minute drive from the Plaza. Tiny's house band is made up of guys and dolls who cut their performing teeth during the big-band era. Don't be surprised if you walk in and see an older guy strolling around the bar playing a thousand-dollar accordion, singing Italian and Spanish torch songs—that's Tiny himself, one of the most politically connected guys in the state and the sort of fellow who smiles whenever he spots a couple making out in one of the booths lining the dance floor.

Life is a cabaret... A few places in the downtown area cater to an older and less dance-crazed crowd, with an emphasis on solo performers. On weekends in the Staab House room at **La Posada**, Chris Calloway sings an impressive and very romantic cabaret routine, with a focus on torch songs from the forties and some of the popular thirties songs written by her famous father, the late orchestra leader and singer Cab Calloway. The Staab House is part of what once was a big Victorian mansion, so the atmosphere is subdued, swoony, and quite unlike what you'd expect to find in the Southwest. Another favorite weekend spot for cabaret lovers is **Vanessie**, a downtown area restaurant with a huge bar and a grand piano plunked down in the middle of it all. This is the year-round domain of singer/pianist Doug Montgomery, who has moved on to a career that has him in and out of town part of the year. Most of the time, he stays put in Santa Fe and draws huge crowds of the people who've been listening to him for years. One of the nicest things about Vanessie, no matter who the talent is behind the keyboard, is that anyone wanting to grab the microphone and do their best Vic Damone or Liza is welcome to come on up and give it a shot. Another great downtown place for piano vocalists is **Mañana**, where the talent's almost always a lot better than this small room deserves. The crowd here is usually made up mainly of tourists and a bunch of state employees from the office buildings just across the street, and they don't pay as much attention to the musicians as they should—they seem to be in and out after a single drink, which is a shame. The piano bar gets cranked up for happy hour weekdays and stays running late on weekends and every night in summer. Mañana rotates a number of pianists in and out of the spotlight, but there's usually a core group of three who take turns on different nights—extraordinarily talented players who have recently moved into Santa Fe after making their livings in places like L.A. or New York.

There's a talented group of waitpersons at **La Casa Sena** who sing Broadway show tunes in the restaurant's bar, an act I only liked the first time I saw it. To this day it draws lots of blue-haired ladies and German tourists. Several of the downtown hotels have lobby or lounge acts that change around quite frequently; the talent tends to be itinerant musicians—competent enough to make a living but burdened with serious wanderlust.

That country twang thang... You can even get a decent country-and-western music fix in the downtown area, especially when local acts like Bill and Bonnie Hearne or South by Southwest are playing at the **Inn at Loretto** or **La Fonda** hotel's La Fiesta Lounge. The crowds tend to be adults who know a thing or two about dancing the Cottoneyed Joe, but nobody will mind if you just get up there and have a good time. The most popular C&W dance hall in town is **Rodeo Nites**, which is several miles south of downtown on Cerrillos Road. It's the kind of place where some gals have teased hair and fistfights break out in the parking lot, men's room, ladies' room, wherever. There are live bands several nights a week and a huge bar scene.

Dance fever... Out on Canyon Road, **Club Dr. No** is the only centrally located place with a real dance floor, and on weekends there's plenty of room to funk out. Lots of R&B goes down here. Across the street at **El Farol**, there's nightly music—rock and blues on weekends, folkier stuff weeknights—but the dancing takes place on a tight, tight space wedged between the bar and the band. There's disco downtown at **Shakers**, a third-floor club where Top-40 hits blare into the night. South of town, **Club Alegria** has a decent-sized dance floor for the nights when up-and-coming national bands play here; other nights, Mexican traditional music is on tap. Both gays and straights pack the tiny dance floor at the downtown gay club **414** on Wednesday and Saturday "trash disco" nights. Couples my parents' age feel right at home dancing to "The Way We Were," "New York, New York," or any of the other standards from the house band at **Tiny's**. If you prefer two-stepping to some C&W, try the postage stamp–size dance floor at the **Inn at Loretto**. The biggest dance floor in town is at **Rodeo Nites**, if country music rings your bells, but watch your manners if you come here—some of the clientele have been known to settle disputes with their bare knuckles.

For a stiff drink... Every once in a while, ya just gotta throw a couple back and let loose. A great place to go for those "I need a martini" moments in life is **Evangelo's**, a downtown bar that's a great place to get lost in space. You sit in some funky, pseudo-tropical surroundings, complete with tubes of bubbling water sliding up and down the wall behind the bar. Downstairs, there are pool tables and young bucks chasing young chicks. Upstairs is where the drinkers sit, listening to the best jukebox in town. On one side of you is a tattooed biker. Next to him is a state worker in a business suit. On the other side of you is an attractive (your choice) man or woman, ready to start a conversation and share a slice of life. A must, if even only for one drink.

If you're looking to sip off of the top shelf, a good bet is **Cafe Escalera**, also in the downtown area. There's French poster art on the walls, Lou Reed on the sound system, artsy metal chairs and tables on the linoleum floor, and a dressy, fashionable crowd smoking Gauloises. Not an especially great place to meet someone, unless you're into starting a conversation at the bar. But the bartenders sure know how to pour a triple Stoli martini with pearl onions. One of the greatest things about the small, fashionable bar at the famous **Coyote Cafe** is its incredible selection of imported tequilas (the $40-a-bottle stuff) and single-malt scotches. **Tommy's Bar & Grill**, which folks around here like to think of as an East Coast–style bar (whatever that means), is another great downtown place to duck into for an expertly poured drink, some back talk from the barkeep, good bar eats, and a sometimes-friendly crowd. Great dirty martinis, great jukebox, nice and dark the deeper in you walk—Tommy's is one of the best meeting places in town, though it does get jammed on weekends. **The Bull Ring** is another surefire downtown bet for a stiff drink. The crowd here tends to be loaded with political types and lawyers, especially when the state legislature's in session from January through March.

Twelve-stepping hot spots... Here in the eternally self-reflective environment of Santa Fe, most of us are on a lifelong quest for self-improvement/-realization/ -enrichment. Drug problems, alcohol problems, rela- tionship problems, sex addictions, parent problems...all those inner meanies seem to be solved (in some part) by going into recovery, joining a 12-step program, and cold-turkeying yourself away from whatever ails you. Those who are journeying into and out of 12-step pro- grams seem to need each other's company; they can find that in the remarkably funky atmosphere of two downtown hangouts. The **Aztec Street Cafe** (my friend calls it the "Prozac Cafe") is one of the best, if not *the* best, coffee joints in the state. Its four cozy, European- feeling rooms are filled with local art, racks loaded with every free arts, entertainment, and music publication in the state, even a *New York Times* vending machine. There's a great bulletin board, a patio for the sun- starved hip, and a crowd that ranges from teenagers to grungy artists pushing 50. Open late into the evening, the Aztec also pours the best latte south of Puget Sound and knows how to treat its clientele with sassy, friendly respect. **Cafe Oasis** is within walking distance of the Aztec but is a world apart. Everything here is a throwback to the glorious 1960s freak show that made this town (as well as Boulder, Eugene, Missoula, and Austin) a favorite for druggies wearing love beads and serapes. Occupying an old house whose walls are paint- ed with everything from wild murals to brilliant pastel shades, Oasis is a little bit coffee shop, a little bit restaurant, a little bit bar, and a whole lot of room for people to spread out. You can sit outside on the enor- mous patio, have a vegetarian lunch, or hang out until past midnight, listening to occasional folksingers and watching the weird and colorful subculture of Santa Fe. You've got to try it, just once, during your visit.

Painting the town pink... It's ridiculous that a town with such a high percentage of gays and lesbians has such limited nightclub options. Go to the opera, go to restau- rants, go to art openings, go to any public event and you find lots of gay and lesbian couples who are thoroughly integrated into Santa Fe's civic, political, business, and cultural life. But go out at night looking for madcap gay bar and club scenes and Santa Fe will disappoint you. I don't know whether the town is too small to support more than one nightclub at a time, or whether it's just the laid-back whatchamacallit that works its way into our Santa Fe psyches. Whatever it is, it's depressing and someone who knows how to fix the situation should move into town and get to work!

The only gay and lesbian club in town is **414**, which is in the downtown area right next to the state capitol. Up until recently, this adobe building was a steak house, and it's sectioned off into a number of what once were dining rooms, and now are rather mundane sitting areas where people converse and drink or play pool. There's a small patio and an even smaller dance floor as well as a long, narrow bar. Wednesday and Saturday nights are set aside as "trash disco" nights, which draw a large crowd of straight couples, gay and lesbian couples, and a flock of gay and straight singles who keep the dance floor packed with sweaty, undulating bodies. Ages range from mid-20s to late 40s. During the rest of the week there's some torch singing, some tea dancing, but mostly it's a fairly sedate crowd. On Wednesday nights in the winter, **Vanessie**, which always has a number of gays frequenting the bar, turns its bar area into something called **Club V**, another trash disco scene that draws a fairly lively crowd of straights and gays.

See-and-be-scenes... Those nice clothes hanging in your travel bag are going to come in quite handy when you hit center stage at the **Double A**, a fancy-schmancy, $5-million restaurant and bar that's been Santa Fe's headquarters for beautiful people since it opened in the summer of '95. At Double A you'll never feel over-dressed, no matter how Euro, Soho, LoDo, or SoMa your tastes run. There's a flavor of the Southwest in Double A's decor, but it's the sort of design note that restaurateurs and interior designers can hit in Miami, Vancouver, or London, provided they've got the big bucks. Another hip place to stop in for a drink or two is the smallish bar at the **Coyote Cafe**, a landmark restaurant best known as the nation's pioneer in developing contemporary Southwestern cuisine. The Coyote's bar can seat a dozen or so on its cowhide bar stools, and the atmosphere is sophisticated in the most upscale sort of Southwestern way. The bartenders here are experts at pouring perfect drinks, the stemware is elegant, the crowd (mostly visitors) is lively, and the atmosphere is intoxicating. **Cafe Escalera**'s crowd tends to be more local than Coyote's or Double A's, but these are the sorts of locals who travel quite a bit, know a thing or two about art, and who have the closet space to make significant fashion statements. The bartenders here seem to know about half the crowd by their first names. There's usually a silly musical chairs game going on—people come in here and hoard a cluster of the artsy metal chairs for their friends, who are supposedly showing up in just a minute or two, but who somehow never arrive until past midnight.

Pickup spots... If you've passed your 30th birthday and know a few things about conversation, try the town's oldest and friendliest bar at the **Pink Adobe**. There's music most nights (a guitar duo), a kiva fireplace in one corner, free popcorn, a row of tables and bancos along one of the walls, an always-lively bar, one of the most eclectic and well-mannered crowds in town, and the Pink's vivacious owner, Rosalie Murphy. Everybody stops in at the Pink, sooner or later. Not everyone becomes a regular, but the place is wide-open and welcoming. The atmosphere is conducive to starting conversations, but even though half the people here are on the make, nobody's going to press their case if the signals aren't right from the other side of the transaction. **The Bull Ring** bar and restaurant downtown is another place known for its high concentration of looking-for-love types—lobbyists, legislators, lawyers, and an older singles crowd hunting for some after-hours action, great steaks, and stiff drinks. **Vanessie** has a friendly bar crowd that's mixed straights and gays; it's an easy place to strike up conversations, whether you're at the bar or sitting at one of the closely packed tables. The crowd at Vanessie is generally older, starting in their late 30s. Even if there are a dozen Harleys lined up by the front door on weekends, **El Farol** is a likely spot for hooking up with someone whose better half is out of town on business, or whose significant other has just moved out of the house. El Farol is perfect for locals who want some measure of anonymity when they're out cheatin' around, thanks to its crowds, many small rooms, and dim lighting.

If you're into hanging with a younger crowd, try the bar scenes at trendy **Tommy's Bar & Grill**, friendly yuppie-ish **Catamount Bar**, **Evangelo's** (downstairs around the pool tables), and (again) crowded old **El Farol**. You'll find pretty much the standard sort of crowd with a fair share of visitors, so don't be surprised if the person you start talking to is also in Santa Fe on vacation... come to think of it, what a great match!

Once you've found that lucky soul, romance him or her with a tête-à-tête at **Geronimo's**, one of the smallest bars in town, but also one of the coziest and most discreet. Copper tables, a kiva fireplace, and pleasant tunes should warm things up nicely. Another suitable setting for batting your eyelashes at each other is the bar at **Vanessie**, where the lights are always dimmed and there are plenty of small tables where you can sit and cozy up to whoever that lucky new friend is. The bar at **La Posada**'s Staab House room isn't set up for lovers to hide behind booths and walls, but the antique-laden setting and deep green walls always work a number on your senses. The crowd here is a little older, a mixed group of locals and out-of-towners.

The more sophisticated and older crowd goes to... The **Hotel St. Francis**'s quirky bar attracts an interesting mix of guests, couples, and an assortment of local folks who stop in for a drink while they're on their way somewhere else. The crowd at **La Fonda**'s rooftop bar is about the same mix, with more people who can remember back to the years when Vietnam was a war zone and not a business opportunity. The **Pink Adobe**'s welcoming Dragon Room bar always has a wide range of souls having a good time; the trendy crowd at the sleek **Double A** restaurant is so sophisticated, you may feel self-conscious if you don't look totally sharp. (If you're trying to meet someone here, steer clear of the bimbos trotting out their newest cosmetic surgeries.)

The bar at **Vanessie** steak house is comfortable and friendly, while the local political and business types make **The Bull Ring** and **Tiny's** come to life after working hours and on weekends.

The wild, young, and ready-for-anything go to... Downtown, you've got **Tommy's Bar & Grill** for drinks and loud conversation; funky, countercultural **Evangelo's** for an insane mix of slackers, suits, dazed tourists, and bikers; and **Catamount Bar** for draft beer and live music. **Shakers**, in its third-floor, urbanesque downtown space, spins disco for a mainstream audience of swinging single straights, slamming down Buds and smoking Kools. On Canyon Road, **Club Dr. No** attracts the same age crowd for dancing. Keep in mind that somebody's bound to open a new club in this town every year, so check the local rags for leads on the latest action.

The big game... Downtown, the only place to watch that big game on the tube is **Pizzazz**, a wood-fired pizza restaurant with a large bar and one of the nicest interiors in town. The pizza's as good as some of the action on the tube...actually, the pizza's always good, even when the game isn't. There are lots of microwbrews on tap, and food's served up to 11pm, late for Santa Fe.

Entertainment

The silver screen... For a city Santa Fe's size, we're lucky to have several theaters regularly showing foreign films, Hollywood revivals, and independent releases. The best selection is what's shown daily at the **Center for Contemporary Arts**, a reasonably comfortable setting a few minutes' drive from the Plaza. One word of caution is in order: CCA doesn't sell popcorn, Cokes, Junior Mints, or anything else that may gum up their clean floors, and they don't permit anything edible or drinkable to be brought into the theater. I've smuggled bags of peanut M&Ms past the ticket-takers on occasion, but it always made me feel as guilty as I used to feel whenever I pocketed a candy bar from the Marx Brothers stationery store in my home town (okay, I've come clean, I was a petty thief at age nine).

The city's smallest theater, the **Jean Cocteau Cinema**, looks like a gem when you first walk inside, but after an hour in its designer seats you'll be shifting from one side of your butt to the other, trying to relieve the pain and cramps these idiotic seats inflict on movie-goers. Named after the French film auteur, this Guadalupe District movie palace would be better off renamed after the Marquis de Sade. It's a damn shame, too, because I really like the dimensions of this movie house. There's a spacious lobby with tables and chairs like you'd find in a French cafe, along with changing art exhibits on the walls. And there's an espresso machine, as well as a popcorn popper that dispenses real butter instead of liquified pig testicles. The theater itself seats around 150 lab rats who invariably jump up and leave as soon as the last frame is screened. We all keep coming back to the Jean Cocteau, however, because the place does show some of the best movies around, especially those independent American releases whose popularity spreads through word of mouth. There's also the **Grand Illusion**, a comfortable, large theater about a 10-minute drive south of the Plaza. Owned by the same people who run the Jean Cocteau, it has excellent munchies and the movies are almost always an intriguing mix of intel-ligent foreign and domestic releases...the sort of flicks that make you go hmmm.

What's opera, doc?... Take those very bestest clothes out of their treasured places in your closet and wear them to the dressiest show this side of Houston: the **Santa Fe Opera**, our own professional, international-class opera-company-under-the-stars. This organization has been around since the mid-1950s, and it performs every sum-mer on some of the most beautiful land in the Southwest, about a 10-minute drive north of the Plaza. The opera's partially covered amphitheater is going to be roofed in before the 1998 season—until then be prepared to occasionally weather nature's elements while you're getting your culture fix. There's always an old standard or two in the five-opera season, so if your tastes run toward *The Barber of Seville* or *Madame Butterfly* you'll be in opera-queen heaven. In recent years, though, Santa Fe has commissioned an annual new work from some of the opera world's most dynamic directors, composers, and librettists, so if you favor new music be sure to catch each season's contemporary operatic showpiece. If you're in town for the season's opening night, be sure to buy at least a $10 standing-room ticket, which will entitle you to show up for the free pre-party (sponsored by a French champagne company) and a free post-party featuring waltzing on the stage accompanied by the opera's 40-piece orchestra.

While you can count on the opera to be a fantastic, professionally presented show, the real reason so many local people love turning out for the opera has little to do with the action on stage. No, what opera means to many of us is a glorious opportunity to dress up in all those killer outfits we've shopped for and lay-awayed all winter long. Come summer we're just damned tired of cowboy boots, Levis, and bolo ties, so the opera's our annual chance to dress up and act like big-city folks. Arrive about 30 minutes before curtain time so you can casually mill about the patio area behind the main doors, checking out who comes in wearing what and whom they've got dangling from their arm. It's a show you don't want to miss.

The play's the thing... The fate of live theater in Santa Fe reminds me of a Dudley Do-right cartoon where Nell seems destined to be tied forever to the railroad tracks, screaming her bloody head off while savior-to-be Dudley dithers away elsewhere. Unlike the cartoon characters, our local theater companies as often as not let the train barrel right over their heads, leaving behind a messy, lifeless body. In the past few years, the two largest theater companies in Santa Fe have gone under. One was an Actors' Equity company whose artistic director has since managed to corral enough backing to start a new company, **Santa Fe Stages**. Its first season was successful enough, with a resident group of actors performing four shows in repertory as well as presenting six touring productions from the U.S., Canada, and Europe. Some of what Santa Fe Stages showcased was better than others, but that's nothing more than the nature of live theater; it's still a group worth watching. No bare-bones alternative stuff—they're well funded and it shows, with staging that's successfully innovative. They tend to pick plays by playwrights you've heard of, past and present, with a healthy sprinkling of big names (your Molières, your Kushners), but their approach is generally irreverent. For now, they perform at the College of Santa Fe's 800-seat theater.

Several local amateur theater groups make regular use of the **Santa Fe Community Theatre** building in the city's historic barrio district. The Community Theatre's own company stages a half-dozen or so annual productions, including a late-summer melodrama that's wildly popular with the local audience as it spoofs and humiliates the local political structure. The Community Theatre group's other productions are standard small-town stuff, though surprisingly well staged, but every now and then there's a failure...just to keep us all human, I suppose. Two other groups, **Southwest Children's Theater Productions** (see "Kidsville," below) and the **Santa Fe Theater Company**, also use the Community Theatre. The Santa Fe Theater Company is the one I'd hook up with if I were a theater professional relocating to Santa Fe. They pick plays with a regional emphasis, including premieres by local playwrights or plays about home-town heroes like Georgia O'Keeffe; there's a lot of talent in the group, which makes all their productions sparkle. On Monday nights they usually do a new play reading.

Sage Repertory Company, another amateur group, presents most of its productions at the **Railyards Performance Center**, which is close to downtown. This intimate brick-walled space really suits Sage's style— dedicated, innovative, low-budget theater that works on sheer talent. They're always worth a look, covering everything from new work by local and national playwrights to some reworked classics. The Railyards is as close as Santa Fe gets to a truly alternative arts center; it's rented out to independent playwrights wanting to stage their own shows, and there have been some killer theatrical events here, ingenious one-artist shows by some of the talents who have moved into Santa Fe from New York and L.A. The **Santa Fe Performing Arts School** is based in one of the city's best theater venues, the Armory for the Arts, a facility that's a few minutes' drive from the Plaza. Originally focused on children's theater productions, the Performing Arts School has started moving into adult theater with its recently remodeled facility, which allows it much more flexibility than did its previous location in an industrial warehouse. They haven't done much adult stuff yet—a couple of comedies and locally produced new plays—but keep an eye on them for solid mainstream fare.

It's a stretch to refer to the **Old Santa Fe Music Hall**'s shows as theater, it's geared so blatantly toward the tourist market. Its spanking-new downtown facility is nice enough, but these no-brainer musicals, while supposedly teaching you a thing or two about Santa Fe, are predictable, boring, and too light for anyone who has actually attended live theater. This is definitely a show for the couch-potato, television-is-my-life crowd.

Bardsville... This is an incredible event you shouldn't miss. From early July to late August, **Shakespeare in Santa Fe** stages one of the best free outdoor events anywhere in the Southwest. Performing on the St. John's College campus, this semiprofessional company contracts with actors who've come up through the ranks of major Shakespeare groups from across the nation; the action here is smooth, clear, funny, and great even for families and seniors. You can either sit on the sloping lawns surrounding the stage at no cost, or you can pay a few bucks to sit in a lawn chair closer to the stage. One of the local natural-food stores sets up a concession selling everything from Caesar salad to grilled chicken. Bring a picnic basket, a bottle of wine, a seat cushion, and maybe even a set of binoculars in case you want to watch the actors sweat (but you'll never be far away from the action).

Kid stuff... Santa Fe has two theater companies regularly staging children's plays, **Southwest Children's Theater Productions** and the **Santa Fe Performing Arts School**, both of which also run theater workshops and summer programs for kids. Both companies use young actors— SCT's are trained kids, while the Performing Arts School stars everyday kids who are taking acting classes at the school. It's all basically light entertainment based on classics, though SCT occasionally mixes in some contemporary pieces. The **Santa Fe Children's Museum** (see

Diversions) has opened its doors to puppetry, classical music, folk music, and theater companies whose work is oriented toward kids.

Classical sounds... The most professionally staged and run music groups in Santa Fe are the city's classical music organizations. We've got a wealth of talented musicians and music professionals living in this area, and this concentration of talent has only led to other music professionals wanting to perform, produce, or conduct for such a savvy local audience. The classical music scene here runs year-round and covers the whole gamut—on any given weekend you can attend a chamber concert, a recital, an orchestra performance, or something entirely new. In fact, there are probably too many presenting organizations working the classical music turf in this town. (If only we could siphon off some of that energy and apply it to the theater scene!) Some very worthy performances are painfully under-attended. There's bound to be some shake-out in the next couple of years—some of the city's most prominent organizations have already announced that their future schedules will be scaled back from what they've done in the past.

The **Santa Fe Chamber Music Festival** is the most prominent and best-financed of the local classical music groups. Its summer season covers a wide range of territory, from classical to jazz and new commissioned works, presented downtown, adjacent to the Plaza, in the St. Francis Auditorium of the Fine Arts museum—a long, narrow adobe shoe box with uncomfortable church-pew seats. (Try not to sit under the balcony, where the acoustics suck.) Major national names are brought into town for these performances, and the organization's resident musicians aren't slouches when it comes to keeping up with the heavyweights. Sitting in the historic setting of the St. Francis Auditorium, wandering outside into a warm summer night afterward, beautiful strains of music still humming in your ears...a performance here is quite an experience.

Choral music from classical European composers as well as more contemporary sounds from American artists form the core of the **Desert Chorale**'s summer program. This mostly a cappella group, which has as many as 15 voices, performs in glorious settings—the Loretto

SANTA FE |. NIGHTLIFE & ENTERTAINMENT

Chapel, the historic adobe surroundings of the Santuario de Guadalupe (see Diversions)—singing the works of Brahms, Handel, Bach, and many others. Romantic, inspirational, and intoxicating.

The most significant drawback to the **Santa Fe Symphony and Chorus** is the venue where it performs. Downtown's Sweeney Center was built as a high school gym, and no matter how much the symphony tries to dress it up, the setting is still more reminiscent of sweat socks than it is of French horns. Still, their performances, which run through the winter months, can be quite captivating, if you can close off your mind to the fact that you're sitting on a basketball court. **Santa Fe Pro Musica** is another major presenter during the winter season, a locally based professional ensemble with nationally touring guest soloists. They play a range of chamber and orchestral programs, both old music and new, in the downtown Lensic Theatre and at the Loretto Chapel. I tend to get more excited about the **Oncydium Chamber Baroque**, which offers an interesting alternative to the normal classical music scene in Santa Fe: First, it performs in alternative venues such as art galleries, restaurants, and shopping malls; second, it generally breaks all the musical rules, doing whatever it takes to shake up the audience and make the music come alive. It's a group of 20 to 25 musicians, constantly shifting personnel according to the pieces they're playing; sometimes they play period instruments, sometimes contemporary instruments. Not surprisingly, the iconoclastic Oncydium gravitates to younger audiences and younger musicians than you'd normally find at classical music programs in this area.

For free—or almost… Everybody loves a great deal, and Santa Fe offers some winners that you'll want to consider no matter how deep your pockets. The best of the lot takes place on opening night of the **Santa Fe Opera**, our primo outdoor summer opera festival. While not exactly a freebie, the season's opening night in late June lets anybody holding at least a $10 standing-room ticket attend a free champagne party before the opera (hosted by one of those fancy-schmancy French wineries whose bubblies sell in the $30-a-bottle range), as well as a black-tie optional waltz held on the opera's stage after the evening's performance, with music by the opera's orchestra. It's an intoxicatingly beautiful and memorable affair, one that will make you wish you paid better attention during high school dance class. Another great freebie is **Shakespeare in Santa Fe**, a two-month summer run of one of the Bard's plays, performed under the stars in the courtyard of St. John's College. Perfect for families who want to have a picnic dinner on the grass, Shakespeare in Santa Fe is surprisingly well performed by a company of semiprofessional actors drawn from across the country, and there's a great concession selling things like grilled chicken, brownies, and iced tea. Yet another no-charge treat is the open rehearsal schedule of the **Desert Chorale**, Santa Fe's professional summer choral company that performs and rehearses in the historic Santuario de Guadalupe. Not all, but enough, of the company's rehearsals are open to the public, an absolutely wonderful experience worth going out of your way for. Two of the city's leading performing arts groups, the **Santa Fe Chamber Music Festival** and the **Santa Fe Opera**, present a series of free lectures to accompany their summer performance calendars. These early-afternoon lectures, which feature actors, musicians, directors, and conductors, take place at the St. Francis Auditorium, downtown at the New Mexico Museum of Fine Arts. Finally, **St. John's College** coordinates a great lecture and performance series that runs year-round, charging either minimal admission or no admission at all, as well as a classic film series that costs only $3 a head.

Rock, reggae, pop, and blues... Big-name national acts rarely make Santa Fe a stop on their touring itineraries. The city doesn't have a suitable indoor venue, and anyway, we just don't turn out to support these sorts of shows when they do come to town. **Club Alegria** will book the sorts of touring acts that play Albuquerque's nightclubs, some of them real up-and-coming groups getting significant airplay; recently, Boxing Ghandis, Charlie Musslewhite, Sonny Landreth, and Tragically Hip have played here. In summer, **Paolo Soleri Amphitheatre** (at the Santa Fe Indian School, on Cerrillos Road) is used for touring national acts, but the number of bands booked in recent years has trickled to near nothing. Still, acts like B.B. King, Shawn Colvin, Blues Traveler, and Santana have appeared here—with luck, someone you like might be playing while you're in town.

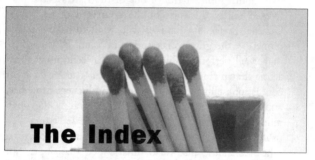

The Index

Aztec Street Cafe. The city's best coffeehouse.... *Tel 505/983–9464. 317 Aztec St.*

Blue Corn Cafe. Part of a fairly popular downtown restaurant; live music weekends.... *Tel 505/984–1800. 133 W. Water St. (2nd floor).*

The Bull Ring. Santa Fe's most popular political hangout.... *Tel 505/983–3328. 125 Lincoln Ave. Closed Sun.*

Cafe Escalera. This sophisticated bar and restaurant attracts a chic crowd.... *Tel 505/989–8188. 130 Lincoln Ave.*

Cafe Oasis. Bizarre, funky old house for coffee, hummus, and great people-watching. Entertainment on weekends.... *Tel 505/983–9599. 526 Galisteo St.*

Catamount Bar. Owned by a young group of entrepreneurs from Martha's Vineyard, this friendly downtown bar tries to be all things to all people, and does a hell of a good job at it.... *Tel 505/988–7222. 125 E. Water St. Cover charge for music.*

Center for Contemporary Arts. Wonderful foreign/independent/art film series runs nightly, with weekend matinees.... *Tel 505/982–1338. Old Santa Fe Trail at Barcelona Rd.*

Club Alegria. The only place in Santa Fe regularly booking touring national bands turns into a Mexican nightclub most nights of the week. Large dance floor.... *Tel 505/471–2324. Lower Agua Fria Rd. Cover.*

Club Dr. No. Part of a Chinese restaurant, this dance club has a decent-sized dance floor and a lively pick-up scene.... *Tel 505/988–7100. 731 Canyon Rd. Cover and minimum on weekends.*

Club V. See **Vanessie**.

Coyote Cafe. The Southwest's original bastion of nouveau-southwestern cooking also has a small, but very fashionable bar drawing a crowd of mostly visitors.... *Tel 505/983–1615. 132 W. Water St.*

Desert Chorale. Professional choir comprised of young and old voices from universities, music schools, and symphonies from across the nation.... *Tel 505/988–7505 or 800/244–4011. Performs at Santuario de Guadalupe (corner of Guadalupe and Agua Fria sts.), Loretto Chapel (corner of Water St. and Old Santa Fe Trail). Box office: 219 Shelby St. Performances Jul–Aug.*

Double A. New upscale restaurant has a busy, stylish bar.... *Tel 505/982–8999. 331 Sandoval St.*

El Farol. One of the oldest nightspots in Santa Fe, a good place to enjoy yourself. Music nightly.... *Tel 505/983–9912. 808 Canyon Rd. Cover.*

Evangelo's. The funkiest drinking place north of Albuquerque.... *Tel 505/982–9014. 200 W. San Francisco St.*

414. The town's only gay and lesbian bar has pool tables, an outdoor patio, a mixed straight and gay crowd on Wednesdays and Saturdays for trash disco, and tea dancing on weekends.... *Tel 505/986–9971. 414 Old Santa Fe Trail. Cover.*

Geronimo's. This Canyon Road restaurant has a small, very romantic bar that's a great place to warm up on cold winter nights.... *Tel 505/982–1500. 724 Canyon Rd.*

Grand Illusion. This large, independent cinema shows great films, including independent Hollywood releases and some foreign flicks.... *Tel 505/471–8935. St. Michaels Drive at Llano St.*

Hotel St. Francis. Restored 1920s downtown hotel has a dark, wood–paneled bar.... *Tel 505/983–5700. 210 Don Gaspar Ave.*

Inn at Loretto. The downtown area's most jumpin' country-and-western scene on weekends and Wednesday nights.... *Tel 505/988–5531. 211 Old Santa Fe Trail.*

Jean Cocteau Cinema. A small, uncomfortable theater that continually books the newest and most interesting foreign and independent films.... *Tel 505/988–2711. 418 Montezuma St.*

La Casa Sena. Broadway show tunes are sung by Casa Sena's Troubadors, the restaurant's talented waiters and waitresses. Routines accompany a piano player in the spacious bar.... *Tel 505/988–9232. 125 E. Palace Ave.*

La Fonda. Downtown hotel offers rooftop bar and La Fiesta Lounge.... *Tel 505/982–5511. 100 E. San Francisco St.*

La Posada. The hotel's Staab House bar is a romantic setting for torch singers, cabaret singers, and an occasional flamenco guitarist.... *Tel 505/986–0000. 330 E. Palace Ave. Two-drink minimum for music.*

Mañana. Dark piano bar located on a busy street corner.... *Tel 505/982–4333. Corner of Alameda St. and Don Gaspar Ave.*

Old Santa Fe Music Hall. Tourist-oriented floor show in a dinner-theater setting.... *Tel 505/983–3311. 100 N. Guadalupe St.*

Old Santa Fe Trail Bookstore & Coffeehouse. A place to meet the literary lovelorn or to just grab a book, sip a cappuccino, and listen to a folkie playing guitar.... *Tel 505/988–8878. 613 Old Santa Fe Trail.*

Oncydium Chamber Baroque. Interesting classical music organization dedicated to new music and refreshing performances of the classics.... *Tel 505/988–0703. No offices. Performances year-round at various venues around town.*

Paolo Soleri Amphitheatre. On the campus of Santa Fe Indian School, this is Santa Fe's outdoor venue for summer rock shows.... *Check* Pasatiempo *for ticket information and show schedules.*

Pink Adobe. The oldest bar in Santa Fe is also one of the city's best pick-up places.... *Tel 505/983–7712. 406 Old Santa Fe Trail.*

Pizzazz. The city's only sports bar is also its newest pizza place. Open late.... *Tel 505/820–0002. 422 W. Water St.*

Railyards Performance Center. A brick-walled space hosting theater, dance, and music performances.... *Tel 505/982–8309. 430 W. Manhattan Ave.*

Rodeo Nites. The city's largest and most authentic country-and-western bar.... *Tel 505/473–4138. 2911 Cerrillos Rd. Cover.*

Santa Fe Chamber Music Festival. Stunning summer performances by international stars of the classical music world. Reservations usually necessary.... *Tel 505/982–1890. Tickets sold at entrance to St. Francis Auditorium of the New Mexico Museum of Fine Arts, 107 E. Palace Ave. Performances Jul–Aug.*

Santa Fe Community Theatre. Home to three of Santa Fe's amateur theater companies: the Santa Fe Community Theatre, the Santa Fe Theater Company, and Southwest Children's Theater Productions.... *Tel 505/988–4262. 142 E. de Vargas St.*

Santa Fe Opera. World-class opera on an outdoor stage, with five productions each summer. Reservations are recommended if you want great seats, but $10 standing-room tickets go on sale each morning for that day's performance, and it's easy to move into an unoccupied seat.... *Tel 505/986–5900. Seasonal box office at Eldorado Hotel (309 W. San Francisco St.), or at the opera grounds, on*

N.M. Hwy 84–285, 7 miles north of Santa Fe. Performances Jul–Aug.

Santa Fe Performing Arts School. Theater company occupies the Armory for the Arts, Santa Fe's newest performing arts space.... *Tel 505/983–7992. Old Santa Fe Trail at Barcelona Rd.*

Santa Fe Pro Musica. Chamber music and orchestral performance during the autumn, winter, and spring. Focuses on both new and old music.... *Tel 505/988–4640. 320 Galisteo St., suite 502 (box office). Open weekdays.*

Santa Fe Stages. Professional theater company performing and presenting touring acts during June and July, with an emphasis on new and exciting developments in American and European theater.... *Tel 505/982–6683. Greer Garson Theatre, College of Santa Fe, 1600 St. Michaels Dr.*

Santa Fe Symphony and Chorus. Large orchestra and choral group plays mostly standard classical repertoire.... *Tel 505/ 983–3530. Sweeney Center, corner of Marcy and Grant Sts. Performances Sept–Apr.*

Santa Fe Theatre Company. See **Santa Fe Community Theatre**.

Shakers. Top-40 club in the downtown area, this place attracts a young crowd of local 20s and 30s.... *Tel 505/986–1814. 135 W. Palace Ave. Closed Sun.*

Shakespeare in Santa Fe. The best summer freebie in town, this Shakespeare company performs outdoors on the campus of St. John's College and features professional actors drawn from Shakespeare companies across the nation.... *Tel 505/982–2910. St. John's College, 1160 Camino de la Cruz Blanca. Jul–Aug, 3 evening performances weekly.*

St. John's College. Summer home of Shakespeare in Santa Fe (see above) and a winter film series.... *Tel 505/984–6000. 1160 Camino de la Cruz Blanca. Southwest Children's Theatre Productions. See Santa Fe Community Theatre.*

Tiny's. A favorite of local politicians and state government workers, it has a bar scene and live music geared to an older set.... *Tel 505/983–1100. 1015 Pen Rd.*

Tommy's Bar & Grill. Good bar eats, frequent live music, dark atmosphere, and stiff drinks.... *Tel 505/989–4407. 208 Galisteo St. Cover charge for music.*

Vanessie. A combination steak house, piano bar, and occasional disco (called Club V), where everyone's friendly as can be.... *Tel 505/982–9966. 434 W. San Francisco St.*

hotlines & other basics

Airport... **Albuquerque International Airport** (ABQ) is a great place for your first taste of the Southwest. Cavernous, with decidedly Southwestern architecture, it's staffed by some of the surliest desk jockeys this side of New Orleans. No trip to New Mexico is complete till you've negotiated the muddle that's ABQ's parking garages. ABQ is served by most major airlines, with **Southwest Airlines** (tel 800/435–9792) being by far the largest and most prominent commercial carrier. The **Santa Fe Airport** is served by a few shuttle flights daily on **Mesa Airlines** (tel 800/637–2247), but in the summer thermal updrafts toss those small planes around like rubber duckies in a bathtub. So save your tummy the turmoil, fly into ABQ just like everyone else, and drive to Santa Fe (which only takes an hour). If you don't plan on renting a car at the airport, take the **Shuttlejack** (tel 505/982–4311) airport limo service, which runs frequently from ABQ to downtown Santa Fe hotels (or even Cerrillos Road hotels, if you call in advance). Shuttlejack has several trips daily during winter months and almost hourly service come summer. The only time I've taken a taxi from ABQ to Santa Fe, the fare was $65; it would have been cheaper just to rent a car for the night.

Babysitters... **Santa Fe Kid Connection** (tel 505/471–3100) or **Magical Happenings Babysitting and Children's Tour Service** (tel 505/982–1570) can have sitters stay with the kids in your hotel room if you want to go out for the night (Magical Happenings charges $8–15 per hour; Santa Fe Kid Connection, $7–15 per hour, depending on the number of kids). Either service can also come to your hotel and pick up your little one, have some kid-friendly fun around town, then return her or him to you later in the day.

Buses... **Santa Fe Trails** (tel 505/438–1464), Santa Fe's small but efficient and inexpensive (50 cents a ride) city bus system, is something that would bring tears of joy to the eyes of your tree-hugging friends. Using buses that run on compressed natural gas, these nearly pollution-free, 35-passenger mini-buses operate frequently (every 30 minutes on most routes) during the day, but also have reduced night schedules that run until 10:30pm (except on Saturdays when service ends at 8pm).

Car rentals... Unless you want to rely on the bus and your feet for transportation, a rental car is a must. You'll get the best rental rates and the best selection of vehicles if you pick up your car (or four-wheel-drive truck) from one of the major rental operators at the Albuquerque airport: **Avis** (tel 505/982–4361, 800/831–2847, fax 505/984–8847), **Budget** (tel 505/984–8028, 800/527–0700, fax 505/768–5927), **Enterprise** (tel 505/473–3600, 800/325–8007, fax 505/473–3603), **Hertz** (tel 800/654–3131), or **National** (tel 505/842–4223, 800/227–7368).

Convention center... What once was the gymnasium for the old Santa Fe High School is unfortunately the best Santa Fe has to offer when it comes to convention facilities. Take one look at the **Sweeney Center** (201 W. Marcy St., tel 505/984–6760) and you'll understand why the city's larger hotels—especially the Eldorado, Santa Fe Hilton, and Picacho Plaza—all have an easy time poaching meetings and convention business away from our converted gymnasium.

Driving around... The main highway into Santa Fe is Interstate 25, which runs north–south through much of the Rocky Mountain region. From the Albuquerque airport, Santa Fe is an hour's drive north on I-25. The road

that takes you the 5 miles into downtown from the interstate is Cerrillos Road, which eventually leads you into
the older parts of town, changing its name to Sandoval
Street when it hits Paseo de Peralta. Driving downtown is
a confusing pain in the
ass, and parking's a
bitch in the summer, so
take time to get to know
your way around. Also
see "Parking," below.

Emergencies... For
ambulance, **fire**, or
police dial 911. **Poison
Control**, tel 800/432–
6866. **Rape Crisis
Center and Domestic
Violence Shelter**, tel
505/473–7818. **Road
Conditions**, tel 800/
432–4269. There's a 24-
hour pharmacy at
Walgreen's (tel 505/
982–9811). The main
hospital is **St. Vincent's**
(tel 505/820–5247 for
emergencies, 455 St.
Michaels Dr.). There are
two locations of the
HMO provider **Love-
lace** (tel 505/995–2900,
901 W. Alameda St.,
and tel 505/995–2400,
440 St. Michaels Dr.).

**Festivals and special
events...**

Winter: Christmas is a big
deal down here: there's a
winter version of the
Spanish Market arts
fair (tel 505/983–4038 or 505/988–1878); **Christmas at
the Palace of the Governors** (tel 505/827–6476) events
at the state historical museum; the religious street proces-
sion known as **Las Posadas**; and **Canyon Road
Christmas Eve Walk** (for information on all these, call

Feliz Navidad

*Santa Fe's annual Christmas
Eve spectacular is one of
those warm and fuzzy traditions that makes you want to
do something really humane,
like patch things up with your
ex (well, maybe not). Christmas in Santa Fe has a decidedly southwestern flavor, from
the traditional bowls of posole
we eat to keep our innards
warm, to the casual strolls we
take down traffic-free streets
illuminated with farolitos—you
know, the candle-in-a-paper-
bag trick. Tens of thousands of
farolitos line the Plaza and
Canyon Road on Christmas
Eve, a gorgeous sight that
turns out everyone in town
who hasn't already hopped a
flight to Puerto Angel. Lumin-
arias, which are burning piles
of cordwood, are built at certain points along Canyon
Road, where the musically
minded gather to sing a few
Santa tunes, desperately trying
to keep warm on what's invariably a below-20-degree night.
The trick is to snag an invitation to a house party somewhere in the Canyon Road
area, so that you have a place
to keep warm—and a parking
spot, since the thousands who
swarm into Santa Fe on Christmas Eve gobble up every possible parking spot downtown.*

the tourist office at 505/827–7400). For information on either the **Celebrity Ski Classic**, in January, or February's **Winter Ski Fiesta**, call the Santa Fe Ski Area at 505/983–9155.

Spring: Easter brings **Easter Dances** at Indian Pueblos—call the Eight Northern Pueblos office (tel 505/455–3144). In May, **Taste of Santa Fe**, sponsored by a different restaurant each year and held in various hotel ballrooms, lines up booths where you can sample various restaurants' food, and the South West Association of Indian Arts holds its **SWAIA Spring Pow-Wow** art festival (tel 505/983–5220).

Summer: Tourist high season begins in June with the **Opening Night of the Santa Fe Opera** (tel 505/986–5900). In July, **Rodeo de Santa Fe** comes to the rodeo grounds (call the parks department at 505/473–7228), and the outdoor **Spanish Market** (tel 505/983–4038 or 505/988–1878) takes over downtown with loads of Hispanic art for sale. In August, there's the historically oriented **Rancho de las Golondrinas Summer Festival** (tel 505/471–2261); the madly popular, long-running outdoor art festival **Santa Fe Indian Market** (tel 505/983–5220); and **Mountain Man Rendezvous** (tel 505/827–6474), a stupid event that turns the Palace of the Governors into an ersatz frontier trading post for Grizzly Adams wannabes.

Fall: **Fiestas de Santa Fe** (tel 505/988–7575) is a huge good-time street fair the weekend after Labor Day; the **Santa Fe Air Show** (tel 505/473–7863) fills the skies later in September. In October, look for the **Wine and Chile Fiesta** in the parking lot of the Santa Fe Hilton. The **Santa Fe Ski Area** (tel 505/983–9155) opens in November, launching ski season and starting winter all over again.

Gay and lesbian resources... The region's umbrella group for everything from AIDS services to gay and lesbian travel tips and restaurant recommendations is **Santa Fe Cares**, which operates an information-loaded, multi-choice hot line (tel 505/982–3301).

Newspapers and magazines... Santa Fe's daily, *The New Mexican*, does a great job of covering the city council, the local arts scene, state government, and *Doonesbury*. Albuquerque's daily, *The Albuquerque Journal*, does a respectable job covering what's happening in Santa Fe, but its emphasis is on statewide events. *The Reporter*, Santa Fe's free weekly, has a very usable calendar section but it's not at all hip, like a weekly should be. *The* magazine, Santa Fe's monthly arts journal, is surprisingly sophisticated, although a bit dry, in its academic reviews of art exhibitions. *The Sun* covers mostly the New Age community's events and personalities. *Crosswinds*, which is especially attuned to environmental issues, also covers entertainment news and events for Santa Fe and Albuquerque; it manages to be both interesting and funny about half the time.

Opening and closing times... Most art galleries as well as clothing stores in both the downtown Plaza area and on Canyon Road open at 10am and close at 5:30pm. Some stores and galleries are closed on Sundays, others on Mondays; some close both days in the winter months, so it's a good idea to call ahead. Restaurants tend to close early, with some serving their last meal at 9pm, most closing at 10, and very few staying open until 11. Most movie theaters have their last show at 9:30pm.

Parking... This is one part of the Santa Fe experience that's slowly improving year by year. While street parking is in short supply during the summer, the city operates several inexpensive downtown parking lots—try the ones at Water Street and Don Gaspar Avenue, at Almeda Street and Cathedral Place, or at San Francisco and Sandoval streets—as well as one on Canyon Road (at Camino Monte Sol). The rates start at 75 cents for 30 minutes and there are maps of the lot locations available at any of the city's visitor centers. Even if you do get a parking ticket, the fine's only $3 (or $10 if you're in a yellow zone).

Radio stations... Most of our radio comes in from Albuquerque, but there are a few Santa Fe radio stations that program news, music, and weather reports specific to the area. **KIOT (102.5 FM)** plays an eclectic mix of world music, jazz, blues, and rock. **KSFR (90.7 FM)**, operated by Santa Fe Community College, programs truly innovative, always modern music; its DJs are locals who have connections to Santa Fe's small music scene. **KVSF (1260 AM)** is the best bet for local news, weather, sports, and talk. Spanish-language station **KDCE (950**

AM) is a welcome relief from what normally passes for radio programming in this corner of the country: The DJs talk in Spanglish, interview mariachis, and play rancheros music. If you're lucky enough to be high on a hill or in a car with a strong antenna, you'll be able to pull in **KTAO (101.5 FM)**, the solar-powered station from Taos that plays music as eccentric as the community it represents.

Restrooms... Public restrooms are located at city-operated parking lots and at visitor centers; there are also facilities in hotel lobbies at **La Fonda**, **Eldorado**, **Santa Fe Hilton**, and the **St. Francis**. All of these are close enough to the Plaza so you can avoid any embarrassing moments. As for Canyon Road, there are public restrooms at the gallery complex at **225 Canyon Road**, or feel free to ask at any gallery if you may step into their potty (almost all will allow you to).

Smoking... We're turning into a town of smoke-free restaurants, but Santa Fe isn't quite there yet. All the bars allow smoking and most of the restaurants have smoke-free sections. The natural-food restaurants go even further—you'll have to step outside to light up.

Taxes... The sales tax around here is 6.25 percent, but most of the local art galleries and clothing stores will ship whatever you buy for free to your home or business, which means (for out-of-state buyers) that you can avoid all state and city sales taxes. When you're purchasing an original painting in the several-thousands-of-dollars range, that can add up to a significant amount of pocket change. For rooms, there's an additional 4-percent hotel occupancy tax, known here as a lodger's tax, which goes to pay for all those Santa Fe ads that show up in national magazines.

Taxis... In Santa Fe you have to order a cab by phone—if you try to flag one down on the street the driver will simply ignore you (or worse). **Capital City Cab Co.** (tel 505/438–0000) is Santa Fe's only taxi operator; be ready to wait as long as 30 minutes before your taxi shows up.

Tipping... Santa Fe's waiters and waitresses may not be the most competent in the world, and they may not even give a damn about your business, but they do know an insult when they see one. A 10-percent tip is what you give someone who has single-handedly ruined your meal. A stiff, on the other hand, is something I reserve for really special occasions when the service, food, and attitude all are deplorable. The average tip in a decent restaurant is somewhere in the 17-percent range, but don't go over 20 percent, even if the server throws in her phone number and a shoe shine. Bartenders get a buck a round, and be sure to tip on the first round if you don't want to be ignored for the rest of the night (they do have memories, you know).

Trains... The **Amtrak** (tel 800/872–7245) *Southwest Chief* stops in Lamy, a wide spot in the road about 20 minutes outside of Santa Fe. Once you get off the train, you'll have to call a taxi to bring you into downtown's hotel district, since there are no services available at Lamy's old-time depot. At least you won't have to worry about getting massacred by Comanches.

Travelers with disabilities... Most of Santa Fe's side-walks have curb cuts, making wheelchair access possible, but it's not always smooth going on our poorly main-tained sidewalks. Most parking lots have spaces reserved for disabled drivers. The City of Santa Fe distributes a guide—to these parking places as well as to shops and restaurants that are wheelchair accessible—called *Access Santa Fe* (tel 505/984–6568). Temporary disabled-driver tags are available for vehicles by contacting the **New Mexico Motor Vehicle Division** (tel 505/827–7601). **Capital City Cab Co.** (tel 505/438–0000) offers dis-counted rides for disabled individuals.

TV stations... None of the local TV stations are worth watching except to make fun of the weather forecasters. If you can't make it through your vacation without watching your favorite shows, here's where to tune your dial: **Channel 2** (KASA) is Fox; **Channel 4** (KOB) is NBC; **Channel 7** (KOAT) is ABC; **Channel 13** (KRQE) is CBS; and **Channel 41** (KLUZ) is Univision.

Visitor information... The State of New Mexico's offi-cial **Welcome Center** across the street from the capitol building at 491 Old Santa Fe Trail (tel 505/827–7400) carries the broadest selection of brochures for Santa Fe attractions, hotels, and restaurants, as well as for areas throughout the state. Be sure to ask for one of the offi-cial (and free) state highway maps before you head out the door. The City of Santa Fe maintains a visitor infor-

mation area at the **Sweeney Center**, an ancient structure that does double duty as the city's convention center (201 W. Marcy St., tel 505/984–6760, 800/777–
2489), but the information available here isn't as comprehensive as what's over at the state's welcome center.
In summer, a kiosk-like visitor information center run
by the City of Santa Fe is located on the west side of
the Plaza, adjacent to the entrance of First National
Bank. Staffed by helpful volunteers, it's downtown's
most convenient info booth.